Corporate Communications
Theory and Practice

Joep Cornelissen

SAGE Publications
London • Thousand Oaks • New Delhi

First published 2004

 SAGE Publications Ltd
1 Oliver's Yard
55 City Road
London EC1Y 1SP

SAGE Publications Inc.
2455 Teller Road
Thousand Oaks, California 91320

SAGE Publications India Pvt Ltd
B-42, Panchsheel Enclave
Post Box 4109
New Delhi 110 017

British Library Cataloguing in Publication data

A catalogue record for this book is available
from the British Library

ISBN 0 7619 4435 4
ISBN 0 7619 4436 2 (pbk)

Library of Congress Control Number: 2004094664

Typeset by C&M Digitals (P) Ltd., Chennai, India
Printed and bound in Great Britain by TJ International Ltd, Padstow, Cornwall

Contents

List of Boxes, Figures and Tables

Tables

Preface

I cannot remember exactly when I first encountered the term 'corporate communications'. I probably reacted to it in much the same way as I did to the various other concepts and terms in the professional communications and marketing fields that have come and gone over the past couple of years, expecting that it would disappear in time or simply lose its allure as a fashionable set of 'new ideas'.

However, it seemed as if the clamour of arguments in favour of corporate communications, or the so-called corporate communications view of an organization's communications practices, increased rather than diminished with time. Deeply connected with structural changes in practice and the allied professions of marketing and public relations – including the need for a make-over term for 'public relations' or 'public relations department' because of their negative 'spin' connotations – and a whole arsenal of other new themes and ideas, most notably stakeholder management and the integrated, holistic perspective on communications practice, corporate communications appeared more and more as a powerful configuration of new sentiments and thoughts. In its early days, at the start of the 1990s, it seemed set fair to play a crucial role in defining communications practice and the trajectories of professional development involved. And in recent years, as this book testifies, the corporate communications concept has in effect come to full gestation and now across many parts of the world defines contemporary communications practice.

Purpose of the book

This book is about corporate communications. Its chief purpose is to provide a comprehensive and up-to-date treatment of the subject of corporate communications – the criticality of the function, strategies and activities involved, and how it can be managed and organized properly. The book incorporates current thinking and developments on these topics from both the academic and practitioner worlds, combining a comprehensive theoretical foundation with numerous practical insights to assist managers in their day-to-day affairs and in their strategic and tactical communications decisions. Illustrative examples and case studies are based on companies in the US, UK, continental Europe and elsewhere.

Specifically, the book provides insights into the nature of the corporate communications profession, the issues that define this profession, the strategies and activities that fall within its remit, and the ways in which it can be managed and organized in companies. It addresses three important questions:

1. What is corporate communications, and how can it be defined?
2. What strategies and activities are central to this profession?
3. What is the organizational location, status and role of this profession?

In addressing these questions, the book is written to deliver a number of benefits. The reader will learn the following:

- The nature of the corporate communications profession, its historical emergence and its role in contemporary corporations.
- The critical role of the corporate communications function in building and maintaining relationships with the stakeholders of a corporation.
- The key issues – corporate social responsibility, reputation management, corporate identity, integrated communications – that dominate this profession, and how to deal with them.
- Different approaches to develop corporate communications strategies and to implement communications programmes.
- Different approaches to measure and monitor the impact of communications upon the images and reputations that stakeholders have of a corporation.
- Different ways of organizing communications practitioners within a corporation and of maximizing their performance.

Approach of the book

In writing this book, the objective was to satisfy three key criteria by which any management text can be judged:

1. *Depth*: the material in the book needed to be presented in a comprehensive and thorough manner, and needed to be well grounded in the academic and practitioner literature and knowledge base.
2. *Breadth*: the book had to cover all those topics that define the field of corporate communications and that practising managers and students of corporate communications management find interesting or important.
3. *Relevance*: the book had to be well grounded in practice and easily related to past and present communications activities, events and case studies.

Although a number of books have been written on corporate communications in recent years, no book has really maximized these three dimensions to the greatest possible extent. Accordingly, this book sets out to fill that gap by accomplishing three things. First, instead of being solely based on practitioner anecdotes (that rashly lead into sound-bite steps to communication success) or simple and normative frameworks that have been developed in recent years, the book provides a more informed and evidence-based account of the corporate communications profession by including insights from academic research. Second, all the contemporary and important themes and topics within the remit of the corporate communications function including 'corporate social responsibility' and 'stakeholder management' are discussed in detail. Particular attention is paid to the central topics of the structuring of the communications function within organizations, communications strategy development, and the professional development of communications managers, which have received little attention in other books. Third, the book not only presents the latest academic thinking and research on the subject, but also features toolkits, management briefs and snappy cases to illustrate the concepts and themes of the book and to meet the 'double hurdle' of rigour and relevance.

Thus, combining theory, research and practitioner accounts on corporate communications, the book provides a comprehensive, realistic and up-to-date overview of the status and playing field of this profession. Important issues in managing and organizing corporate communications are discussed, providing practising managers with appropriate concepts, theories and tools to make better management and communications decisions. Readers will gain a greater appreciation and a more in-depth understanding of the range of topics covered in corporate communications management as well as a means to organize their thoughts about those topics.

Readership of the book

A wide range of people can benefit from reading this book, including the following groups:

- Students at the graduate level enrolled on a business, management, marketing, corporate communications, public relations or business communications course interested in increasing their understanding of the theory and practice of corporate communications.
- Managers and analysts with a professional interest in the area of corporate communications (and with responsibility for a slice of the corporate communications cake), concerned with making informed decisions that maximize their day-to-day performance.
- Senior executives looking for an understanding of corporate communications, and what it can do for their business.
- Academics researching and reading in the areas of corporate communications, public relations, marketing and strategic management looking for a resource guide that circumscribes the themes and development of the corporate communications profession in a single volume.

Organization of the book

As mentioned, the purpose of this book is to present a major retrospective and prospective overview of the *academic discipline* and *practice* of corporate communications. The distinction made between the 'discipline' and 'practice' of corporate communications is intentional and implies that the book aims to draw out and integrate conceptual and intellectual accounts of the evolution of the corporate communications field with more hands-on, practice-based insights and skills from the profession. Mindful of the differences between academic reflections upon corporate communications and practitioner approaches to it, conceptual and practitioner accounts are integrated into a comprehensive and contemporary overview of the corporate communications field.

The book takes the view that corporate communications is a field of management within organizations, and that not only our understanding of it but also the development of the field (as both a discipline and practice) is best served by a *management* spectre. This means that alternative perspectives on corporate communications such as the critical and rhetorical accounts that consider the role and effect of communications at the macro level, at the level of society, are included in the book's ruminations of the field, yet are considered of secondary importance in view of the core management perspective and theme of the book.

In framing, addressing and synthesizing corporate communications as an area of management, the book starts with the existing academic and practitioner works and their respective accounts of the current status and role of the profession. However, in addressing issues about the future shape and development of the field of corporate communications (as a discipline and practice), the book will be more aspirational and adventurous. In organizing the chapters in three parts, the book not only includes state-of-the-art descriptions of corporate communications from both the theory and practice ends, but also addresses professional challenges for the future.

Part 1, Mapping the Field, provides a theoretical characterization of the historical, conceptual and practical roots of the field of corporate communications, frames the strategic management perspective upon the field, and is aspirational about the need to broaden and anchor this perspective to further the study and practice of corporate communications. Part 2, Corporate Communications in Practice, includes three chapters that focus on the practice of corporate communications; discussing subjects such as how corporate communications strategy is developed, how communications disciplines and activities are organized within companies, and the skills and competencies that are required of communications practitioners. Part 3, Retrospect and Prospect, consolidates many of the book strands with a range of theoretical, historicist and professional arguments about the future development of the field.

Acknowledgements

In writing this book I have had a lot of help and encouragement. Andrew Lock, Phil Harris, Danny Moss and Hanne Gardner were influential in shaping my early thinking and research in the corporate communications field. I have also benefited from the wisdom of my colleagues and graduate students at the various institutions to which I have been associated: the Manchester Metropolitan University, the Amsterdam School of Communications Research and the Leeds University Business School. I would also like to thank my reviewers: Ian Blackhall of the University of Sunderland and Professor Betteke van Ruler of the University of Amsterdam. At Sage, Delia Alfonso was an enthusiastic supporter from start to finish, providing invaluable editorial guidance and pulling me through the writing process. Keith Von Tersch and Rosemary Campbell have also been a great help in proofreading the material and getting the artwork ready. Finally, I would like to thank Mirjam for her support, and for her understanding and forbearance (all those lost summer days!).

About the author

Dr Joep Cornelissen is a Lecturer in Corporate Communications at the Leeds University Business School, and previously taught at the Amsterdam School of Communications Research, the University of Amsterdam. He currently teaches corporate communications and marketing communications on the MBA and MA programmes at Leeds. Dr Cornelissen has contributed many conference papers and journal articles to the field, with his work appearing in leading management, marketing and communications journals including the *Academy of Management Review, Organization Studies, Journal of Advertising Research, British Journal of Management, Psychology & Marketing, Journal of Business Communications, Journal of Marketing Management, International Journal of Advertising* and the *Public Relations Review*. He has been a corporate communications consultant to Novartis, KPN (Dutch Telecom), the National Health Service and to other companies in the United Kingdom and the Netherlands.

PART 1
MAPPING THE FIELD

This book is about organizations and the way in which they respond and adapt (or fail to adapt) to the world around them through the use of communications. The things they communicate to adapt over time fall within the remit of corporate communications programmes, and the process of organizing and planning for these programmes as well as executing them is called *management*. Although the word 'management' often calls to mind a deliberate, rational process, communications programmes of organizations are not always shaped in that way. Sometimes, they come about by reactions to sudden crises, or as the result of political activity within the organization. The management of corporate communications, and how organizations can do this in a *strategic* manner – that is, by supporting and organizing the corporate communications function in such a way that corporate objectives are met and the organization as a whole is served – is the subject of this book.

In Part 1, we explore the basic themes and concepts that are used in discussing corporate communications, and provide a framework for the strategic management of corporate communications that will serve as a guide to the field (and the remainder of this book). Themes addressed include theory and practice perspectives on corporate communications, the definition of corporate communications *vis-à-vis* concepts such as business communications, public relations and marketing, and the centrality of the stakeholder, corporate identity and reputation concepts to the corporate communications function.

After reading Part 1, the reader should be familiar with the basic vocabulary and concepts of corporate communications, the strategic management perspective on it, and the importance of stakeholder management for contemporary organizations.

Chapter 1
Circumscribing Corporate Communications: Theory and Practice

Central themes

- Corporate communications is an area of both professional practice and theoretical inquiry; and naturally the two domains should be linked in a way that advances both.

- Different theoretical perspectives from communications and management theory have been brought to bear upon the field of corporate communications through reflections and research.

- Seemingly in contrast with theoretical perspectives, practitioner views on the corporate communications field place an emphasis on the vocational skills and management competencies needed for the corporate communications job.

- The strategic management view of corporate communications is the most relevant and useful perspective for advancing our understanding of corporate communications as a professional area of practice.

- Corporate communications can be distinguished from other forms of professional communications (including business communications and management communications) by the corporate perspective on which it is based, the stakeholders that it addresses, and the management activities that fall within its remit.

1.1   Introduction

There is a widespread belief in the management world that in today's society the future of any one company depends critically on how it is viewed by key stakeholders such as shareholders and investors, customers and consumers, employees and members of the community in which the company resides. Public activism, globalization and recent accounting scandals have further strengthened this belief, and have also brought the work of communications practitioners into closer orbit.

   This book is about the activities that are carried out by these communications practitioners; how these practitioners build and nurture relationships with stakeholders; and how their activities can be strategically managed and organized. It concentrates on strategic and management issues around corporate communications because corporate communications is essentially a management function that is used by companies in a strategic and instrumental manner. As the book will outline, companies need to be judged as 'legitimate' by most, if not all, of their stakeholders in order to survive and prosper, and corporate communications is the management function that works the hardest to achieve that.

Understanding corporate communications

As a result of the greater importance that is now attributed to corporate communications in the world of management, the numbers of professionals working in the area, and equally the numbers of university courses and professional training programmes that cater for their development, have mushroomed in recent years. Even Master of Business Administration (MBA) students, who in the past have been reluctant to follow business communications and corporate communications courses, are now in the wake of the corporate scandals and economic turmoil in the US calling for taught modules on corporate communications and corporate social responsibility.[1] Of course, communications practitioners need to know how to recognize, diagnose and solve communication-related management problems, but more and more it appears that the need for understanding corporate communications spirals to other management areas, including senior management and the Chief Executive Officer (CEO). It is indeed useful for managers of all ranks to know what the corporate communications function entails; what it can do for their business; and also how conditions can be created in which communications practitioners can work to the best effect.

Understanding corporate communications management has, however, advantages above and beyond corporate success and career advancement. In many companies, the role and contribution of corporate communications is far from being fully understood. In such companies, communications practitioners feel undervalued, their strategic input into decision making is compromised, and senior managers and CEOs feel powerless because they simply do not understand the events that are taking place in the company's environment and how these events may affect the company's operations and profits. Communications practitioners and senior managers therefore need to be able to take a *critical* perspective on corporate communications; that is, they need to be able to recognize and diagnose communication-related management problems, and have an understanding of appropriate strategies and courses of action for dealing with these. Such an understanding (and the learning and application in practice that it triggers) is not only essential to an effective functioning of the corporate communications function, but also is in itself empowering – it allows communications practitioners and managers to understand and take charge of events that fall within the remit of corporate communications; to determine which events are outside their control; how communications practitioners can contribute to other functional areas within the company; and discover new strategies that the company could have used successfully and will be able to use in the future.

The primary goal of this book is to give readers a sense of how corporate communications is used and managed *strategically*; and how professional and organizational conditions are created that facilitate and support communications practitioners in their work. The book merges reflections and insights from academic research and professional practice, with the aim of providing a comprehensive overview of the status and playing field of the corporate communications profession. In doing so, the book also provides armoury to communications practitioners and senior managers by providing valuable concepts, insights and tools that can be used in their day-to-day practice.

In this chapter, I will start by circumscribing the field of corporate communications and will introduce the strategic management perspective that underlies the rest of the book. First, I will discuss how corporate communications is an area of both professional practice and theoretical inquiry, and outline how the linking of these two domains advances our understanding of the profession. Then I will explain that corporate communications is a multidisciplinary field with different theoretical disciplines (e.g. mass communications, rhetorics, management) offering different lenses for looking at it; and subsequently start defining the strategic management perspective on corporate communications that is central to this book. This perspective suggests a particular way of looking at the corporate communications profession, and indicates a number of management areas and concerns that will be covered in the remaining chapters. As the book progresses, each of these areas will be explained in detail, and the strategic management perspective as a whole will become more and more clear. Good things will thus come to those who wait, and read.

1.2   The intersection of theory and practice

As with every other business and management discipline that is not only an area of professional practice, but also the subject of theoretical inquiry, one way to start circumscribing corporate communications is by considering theory and practice and how both these domains relate to one another. Academics concerned with building theories and communications professionals who are more immediately involved in the nitty-gritty detail of executing communications programmes, obviously have very different orientations to the corporate communications field. Yet, as I will suggest, combining theoretical and practitioner orientations will be advantageous in that it leads to theory and practice informing each other and ultimately will advance our understanding of the field of corporate communications as a whole.

Traditional views of theory and practice in corporate communications

Traditionally, however, this view of linking theory and practice was not widely shared within corporate communications or adjacent management fields. Many academic commentators in these fields traditionally have been 'on the defensive' in that they have argued against closer links between theoretical inquiry and practice. In fact, some academics have even considered virtually all kinds of practitioner intervention and mediation in academia, including applied research and consultancy, as detrimental to the academic enterprise of basic, fundamental research.[2] In the view of these academics, theorizing and academic research are naturally directed at fundamental

Table 1.1 Academic and practitioner orientations to corporate communications

	Academic orientation	Practitioner orientation
Value assumptions		
(1) Objective	Basic understanding	Accomplishment
(2) Criteria of excellence	Validity	Effectiveness
(3) Application	Abstract/general	Concrete/specific
(4) Relation to subject area	Reflection (independent and objective)	Action and creation (involved and subjective)

understanding per se, rather than understanding for use by professionals;[3] and the academic orientation to corporate communications in theorizing and research is as a result distinct and far removed from practitioner reflections on the profession. This distinction in academic and practitioner orientations is based upon the idea that, typically, the academic researcher sacrifices a detailed description and analysis of the specific features of a subject in order to illustrate the general and abstract relations among theoretical concepts – rather than to provide a comprehensive understanding of the subject – while the practitioner focuses on a single and specific problem with the purpose of designing strategies and courses of action for dealing with it (Table 1.1). From this perspective, and as Table 1.1 outlines, knowledge is constituted differently in the academic and practitioner realms according to varying interests, purposes, conventions and criteria of adequacy, and consequently theory (as the outcome of academic deliberations and research) and practice are seen as disparate, with the two domains being too far removed and insulated to have any direct and sustained impact on one another.

As a result of this rift between the academic and practitioner domains many communications practitioners for their part have often turned their back upon theory and research, as they feel that it does not appear to provide anything useful or relevant to their day-to-day affairs.[4] Communications practitioners, it needs to be understood, are, like managers in other fields, typically concerned with short-term actions in response to the specific pressing problems that they are confronted with, and their primary reason for informing their practice with theory would be that it would help them understand their own specific problems better or aid them in identifying scenarios and available courses of action to address them. As much theory and research is pitched at a high level of abstraction, many communications practitioners often have not resorted to theory, as most of it read to them as a paean to inutility.

Towards a theory-informed practice of corporate communications

Yet, while recognizing the apparent differences between the academic and practitioner orientations, I (and others with me) do not favour a juxtaposing or strict separation of both the academic theory and practice domains. In fact, a closer link between both domains will have a number of benefits and not only will aid our overall knowledge of the field, but also will advance professional practice (Figure 1.1). Our knowledge of the field will be enlarged when academic theorizing and research

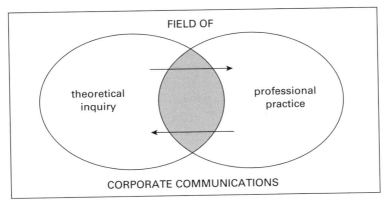

Figure 1.1   The intersection of theory and practice in corporate communications

are more closely related to practice. New insights and knowledge will in fact come from well-established collaborative links between academics and practitioners, which ensures validity in the collection and codification of data, offers anchorage for abstractions and data and tests for hypotheses, and also provides for new understandings that may arise from putting academic knowledge into practice. A good example of such conjoining of academic and practitioner forces is the Reputation Institute, an organization committed to the development of reputation measures that are academically rigorous and valid, but at the same time practical enough to be used by communications consultancies and market research agencies in practice.[5]

In essence, I believe that combining the specific and localized knowledge that comes out of the intelligent reflection and applied research of professionals in practice with academic research that is generally more conceptual and global in outlook will enlarge our overall knowledge base of the corporate communications field. Brinberg and Hirschman have made a similar point with their claim that academic research should be laid next to more applied practitioner reflections and research so that the knowledge coming out of both can inform and complement one another.

> The net result is that our overall base of knowledge is enriched because each study addresses it from an alternative orientation. The strengths of one orientation (e.g. the relative emphasis on the development of the conceptual model in academic research) compensate for the weaknesses of another orientation (e.g. the lack of emphasis on the conceptual model in practitioner research).[6]

At this point, it will have become clear that I favour a close link between theory and practice in order to enhance our overall knowledge and understanding of the field (see Figure 1.1); and I have also taken this principle at heart in writing this book so that the most comprehensive overview available of the corporate communications field is provided to the reader. But there is also a second reason for favouring this mutually supportive interplay of the theoretical and the practical; namely that such an interplay can advance the day-to-day practice of communications practitioners.

In 1945, the Chicago psychologist Kurt Lewin claimed that 'nothing is as practical as a good theory'.[7] Lewin's dictum has often been referred to in discussions about the practical utility of academic theory within many professional contexts, including the field of corporate communications. Given the considerable differences in orientations of both academics and professionals that I have outlined (Table 1.1), there are, however, doubts about the *direct* and *instrumental* applicability of corporate communications theories in practice, as Lewin's dictum would suggest. That is, because of their academic orientation theorists do not generally produce techniques that can be directly applied to specific situations within practice. A more realistic (and helpful) image, therefore, is the view that practitioners nonetheless can be informed and shaped by theories and research in their work, with theories providing them with ideas, concepts and frameworks that may explain, contextualize or otherwise help them understand what they do on a day-to-day basis (see Box 1.1 below). That is, the real-world situations and problems with which practitioners are confronted are often characterized by uncertainty, complexity and instability, and, as unique cases, cannot be directly solved by general theoretical principles (nor does academic theory yet possess many of these principles!).[8] Theory and academic research, however, can act as a source of knowledge, soundboard or interpretive framework to provide practitioners with a better understanding of their day-to-day work, and together with the intelligence, experiences and applied research that practitioners otherwise rely on will provide them with the 'suitable' knowledge to understand and act upon the situation or problem in hand.[9]

Box 1.1 Management brief: how to 'use' corporate communications theory in practice[14]

There are a number of ways in which one can look at the concept of 'using' theory (or theoretical knowledge) in a professional context. From empirical observations, we know that three types of 'uses' can be distinguished:

1. *Instrumental use*: the instrumental type of theory use concerns the traditional view of theory use, where academic theory and research are seen to provide rational solutions to managerial problems in a direct and instrumental way. This type of use is very rare within corporate communications or adjacent management and social science fields because very few of the theories within these fields are in such a formal and elaborate shape that they can directly prescribe actions in practice without requiring any interpretation or adaptation by the practitioner (this type of theory use does, however, have its currency in scientific fields such as physics and engineering where theories contain more procedural, rule-based knowledge).
2. *Conceptual use*: using theories conceptually means that theory offers ideas, problem definitions and interpretative schemes as a set of intellectual tools to practitioners for understanding and anticipating real-world problems. The impact of conceptual use may be more indirect and diffuse than instrumental use, but has nonetheless been found to make up for the bulk of theory use within corporate communications and allied management fields (and should, I believe, even be increased in the light of the notion of 'reflective practice'). For example,

rather than having had a direct and instrumental impact upon practice, the now commonplace concept of integrated marketing communications (IMC) has provided communications practitioners with a metaphor or idea that they have interpreted in the context of their own organizational setting and market environment. The concept of IMC has, for instance, been variously found to have refocused practitioner attention on the link between the marketing communications and marketing functions within strategic management, and to have served as a catalyst in shaking the advertising industry from its enduring myopic view by highlighting a more symbiotic relationship between the public relations and marketing functions.

3. *Symbolic use*: this involves the use of terms from corporate communications theories by practitioners for their symbolic or rhetorical value to legitimize courses of action and to appease senior management. The current craze about 'reputation management', for instance, suggests that this concept is, at least in part, used by practitioners for its symbolic leverage to acquire esteem and to help them step up to a more senior and strategic level in companies.

Taken together, these different types of theory use provide an overview and guidelines for professionals in selecting theoretical concepts, and for considering how these concepts may be used. Although it is a trite saying, determining the actual relevance and currency of theories is up to the individual communications practitioner. As with most management problems, corporate communications does not involve 'right' or 'wrong' answers or general principles, and practitioners should therefore question whatever theorizing and research there is on the subject and judge for themselves how it applies (conceptually or symbolically) to their own day-to-day practice. At the end of the day, the ideas and guidelines from theory – including the ones presented in this book – will become useful only when blended with what a professional already knows and believes.

By informing their practice with theory and research, practitioners can render some plausible account of how they perform, in other words, articulate a more detailed understanding of their own practice, and become *reflective practitioners* in the process.[10] Among the advantages of being a *reflective practitioner* is the ability to transfer skills to others – as one is conscious or aware of the conceptual insights and skills that one bears upon in practice – and the possibility of working out how to adapt one's practice and actions to changed circumstances rather than relying on intuition and trial and error (the so-called 'fly-by-the-seats-of-the-pants' approach),[11] the only route available to the practitioner who cannot reflect upon his/her practice. Theory serves as a resource for practitioners to question continuously and revise their views, and make sense of their situation and experiences that were not easily understood before. This *critical* and *reflective* ability that comes from practice informed by theory leads to more sophistication not only in the professional's understanding of the instrumental aspects of the work – what actions lead to what outcomes in what circumstances – but also in the interpreting of the broader economic, social and political context of which it is part; and in the understanding of the kind of society that their work is reproducing or changing.

The importance of theory-informed practice is further strengthened by observations from communications practice that suggest that informed reflection and the use of established concepts from the theoretical body of knowledge are needed to bolster the professional development and status of the corporate communications profession. Such professional development not only would lead to skill development and empowerment of communications practitioners (moving practitioners beyond a mere 'craft' orientation),[12] but also would enhance the perceived value and accountability of the corporate communications function in the eyes of others (notably the CEO and senior management) and substantially increase the likelihood of the function having an input into decision making and the strategic direction of companies.[13] This book responds to this need for reflective practice, or theory informed practice, by providing concepts, insights and findings from theory and research and stipulating through cases and management briefs how these might inform and guide professional practice.

1.3   Theory and practice perspectives on corporate communications

The preceding section has clarified the very different orientations of academics and practitioners to the corporate communications field, but stressed that, amid these differences, there needs to be an interplay of the theoretical and the practical to advance our knowledge of the field and the professional development of practice. In this section I continue outlining the various perspectives that have been brought to bear upon corporate communications from both the academic and practitioner ends, and provide an overview of the different ways in which one can look at the field.

At the theoretical end, as Figure 1.2 indicates, perspectives on corporate communications have been informed and guided by both communications theory and management theory, offering academic researchers various theoretical frameworks to describe, map and explain how organizations communicate and manage relationships with individuals and groups within their environments. Practice has, perhaps understandably, been more concerned with the question of what competencies and skills are needed to 'do the job' and with the trajectories of professional development involved.

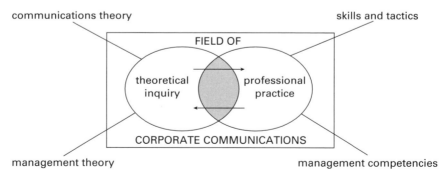

Figure 1.2   Theory and practice perspectives on corporate communications

Theory perspectives on corporate communications

The past decades have witnessed a marked increase in the volume of research into corporate communications. Initially, and until well after 1950, research on the management of communications between an organization and its stakeholders was scattered out among scientific disciplines and mainly completed by researchers working in areas such as social psychology, sociology and even economics and industrial relations.[15] More recently theoretical strands and research activities that previously were disparate have been woven together and integrated into a single theoretical discipline of corporate communications. This theoretical discipline, which in large parts of the world, particularly the US, is still labelled as 'public relations', has started to bring together a considerable amount of research and, as the nexus for these researches, added them up to a coherent whole. In doing so, the corporate communications field has increasingly started to grant itself credibility and independent status as a field of theoretical inquiry (instead of being defined as a subset of mass communications theory, for instance) and is now seen by many as 'maturing' in its theoretical scope, sophistication of its analysis and the many new insights that it has brought.[16]

As a result of this consolidation, two dominant theoretical strands can now be seen to form the foundation of the theoretical field of corporate communications: (1) theoretical perspectives informed by *communications theory*; and (2) theoretical perspectives informed by *management theory*. Both these theoretical strands subsume a huge variety of academic research that employs very different theoretical frameworks and focuses by and large on different areas of the corporate communications field (Table 1.2). The rhetorical and critical perspectives on corporate communications, the dominant theoretical perspectives within the communications strand, for their part, primarily focus on the rhetorical strategies and symbolism within messages issued by an organization, and the effects that these rhetorics and symbolism have on individuals and society as a whole.[17] Rhetorical analysis, dwelling upon communications theory, thus concerns itself principally with the phenomenon, process and effects of communications as rhetorical scholars believe that symbolic behaviour is the essence of how relationships between organizations and stakeholders or publics are created and influenced. Cheney and Dionisopoulous illustrate this claim for the centrality of communications by arguing that symbolism 'must be considered as the substance of organization', and that 'corporate communications must be self-conscious about its role in the organizational process (which is fundamentally rhetorical and symbolic) in responding to and in exercising power (in public discourse) and in shaping various identities (corporate and individual)'.[18]

The management strand of theory and research on corporate communications is in contrast with the rhetorical and critical perspectives not so much concerned with the act or process of communicating by organizations and its influence upon targeted groups and society at large, but with the management processes that professionals engage in to build relationships with stakeholders. From this management perspective, the focus is thus not on the symbolic act of communicating, as this is only seen as a means to an end (the end being the building and maintaining of favourable reputations and relationships with key stakeholders), but on the analysis, planning,

Table 1.2   Theoretical perspectives on corporate communications

Perspective	Theoretical frameworks used	Focus of inquiry
Communications theory: rhetorical and critical perspectives	Critical theory, social exchange theory, attitudinal change/persuasion theory, discourse theory, semiotic theory, co-orientation theory	Rhetorical analyses of organizational speech in mass media accounts Effects (including crisis and disruption) of corporate communications on social systems
Management theory: managerial and organization perspectives	Decision-making theory, stakeholder theory, resource dependency theory, systems theory, power-control theory, contingency theory, conflict theory, organization theory	Management of communication and relationships between organization and stakeholders in its environment Organizational context (role, location, structuring, professional development) of the corporate communications function

programming, tactical and evaluative activities engaged in for communications campaigns. Systems theory, for example, has suggested that for organizations to be effective they must concern themselves with the environment if they are to survive; and that corporate communications can be seen as the critical subunit of the management function of organizations, which is committed to that task. Following a systems perspective, Grunig and Hunt articulate the role of corporate communications as follows: 'they (the [corporate communications] managers) must control conflict and negotiate between the demands of the environment and the need for the organization to survive and prosper'.[19] Importantly, the management spectre through systems theory, or alternative theoretical frameworks within the management strand for that matter, focuses on the corporate communications function from the perspective and interest of the organization (not of individuals or society), and has as such been criticized by rhetorical and critical theorists as being too narrowly focused on corporate communications as a managerial profession, and on the organizational issues that have come to define it.[20]

On the whole, both the communications and management research traditions are strikingly different in the theoretical frameworks used, units of analysis and even the definition of corporate communications that each has put forward. Yet, these traditions need not be seen as in competition, but should rather be considered as alternative and complementary perspectives for advancing our theoretical knowledge of the field.[21] Rather than accepting one research tradition or arguing for one approach, it is because there are differing theoretical perspectives with different assumptions and directions that our overall knowledge of corporate communications is enriched. Nonetheless, as I have already started to suggest, the particular approach of this book is to advance a view of corporate communications from a strategic management perspective. The bulk of theory and research that is sourced to support this view is effectively from the management research tradition. This is not to devalue the communications tradition, or dismiss its currency, but the management tradition will, I believe, have greater value and a more immediate input into the perspectives of practitioners and their professional development.

Practice perspectives on corporate communications

Practitioner perspectives on corporate communications have invariably been at odds with theoretical and academic reflections on the field, as practitioners have always been more immediately concerned with the 'tricks of the trade', or, put differently, the skills and competencies needed by a practitioner to carry out the tasks that fall within the corporate communications remit. At the very start, at the turn of the twentieth century and right up until the 1960s, the period when press agents and public relations officers were employed by corporations to channel and disseminate information into the public realm, emphasis was laid within practice on the vocational skills that were needed to do the job. Communications as an area of professional practice was in itself seen as a vocation and in need of talented individuals who not only possessed a number of 'personality characteristics' such as charisma, patience, discretion and honesty, but had also acquired a talent for handling people and for coming up with startling new ideas. Sam Black, for instance, commented in 1954 that 'it is not necessary to have had any specialized training to possess a good public relations outlook', as 'so much depends on natural common sense and good taste'.[22] Edward Bernays, one of the most influential figures in the field, equally emphasized in 1952 that communications management 'rests fundamentally on ideas', generated by a practitioner who is a 'man of character and integrity, who has acquired a sense of judgment and logic without having lost the ability to think creatively and imaginatively'.[23]

This *vocational perspective* on practice, which alongside the important personality characteristics of a practitioner also emphasized a whole range of writing and presentational skills, has, primarily due to professional pressures, been complemented with a management view since the early 1970s. Embedded in new understandings and applications of analysis and planning for communications programmes, the management view emphasizes that a whole range of new competencies or abilities need to be acquired by the practitioner including the ability to conduct research, develop strategy and plan for communications programmes.[24] Communications itself needs to be seen as a management function (alongside the other management functions of finance, human resources, marketing, research and development, and operations) within the organization. And practitioners, it has been suggested, need to approach their work not so much as 'technicians', who are merely concerned with producing communications materials and disseminating information, but as more rounded 'managers' who use research and planning as the bedrock for their communications programmes and are able to think strategically about the use of communications for organizational problems.[25]

The *management perspective* has now, at the start of the twenty-first century, come to full gestation within practice. The 'management mindset' has become ingrained in the heads of many communications practitioners, influencing how these professionals approach their work, and the higher education sector that caters for their development has increasingly shown a preoccupation with communications as a management function. In fact, the traditional location of under- and post-graduate courses on communications in schools of communications and journalism in the US, UK and Europe (e.g. Annenberg School of Communications UCLA, Amsterdam School of Communications Research), following a vocational view of the profession, has over the past decade been rivalled by an increased uptake of corporate communications (as a separate degree or module) in management departments and business schools worldwide (e.g. the Tuck School of Business, Leeds University Business School and the Rotterdam School of Management). Paul Argenti, a professor who teaches corporate communications on the MBA programme at Tuck School of Business, Darthmouth College, gives the following explanation for this trend:

> business schools are the most appropriate home for the discipline, because like other functional areas within the corporation (such as marketing, finance, production and human resource management), corporate communications exists as a real and important part of most organizations. As such, it should rightfully be housed in that branch of the academy that deals with business administration or graduate schools of business.[26]

In 1996, the Education and Training Committee of the Institute of Public Relations in the UK struck a similar chord when it suggested that on the whole it preferred to see corporate communications located in business and management curricula rather than in schools of communications and journalism, from the perspective that the standing of corporate communications needs to be protected and promoted 'as a strategic and vigorous *management* discipline.[27]

While not ignoring the importance of vocational skills to past and present communications practitioners, the current view in practice is indeed very much geared towards promoting and adopting communications as a management discipline. Recent surveys indicate, however, that despite this interest, and the related understanding among practitioners that new sets of management competencies need to be learned, the large majority of them are still lagging behind in their professional development.[28] The need for an understanding of corporate communications as a management function is thus timely, requiring first of all a greater understanding of the strategies and activities that it involves as well as the competencies and skills that it requires from practitioners. The following section outlines this strategic management perspective on corporate communications, and the themes and topics that will be discussed in the remainder of the book.

1.4   The strategic management perspective on corporate communications

Corporate communications can be seen as a management function; a perspective favoured and aspired to by communications practitioners, and a view central to much corporate communications theory and research.

Corporate, management and business communications

When seen in such a manner, corporate communications can, for definitional purposes, be further distinguished from other professional forms of communications within organizations, including business communications and management communications. Corporate communications focuses on the organization as a whole and the important task of how an organization is presented to all of its key stakeholders, both internal and external. Business communications and management communications are more technical and applied[29] – focusing on writing, presentational and other communications skills – and their focus is largely restricted to interpersonal situations, such as dyads and small groups *within* the organization. Business communications, for its part, tends to focus almost exclusively on skills, especially writing, and looks towards the communicator himself or herself for its focus, while corporate communications focuses on the entire company and the entire function of management.[30] The corporate communications function, as I have already started to suggest above, is also broader than vocational, technical skills alone because of the concepts, principles and management approaches that fall under it. More specific, the function's central concepts of stakeholder, corporate identity and reputation (see below), cannot be understood, approached, let alone managed, by mastering communications skills alone. Communications practitioners, or rather 'managers', thus need management competencies to analyse the position and reputation of their own organization with all of its stakeholders, determine the corporate profile or 'identity' (i.e. the corporate values, messages, images and stories) that needs to be projected, develop and plan communications programmes for it, and evaluate the results that these programmes have achieved afterwards.

Corporate communications as a management function

A central concern stemming from this understanding of corporate communications is the need for organizational structures, rules, routines and effective procedures that actually facilitate this process of decision making and execution concerning corporate communications.[31] Having such structures, routines and procedures in place becomes even more pertinent in consideration of the many communications practitioners, working across all areas of internal and external communications, that need to be coordinated in their work so that a clear, forceful and consistent image of the organization is projected to each and every one of its stakeholders. In other words, corporate communications is not just a catchy umbrella term for the many different communications disciplines in an organization, but, as a management *function*, is actively charged with overseeing and coordinating the work done by practitioners within each of them. Van Riel, in his book on corporate communications, equally suggests that corporate communications is 'an *instrument* of management by means of which all consciously used forms of internal and external communications are harmonized as effectively and efficiently as possible', with the overall objective of creating 'a favorable basis for relationships with groups upon which the company is dependent'.[32]

Together with this view of corporate communications as a management function comes the understanding that corporate communications is at the same time a managerial profession from the perspective of practitioners, suggesting that a number of management competencies need to be acquired by practitioners (alongside the requisite vocational skills) to work and survive within it. The concept of *strategic management* enters into, and elaborates on, both these levels. At the level of the profession,

Table 1.3 Characteristics of strategic management and operational management

	Strategic management	Operational management
Scope	Organization-wide/fundamental (strategic)	Operationally specific and tactical (craft)
Nature of strategies	Changing and varied (in response to environment and changing corporate objectives)	Routinized and programmed (executing and fine-tuning existing strategies)
Time-frame	Long-term implications	Short-term implications
Role of practitioner	Reflective and strategic	Pragmatic and tactical

the adjective 'strategic' in strategic management suggests that professionals need to be able to reflect upon their practice and critically understand their actions, and need to manoeuvre and devise communications programmes in the light of (changing) corporate objectives. A second sense in which the adjective 'strategic' plays a part is in the way in which corporate communications, as a management function, is put to use in and for organizations. Organizations need to understand, from a strategic perspective, how corporate communications can work most effectively; and how it can be used for corporate objectives and to increase organizational performance.[33] In other words, from an organizational perspective, the interest is in knowing how the management function of corporate communications can be used to meet corporate objectives, how the function therefore needs to be organized, and with what resources it needs to be vamped to fulfil its potential. The nature of 'strategic management' in this sense also suggests that corporate communications is valued for its strategic input into decision making and the overall corporate strategy, and not just for its operational excellence in managing communications resources and programmes already deployed within the context and guidance of an existing strategy. The strategic management of corporate communications – as opposed to the mere operational management of the function – thus implies a more organization-wide or corporate scope and involvement where communications is integrally linked to corporate objectives and with generally more long-term implications, instead of an operationally specific scope with more short-term and tactical implications. Table 1.3 summarizes some of these differences between the strategic and operational management of corporate communications.

Characteristics of corporate communications as a management function

The previous sections of this chapter have already started to suggest that corporate communications can be characterized as:

1. A *management function* that requires communications practitioners to look at all communications in a holistic manner, and to *link the communications strategy to the corporate strategy and corporate objectives*. Communications is as such not seen as a

fragmented range of tactics that are employed impromptu, but as a strategic and planned set of actions that follow from the overall corporate strategy.

2. A *managerial framework* for *managing all communications* used by an organization to build reputations and relationships with stakeholders in its environment. This does not necessarily mean that communications disciplines, and the practitioners responsible for them, are integrated into one and the same department. Corporate communications offers a managerial framework that goes above and beyond departmental boundaries, and enables the coordination of the work of the communications practitioners involved.

3. A *vocabulary of concepts and sets of techniques* for understanding and managing communications between an organization and its *stakeholders*. Rather than considering the outside environment of an organization primarily in terms of markets or publics, many organizations and the communications practitioners who work within them now view the environment in terms of the various stakeholder groups upon which the organization is dependent.

Overall, if a definition of corporate communications is required, these characteristics can provide a basis for one:

> **Corporate communications is a management function that offers a framework and vocabulary for the effective coordination of all means of communications with the overall purpose of establishing and maintaining favourable reputations with stakeholder groups upon which the organization is dependent.**

A consequence of these characteristics of corporate communications is that they are likely to be *complex in nature*. This is especially so in organizations with wide geographic scope, such as multinational firms, or with wide ranges of products or services, where the coordination of communications often appears to be a balancing act between corporate headquarters and the various divisions and business units involved. However, there are other significant problems in developing effective corporate communications strategies. Corporate communications demands an *integrated approach* to communications management. Unlike functional problems and a more specialist frame of reference, corporate communications transcends the specialties of individual communications practitioners (e.g. advertising, direct marketing, media relations, etc.) and crosses functional boundaries to harness the *strategic interests of the organization at large*. When attuned to the strategic direction and scope of the organization as a whole, corporate communications is also a way of managing communications that is *relevant for all types of organizations*, however large and whatever sector they operate in. It has often been thought that only large organizations in the private sector (e.g. Fortune 500 companies) need a vocabulary and tools for orchestrating their communications. Smaller companies, including small manufacturing companies and family-owned businesses, as well as larger organizations in the public sector such as hospitals and universities, may indeed have less communications resources and little fully-fledged communications disciplines when compared to large private firms. However, communications to the various stakeholder groups of these kinds of organizations still needs to be aligned and integrated: a need that can be met by corporate communications as a guiding philosophy.

A definition of corporate communications has been given. Of course, any definition has limitations and may lead to lengthy discussions about its exact scope and precision, and whether everyone would agree with it. In fact, there are different definitions according to different authors. There is also a variety of terms used in relation to corporate communications, so it is worth devoting a little space to clarifying some of them. Table 1.4 defines the key terms that readers will come across in this and other books on corporate communications, and that form the vocabulary of the management function of corporate communications, and also shows how these relate to a specific organization – in this case British Airways.

Not all of these terms are always used in corporate communications books. Moreover, it may or may not be that mission, objectives, strategies and so on are written down precisely or indeed formally laid down within an organization. As will be shown in Chapter 4, a mission or corporate identity, for instance, might sometimes more sensibly be conceived as that which is implicit or can be deduced about an organization from what it is doing and communicating. However, as a general guideline the following terms are often used in combination with one another.

A *mission* is a general expression of the overriding purpose of the organization, which, ideally, is in line with the values and expectations of major stakeholders and concerned with the scope and boundaries of the organization. It is often referred to with the simple question 'what business are we in?'. A *vision or strategic intent* is the desired future state of the organization. It is an aspirational view of the general direction in which the organization wants to go, as formulated by senior management, and requires the energies and commitment of members of the organization. *Objectives and goals* are the more precise (short-term) statements of direction in line with the formulated vision, which are to be achieved by strategic initiatives or strategies. *Strategies* involve actions and communications that are linked to objectives, and are often specified in terms of specific organizational functions (e.g. finance, operations, human resources, etc.). Operations strategies for streamlining operations and human resource strategies for staff support and development initiatives are common to every organization as well as, increasingly, full scale corporate communications strategies.

Key to having a corporate communications strategy is the notion of a *corporate identity*: the basic profile that an organization wants to project to all of its important stakeholder groups and how it aims to be known by these various groups in terms of the *corporate images* and *reputations* that they hold. To ensure that different stakeholders indeed conceive of an organization in a favourable and broadly consistent manner, and also in line with the projected corporate identity, organizations need to go to great lengths to *integrate* all of their *communications* from brochures to websites in tone, themes, visuals and logos.

The *stakeholder* concept takes centre stage within corporate communications management at the expense of considering the environment just in terms of markets and publics. This is not so much the result of a different way of thinking about markets and publics, as these are still important groups to be addressed by the organization, but concerns a shift towards a more inclusive view in which the organization recognizes a larger number of groups upon which it is dependent (and that literally hold a 'stake' in the organization). Stakeholders include groups that have primarily an economic or contractual relationship with the organization such as employees,

Table 1.4 The vocabulary of corporate communications

Concept	Definition	Example: British Airways*
Mission	Overriding purpose in line with the values or expectations of stakeholders	'British Airways is aiming to set new industry standards in customer service and innovation, deliver the best financial performance and evolve from being an airline to a world travel business with the flexibility to stretch its brand into new business areas'
Vision/strategic intent	The long-term aims and aspirations of the company for itself.	'To become the undisputed leader in world travel by ensuring that BA is the customer's first choice through the delivery of an unbeatable travel experience'
Corporate objectives and goals	(Precise) statement of aims or purpose	'To be a good neighbor, concerned for the community and the environment', 'to provide overall superior service and good value for money in every market segment in which we compete', 'to excel in anticipating and quickly responding to customer needs and competitor activity'
Strategies	The ways or means in which the corporate objectives are to be achieved and put into effect	'Continuing emphasis on consistent quality of customer service and the delivery to the marketplace of value for money through *customer-oriented initiatives* (on-line booking service, strategic alliances) and to arrange all the elements of our service so that they collectively generate a particular experience – building trust with our shareholders, employees, customers, neighbors and with our critics, through commitment to good practice and societal reporting'
Corporate identity	The profile and values communicated by an organization	'The world's favorite airline' (this corporate identity with its associated brand values of service, quality, innovation, cosmopolitanism and British-ness is carried through in positioning, design, livery, and communications)
Corporate image	The immediate set of meanings inferred by an individual in confrontation/response to one or more signals from or about a particular organization at a single point in time	'Very recently I got a ticket booked to London, and when reporting at the airport I was shown the door by BA staff. I was flatly told that the said flight in which I was to travel was already full so my ticket was not valid any further and the airline would try to arrange for a seat in some other flight. You can just imagine how embarrassed I felt *at that moment of time*. To add ghee to the fire, the concerned official of BA had not even a single word of apology to say' (customer of BA).
Corporate reputation	An individual's collective representation of past images of an organization (induced through either communication or past experiences) established over time	'Through the Executive Club program, British Airways has developed a reputation as an innovator in developing direct relationships with its customers and in tailoring its services to enhance these relationships' (longstanding supplier of BA).

(Continued)

Table 1.4 (Continued)

Concept	Definition	Example: British Airways*
Stakeholder	Any group or individual that can affect or is affected by the achievement of the organization's objectives	'Employees, consumers, investors and shareholders, community, aviation business and suppliers, government, trade unions, NGOs, and society at large'
Public	People who mobilize themselves against the organization on the basis of some common issue or concern to them	'Local residents of Heathrow Airport appealed in November 2002 against the Government and British Airways concerning the issue of night flights at Heathrow airport. The UK Government denied that night flights violated local residents' human rights. British Airways intervened in support of the UK Government claiming that there is a need to continue the present night flights regime'
Market	A defined group for whom a product is or may be in demand (and for whom an organization creates and maintains products and service offerings)	'The market for British Airways flights consists of passengers who search for superior service over and beyond the basic transportation involved'
Issues	An unsettled matter (which is ready for a decision) or a point of conflict between an organization and one or more publics	'Night flights at Heathrow Airport: noise and inconvenience for local residents and community'
Communications	The internal and external communications techniques and media that are used towards internal and external groups	'Newsletters, promotion packages, consultation forums, advertising campaigns, corporate design and code of conduct, free publicity/public relations …'
Integration	The act of coordinating all communications so that the corporate identity is effectively and consistently communicated to internal and external groups	'British Airways aims to communicate its brand values of service, quality, innovation, cosmopolitanism and British-ness through all its communications in a consistent and effective manner'

*extracted from British Airways annual reports and the world wide web.

unions, distributors, suppliers, shareholders and customers, as well as groups whose relationship is more diffuse and also primarily societal or moral in nature, such as the media, special interest groups, non-governmental organizations (NGOs), community members and the government. A breaking point for the stakeholder concept is that organizations have increasingly become aware of the need for an 'inclusive' and 'balanced' stakeholder management approach that involves actively communicating with and being involved with all stakeholder groups upon which the organization is dependent and not just with shareholders or customers.[34] Such awareness stems from high profile cases where undue attention to certain stakeholder groups led to crisis and severe damage for the organizations concerned, government initiatives in the US, UK and the European community that favour stakeholder management and social reporting, and influential think-tanks such as Tomorrow's Company and management consultancies that continue to stress its importance.

All of these terms will be discussed in detail in the remainder of the book, but it is worthwhile already to emphasize how some of them hang together. The nub of what matters in Table 1.4 is that corporate communications is geared towards establishing favourable corporate images and reputations with all of its stakeholder groups, so that these groups act in a way that is conducive to the organization. In other words, through favourable images and reputations existing and prospective customers will purchase products and services, members of the community will appreciate the organization, investors will grant financial resources, and so on. It is the spectre of a favoured or damaged reputation – of having to make costly reversals in policies or practices as a result of stakeholder pressure or, worse, as a consequence of a self-inflicted wound – that overhangs the urgency with which integrated stakeholder management now needs to be treated.

The definitions and vocabulary presented furthermore point to a number of topics that define this strategic management perspective on corporate communications. Each of these topics is discussed in more detail in the remaining chapters of this book. A first central topic involves the process of developing *communications strategy* in line with the overall corporate strategy of an organization, and in account of the important stakeholders and issues that are of concern to that organization. As Chapter 4 outlines, this requires an understanding of the strategic value and contribution of corporate communications to the organization and a grounded insight into how strategy is developed, how the organizational environment and its stakeholders can be analysed and mapped, how strategic action is taken, how communications programmes are developed, and how the effects of communications can be identified and tracked. Another important topic involves the question of how communications practitioners and their work can be best organized. The *organization of communications* in terms of the hierarchical position of communications within the organization, and the integration and coordination of communications work, is covered in an in-depth manner in Chapter 5. Viewing corporate communications as a management function also involves an understanding of the various competencies and skills that it requires of different communications practitioners, and the 'manager' and 'technician' roles that these practitioners fulfil within the corporation. Chapter 6 deals with the subject of *professional roles and competencies* and suggests ways in which communications practitioners can be supported in their work and development. Each of these topics is, as mentioned, covered in an in-depth manner in the remaining chapters of the book by combining knowledge from the theory and research domain with insights from best practice cases from organizations in the US, UK, continental Europe and elsewhere. In all, corporate communications thus represents a particular view and philosophy of communications management and embodies a number of strategic, structural and professional changes. In the remainder of the book, the term 'corporate communications' is explicitly used when referring to this particular perspective of communications, while the terms communications, public relations, public affairs and marketing communications are used as general and more descriptive terms for talking about and characterizing communications practice.

1.5   Chapter summary

All organizations, of all sizes, sectors and operating in very different societies, must find ways to successfully establish and nurture relationships with their stakeholders upon which they are economically and socially dependent. The management function that has arisen to deal with this task is corporate communications; and this chapter has made a start with circumscribing the importance and key characteristics of it. For one, as we have seen, depending on whether one is looking at corporate communications through the eyes of a theorist or practitioner, the spectacle is rather different. Yet, despite this divergence in views, both the 'theory' and 'practice' camps now appear to converge on their view of corporate communications as a management function. The remaining chapters in Part 1 of the book describe in more detail how corporate communications historically emerged and how it has grown into the management function that it is today. Chapter 2 discusses the changing socio-economic conditions that led to the emergence and increasing importance of corporate communications. Chapter 3 discusses three key theoretical concepts within the strategic management view of corporate communications: stakeholder management, corporate identity and reputation. Each of these concepts has also amassed huge interest in recent years in the world of organizations.

   An organization, as mentioned, needs to have a public profile and favourable reputation with most, if not all, of the stakeholder groups upon which it is dependent, and a challenging – at times daunting – task is to develop an integrated communications strategy that clearly signals the strategic direction of the organization and demonstrates a commitment to its stakeholder groups. The many layers that are involved in communications strategy, including decision making concerning communications strategy, the analysis of the organizational environment and its stakeholders, the development of communications programmes, and the measurement of communications effects (i.e. corporate reputations) are covered in detail in Chapter 4 in Part 2 of the book. Communications strategy and the overall responsibilities of corporate communications also cut across different domains and departments (e.g. marketing, public relations) of the organization, making the question of how organizations can design structures that facilitate interaction between communications practitioners and the integration of their work a very significant one indeed.[35] Chapter 5 answers this question in detail. Chapter 6, the last chapter in Part 2 of the book, zooms in on the person of the communications practitioner in terms of the required competencies and skills for enacting particular roles within the organization.

The issue of training and development of these practitioners is in part covered in Chapter 6, but is also carried over and further discussed in Chapter 7, the last chapter of the book. Chapter 7 also provides a number of directions and recommendations for the function and profession of corporate communications in the future.

At this point, all of these themes and issues may seem a little overwhelming. I hope that most readers feel a little overwhelmed. Corporate communications is an exceptionally complex management function, and up until now the intricate strategic, structural and political ideas and issues that characterize the function have been largely uncharted territory. True, there is a large number of books, training programmes, and consultant gimmicks out there that depict effective corporate communications as the simple application of a number of 'proven' tools and techniques. Unfortunately, these depictions are as glib as they are misleading. There are a number of principles, insights and tools that can be turned to in most corporate communications situations, but they are neither simple, foolproof, nor generally applicable to every case. My goal in the remaining chapters of this book is to explain those principles, insights and tools and indicate how communications practitioners can analyse and understand the complexities that they face in their day-to-day work and choose appropriate strategic responses.

Key terms

Business communications	Operational management
Corporate communications	Practice
Corporate identity	Professional development
Corporate image	Public
Corporate reputation	Reflective practitioner
Integration	Stakeholder
Issues	Strategic management
Management communications	Strategies
Market	Theory
Mission	Vision

Notes

[1] *Financial Times* (2003), 'Schools look at ways to put their house in order', special report on business education, 20 January.

[2] See for instance Holbrook, M.B. (1985), 'Why business is bad for consumer research', in Hirschman, E.C., and Holbrook, M.B. (eds), *Advances in Consumer Research* (volume 13). Ann Arbor, MI: Association for Consumer Research, pp. 145–156; Botan, H. (1989), 'Theory development in public relations', in Botan, C.H., and Hazleton, V. (eds), *Public Relations Theory*. Hillsdale, NJ: Lawrence Erlbaum Associates, pp. 99–110.

[3] Kover, A.J. (1976), 'Careers and non-communications: the case of academic and applied marketing research', *Journal of Marketing Research*, 13 (November), 339–344.

[4] Cornelissen, J.P. (2000), 'Toward an understanding of the use of public relations theories in public relations practice', *Public Relations Review*, 26 (3), 315–326.

[5]The Reputation Institute is a private research organization founded by Charles Fombrun (Stern School of Business, New York University) and Cees van Riel (Erasmus University, Rotterdam), bringing together a global network of academic institutions, market research agencies, communications consultancies and corporations, with the purpose of advancing knowledge about corporate reputation measurement (see http://www.reputationinstitute.com/).

[6]Brinberg, D., and Hirschman, E.C. (1986), 'Multiple orientations for the conduct of marketing research: an analysis of the academic/practitioner distinction', *Journal of Marketing*, 50, 161–173, p. 168.

[7]Lewin, K. (1945), 'The research center for group dynamics at Massachusetts Institute of Technology', *Sociometry,* 8, 126–136, p. 129.

[8]Armstrong, J.S., and Schultz, R. (1994), 'Principles involving marketing policies: an empirical assessment', *Marketing Letters*, 4, 253–265, and Cornelissen, J.P., and Lock, A.R. (2002) 'Advertising research and its influence upon managerial practice', *Journal of Advertising Research*, 42 (3), 50–55.

[9]Schön, D. (1983), *The Reflective Practitioner: How Professionals Think in Action.* New York: Basic Books.

[10]Ibid.

[11]Broom, G.M., and Dozier, D.M. (1990), *Using Research in Public Relations: Applications to Program Management.* Englewood Cliffs, NJ: Prentice Hall.

[12]Grunig, J.E. (ed.) (1992), *Excellence in Public Relations and Communications Management.* Hillsdale, NJ: Lawrence Erlbaum Associates.

[13]See for instance Lauzen, M.M. (1995), 'Public relations manager involvement in strategic issue diagnosis', *Public Relations Review*, 21, 287–304; and Moss, D., Warnaby, G., and Newman, A.J. (2000), 'Public relations practitioner role enactment at the senior management level within UK companies', *Journal of Public Relations Research*, 12 (4), 277–307.

[14]This management brief is based on insights from Astley, W.G., and Zammuto, R.F. (1992) 'Organization science, managers, and language games', *Organization Science,* 3, 443–460; Cornelissen, J.P. (2000), 'Toward an understanding of the use of public relations theories in public relations practice', *Public Relations Review*, 26 (3), 315–326; and Cornelissen, J.P., and Lock, A.R. (2002), 'Advertising research and its influence upon managerial practice', *Journal of Advertising Research*, 42 (3), 50–55.

[15]Redding, C.W. (1985), 'Stumbling towards identity: the emergence of organizational communications as a field of study', in McPhee, R.D., and Tompkins, P.K. (eds), *Organizational Communications: Traditional Themes and New Directions.* Beverly Hills, CA: Sage, pp. 15–54; Grunig (1992).

[16]Grunig (1992).

[17]Toth, E.L. (1992), 'The case for pluralistic studies of public relations: rhetorical, critical and systems perspectives', in Toth, E.L., and Heath, R.L. (eds), *Rhetorical and Critical Approaches to Public Relations.* Hillsdale, NJ: Lawrence Erlbaum Associates, pp. 3–15.

[18]Cheney, G., and G.N. Dionisopolous (1989), 'Public relations? No, relations with publics: A rhetorical–organizational approach to contemporary corporate communications', in Botan, C.H., and Hazleton, V. (eds), *Public Relations Theory.* Hillsdale, NJ: Lawrence Erlbaum Associates, pp. 135–157. p. 137.

[19]Grunig, J.E., and Hunt, T. (1984), *Managing Public Relations.* New York: Holt, Rinehart & Winston, p. 9.

[20]Dozier D.M., and Lauzen M.M. (2000), 'Liberating the intellectual domain from the practice: public relations, activism, and the role of the scholar', *Journal of Public Relations Research,* 12, 3–22.

[21]Toth (1992), p. 12.

[22]Black, S. (1954), 'The need for mutual understanding', *Public Relations*, 6 (4), 35.

[23]Bernays, E. (1952), *Public Relations.* Norman: University of Oklahoma Press, VII, p. 126.

[24]See Cutlip, S.M., and Center, A.H. (1978), *Effective Public Relations*. Englewood Cliffs, NJ: Prentice Hall; White, J., and Mazur, L. (1995), *Strategic Communications Management: Making Public Relations Work*. Wokingham: Addison-Wesley.

[25]Dozier, D.M. (1992), 'The organizational roles of communicators and public relations practitioners', in Grunig, J.E. (ed.), *Excellence in Public Relations and Communication Management*. Hillsdale, NJ: Lawrence Erlbaum Associates, pp. 327–356.

[26]Argenti, P.A. (1996), 'Corporate communications as a discipline: toward a definition', *Management Communications Quarterly*, 10 (1), 73–97, p. 74.

[27]Institute of Public Relations (1996), *Criteria and Procedures for IPR Recognition of Public Relations Programs*. London: IPR.

[28]Moss, Warnaby and Newman (2000); Marion, G. (1998), 'Corporate communications managers in large firms: new challenges', *European Management Journal*, 16 (6), 660–671.

[29]Shelby (1993), 'Organizational, business, management and corporate communications: an analysis of boundaries and relationships', *Journal of Business Communications*, 30 (3), 241–267.

[30]Argenti (1996), p. 84, Shelby (1993), p. 254.

[31]Van Riel, C.B.M. (1995), *Principles of Corporate Communications*. London: Prentice Hall, p. 22.

[32]Ibid., p. 26.

[33]Van Riel, C.B.M. (1997), 'Research in corporate communications: overview of an emerging field', *Management Communication Quarterly*, 11 (2), 288–309.

[34]Tomorrow's company (1996), *The Role of Business in a Changing World*. London: The Royal Society for the Encouragement of Arts, Manufactures and Commerce.

[35]Gronstedt, A. (1996), 'Integrated communications at America's leading total quality management corporations', *Public Relations Review*, 22 (1), 25–42.

Chapter 2
Corporate Communications in Historical Perspective: Marketing, Public Relations and Corporate Communications

Central themes

- By the early 1900s, every organization realized (albeit at first rather reluctantly) that it had to engage through communications with a number of groups in its environment, including the general public and consumer markets, to remain economically afloat.

- The task of managing communications between an organization on the one hand, and the general public and consumers on the other, was for the majority of the twentieth century defined by the public relations and marketing functions.

- Through socio-economic developments, and the practical need to coordinate and draw communications disciplines together, disciplines previously falling under marketing and public relations headings have increasingly been integrated into the corporate communications function.

- Many organizations around the globe have experienced a shift from being in markets characterized by rigid systems of mass production and consumption to more flexible and increasingly competitive marketplaces. This, together with a greater call from society for 'corporate citizenship', has pushed many organizations into stakeholder management strategies.

- Corporate communications is the management function that has come to fruition in this stakeholder era, and caters for the need to build and manage relationships with stakeholder groups upon which the organization is economically and socially dependent.

2.1 Introduction

The evolution of communications disciplines and techniques that are used by organizations to promote, publicize or generally inform relevant individuals and groups within society about their affairs began at least 150 years ago. It is the product of the dependencies and ties between business and society, with communications having changed over time in its scope and practices because of altered perspectives on the role of business in society. Starting with the Industrial Revolution and continuing right up until the 1930s, an era predominantly characterized by mass production and consumption, the type of communications that were employed by organizations largely consisted of publicity, promotions and selling activities towards buoyant markets. The move towards less stable, more competitive markets, coinciding with greater government interference in many markets and harsher economic circumstances, led from the 1930s onwards to a constant redefining of the scope and practices of communications in many organizations across the Western world. Ever since, changing socio-economic dynamics have guided organizations, and over the years have not only forced communications professionals to rethink their discipline and develop new practices and areas of expertise (such as issues management and corporate identity), but have also in many cases changed the nature of the communications process itself from down-right persuasion and propaganda to a more open and symmetrical dialogue between an organization and important groups in its environment.

Communications management in historical perspective

This chapter is about the changing definition, scope and practices of communications management, and the socio-economic dynamics that challenged and triggered its evolution. The central argument is that the nature of communications management as we now know it, in terms of the way in which it is practised in contemporary organizations, is steeped in historical circumstances and developments. Disentangling the historical forces that have informed and shaped contemporary communications practice is therefore considered here as a crucial first step towards contextualizing, understanding and framing corporate communications, the most recent and widespread embodiment of communications management. To do this, a brief historical sketch will be provided of the two dominant perspectives (or rather colonizations) of communications management that preceded the corporate communications view: public relations and marketing. The central tenets of each of these perspectives, and their historical development, are first outlined in this chapter, followed by a discussion of the market dynamics and organizational drivers that provoked changes in the way in which organizations approached their communications.

As the chapter outlines, it is now increasingly common in communications practice to see communications disciplines and associated activities not so much from the particular, rather narrow, perspectives of public relations and marketing alone, but from a more integrated conception that advocates seeing the whole range of communications disciplines and activities in conjunction. Corporate communications is a perspective upon communications management, and a way of practicing it, that departs from this integrated perspective. The final section of this chapter is concerned with outlining the key changes that corporate communications has brought to the practice of communications management. By the time this chapter draws to an end, the reader should thus be able to understand the historical conditions and circumstances that led to the corporate communications view of managing and practising communications and to see corporate communications as a vital part of the total management effort of organizations in today's business climate and society.

2.2 The birth of communications management

As the words at the beginning of this chapter suggest, communications management – any type of communication activity undertaken by an organization to inform, persuade or otherwise relate to individuals and groups in its outside environment – is not terribly new. Whenever people have depended on one another to complete tasks or meet their needs, they have formed organizations. The act of organizing, at first in clans, families and feudal structures, already required people to communicate with other workers, as well as (prospective) buyers. The modernization of society, first through farming and trade, and later through industrialization, created ever more complex organizations with more complicated communications needs. The large industrial corporations that emerged with the Industrial Revolution – predominantly at the turn of the twentieth century, first in the United States (US) and the United Kingdom (UK), and from there spreading out over the rest of the Western world – in particular required, in contrast to what had gone before, professional communications officers and a more *organized* form of handling publicity and promotions. These large and complex industrial firms, and the support of society that they sought, made it clear that effective communication techniques and campaigns needed to be developed by expert professionals to gain and maintain that support. Walter Lippmann in his famed book *Public Opinion* (1922) wrote in the early years of the twentieth century about this need of modern industrial organizations for publicity makers and press agents to inform and persuade the general public and to sell their wares:

> The development of the publicity man is a clear sign that the facts of modern life do not spontaneously take a shape in which they can be known. They must be given a shape by somebody, and since in the daily routine reporters cannot give a shape to facts, and since there is little disinterested organization of intelligence, the need for some formulation is being met by those interested parties.[1]

In the first instance, and right up until the early 1900s, organizations hired publicists, press agents, promoters and propagandists to this end. These press agents played on the credulity of the general public in its longing to be entertained, whether deceived or not, and many advertisements and press releases in those days were in fact exaggerated to the point where they were outright lies. While such tactics can perhaps now be denounced from an ethical standpoint, the 'press agentry' approach to the general public (see Table 2.1) was taken at that time, simply because organizations and their press agents could get away with it. At the turn of the nineteenth century, industrial magnates and large organizations in the Western world were answering to no one and were immune to pressure from government, labour or public opinion. This situation was aptly illustrated at the time by a comment made by William Henry Vanderbilt, head of the New York Central Railroad, when asked about the public rampage and uproar that his company's railroad extensions would cause. 'The public be damned', he simply responded. Yet, the age of unchecked industrial growth soon ended, and industrial organizations in the Western world faced new challenges to their established ways of doing business. The new century began with a cry from 'muckrakers' – investigative journalists who exposed scandals associated with power,

Table 2.1 Historical models of public relations

Characteristic	Press agentry/publicity	Public information	Managerial discipline
Purpose	Propaganda	Dissemination of information	Persuasion and/or mutual understanding/accommodation
Nature of communication	One-way complete, truth not essential	One-way, truth important	Two-way, (im)balanced effects
Communications model	Source → receiver	Source → receiver	Source → receiver ← feedback, actor ↔ actor
Nature of research	Little if any	Little, readership readability	Formative attitude evaluation
Quote	'public be damned'	'public be informed'	'public be influenced, involved and/or accommodated'
Communications disciplines involved	Publicity (propaganda)	Publicity, media relations	Publicity, media relations, employee communications, investor relations, general counsel, government affairs…
Period	1800–1899	1900–1940	1940–1990

capitalism and government corruption, and raised public awareness of the unethical and sometimes harmful practices of business. To heed these 'muckrakers', many large organizations hired writers and publicists to be spokespeople for the organization and to disseminate general information to these 'muckraking' groups and the public at large so as to gain public approval of its decisions and behaviour (the 'public information' period mentioned in Table 2.1).[2] At the same time, while demand still outweighed production, the growth of many markets stabilized and even curtailed, and organizations also started to hire advertising agents to promote their products to existing and prospective customers in an effort to consolidate their overall sales.

In the following decade (1900–1910) economic reform in the US and UK and intensified public scepticism brought it home to organizations that these writers, publicists and advertising agents were needed on a more continuous basis, and should not just be hired 'on and off' as press agents had been in the past. These practitioners were therefore brought 'in-house', and communications activities to both the general public and the markets served by the organization as a result became credited as more fully-fledged functions, rather than just as fragmentary, ad hoc publicity stunts.[3] This development effectively brought the first inkling of expertise in the area of communications and planted the seeds for the two professional functions that were to define for the majority of the twentieth century how communications management was approached and understood in organizations: *public relations* and *marketing*.

Both the public relations and marketing functions have sprung from the understanding that has ever since become established in the industrialized world; namely that an organization, in order to prosper, needs to be concerned with issues of public concern (i.e. public relations), as well as with ways of effectively bringing products to markets (i.e. marketing). Starting from this understanding, both the public relations and marketing functions have gone through considerable professional

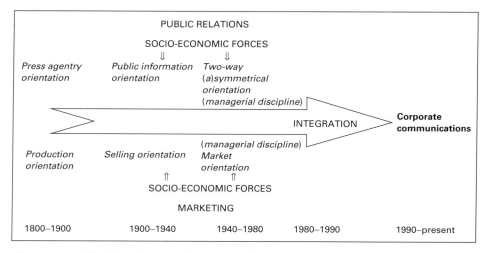

Figure 2.1 The historical development of public relations and marketing

development, shaped and guided by changing socio–economic conditions (see Figure 2.1), yet largely in their own separate ways. Figure 2.1 displays the route that each of these two functions has followed in the twentieth century, largely independently, but with a trend emerging in the 1980s, and carried on through the 1990s and beyond, that both functions should be brought together, integrated, linked, conjoined or in any way connected under the flag of a new discipline that we now know as corporate communications. This trend towards 'integration' was noted by many in the field, including Philip Kotler, one of the most influential marketing figures of modern times, who commented in the early 1990s that 'there is a genuine need to develop a new paradigm in which these two subcultures [public relations and marketing] work most effectively in the best interest of the organization and the publics it serves'.[4]

The professional development of public relations

Public relations developed, expanding in its scope and activities, because of public scepticism, political reform, turmoil and activism throughout the twentieth century, which gradually created a climate in which organizations could no longer suffice with simply engaging in what could be called 'private relations' – that is, making business decisions without regard to governmental or public opinion.[5] Whereas power had previously, at the height of the Industrial Revolution, been largely concentrated with big business, the balance had gradually been shifting towards powerful groups in society including governments, trade unions, investors and stockholders, so that organizations could no longer 'survive while ignoring the impact of social, political, technical and economic changes on its relationships [with public groups]'.[6] In direct response to the increased saliency and power of such groups, new areas of expertise such as investor relations, government affairs and employee communications were added to the existing speciality of media relations under the umbrella of public relations, and public relations gradually developed into a fully-fledged 'managerial discipline' (see Table 2.1). Ever since this development, the process of communications from organizations to these powerful publics has been based to a lesser extent on downright persuasion, and more on dialogue and relationship building. The many NGOs and environmental lobby groups, for instance, that mobilized themselves in the 1980s against big business, forced many organizations to enter into a dialogue about environmental issues and often to accommodate these groups.

The professional development of marketing

Marketing developed as a result of expanding mass communications opportunities and increased competition after the stable period of mass production and consumption ('production era') that had characterized the early years of the twentieth century. Although the century had started with very little promotional activity, with supply, promotions and distribution of secondary concern (and largely left to independent wholesalers and retailers), greater competition and saturated demand in many markets led in subsequent years to the understanding that the 'belief in the sanctity of "I sell, you buy" became simplistic'[7] and increasingly outdated. The production era had been characterized by mass production as demand exceeded supply; the conception and design of product lines had therefore also reflected production requirements more than research into customer needs. And because of the little competition in each product market at that time, businesses, wholesalers and retailers had made little effort to promote their wares because products effectively 'sold themselves'. The greater competition forced organizations to initiate energetic personal selling, backed by research, promotions and advertising, which came to be known as a 'sales orientation' (see Figure 2.1). Around the 1950s, again because of a surge in competition and the emergence of an individualistic consumer ethic (that broke up the homogeneous mass markets of the past), a sophisticated market orientation was adopted by many organizations emphasizing a focus on product branding and positioning, and customer wants and needs as the engine of the marketing process.[8] Marketing thus matured into a full-blown managerial discipline as a result of changing economic conditions and advances in media and technology, and, like public relations, has moved from an 'inside-out' to an 'outside-in' approach in its handling of the relationships between an organization on the one hand and existing and prospective customers on the other. That is, marketing thinking, and the use of the marketing communications tools of advertising, sales promotions, direct marketing and publicity have moved from direct persuasion and transaction to indirect means of exerting power in the creation of favourable conditions and mutuality within relationships with existing and prospective customers and consumers.[9]

So far, the chapter has sketched the historical development of public relations and marketing, and has started to outline how both these functions have changed in their orientation and practices as a result of socio-economic forces in the Western hemisphere. While such a sketch is rather broad-brushed – as the actual changes in scope and practices have obviously been more complex, turbulent and a matter of contestation – it does, however, roughly draw out the stages of development of both public relations and marketing. Importantly, Figure 2.1 also indicates the trend from a view of marketing and public relations as largely separate functions to a more integrated perspective that combines them into a new vision of the practice of communications management. This 'integration' trend was already noted in a landmark article in 1978 by Philip Kotler and William Mindak, which highlighted the different ways of looking at the relationship between marketing and public relations. The view of public relations and marketing as distinct functions had characterized much of the twentieth century, the 1978 article emphasized, yet it predicted that a view of an integrated paradigm would dominate the 1980s, 1990s and beyond as 'new patterns of operation and inter-relation can be expected to appear in these [marketing and public relations] functions'.[10]

Marketing and public relations as distinct functions

Traditionally, before the 1980s, the marketing and public relations functions had been considered as rather distinct in their perspectives and activities, as having very differ-ent objectives and value orientations and with each function going through its own trajectory of professional development.[11] Central to this traditional view was the simple point that marketing deals with markets, while public relations deals with all the publics (that excludes existing and prospective customers and consumers) of an organization. Markets, from this perspective, are created by the identification of a segment of the population for which a product or service is or could be in demand, and involves product or service-related communications; while publics are seen as *actively* creating and mobilizing themselves whenever companies make decisions that affect a group of people adversely. These publics are also seen to concern themselves with more general corporate, rather than product-related, news and communica-tions. Kotler and Mindak articulated this traditional position by saying that 'market-ing exists to sense, serve, and satisfy customer needs at a profit', while 'public relations exists to produce goodwill with the company's various publics so that these publics do not interfere in the firm's profit-making ability'.[12] This split in publics versus markets was further perpetuated by the view that publics need to be addressed by organizations rather differently from markets, through a more balanced or symmetri-cal process of dialogue and accommodation. Markets, it was suggested, are then primarily approached by unidirectional and asymmetrical message flows from orga-nizations, with a strict aim of persuasion to boost sales or increase a company's market share.[13] Following this line of analysis, many industry commentators, academics and communications experts concurred that while both the marketing and public rela-tions functions are needed in the world of organizations, they have very different objectives and target groups, and also use very different ways of communicating. As a result, the conclusion was that both functions are distinct and should remain largely separate from one another in their scope and operations.

Marketing and public relations as distinct but complementary functions

Cracks, however, time and again appeared in this view of public relations and marketing as two functions that are completely distinct in their objectives and tactics. For one, it had

Table 2.2 Examples of marketing public relations worldwide

United States	United Kingdom	Global
Starbucks initially built its brand without any advertising but used public relations efforts (free publicity, features in general interest magazines) to catch attention and to establish a brand experience that was backed up by each Starbucks location.	The success of the Virgin brand is based on the serious self-promotion of its CEO Richard Branson through his hot air ballooning exploits, and environmental and community programmes.	Sony first aroused public interest for Walkman by giving Walkmans to Japan's leading musicians, teen idols and magazine editors.
McDonalds achieves product awareness for its promotions and products because of effective media relations campaigns that are run alongside advertising campaigns.	The Body Shop uses public relations and grass roots campaigning as a model for linking a brand to the advancement of public awareness and customer support for positive social change.	Kodak, keen to 'deepen its roots in the Chinese market', used public relations as support for new product launches, sponsorship and events, as well as for 'executive visits' to China.

become apparent over and again that there was at least some common ground or overlap between them. In the 1980s, for instance, concern over the rising costs and impacts of mass media advertising encouraged many companies to examine different means of promoting customer loyalty and of building brand awareness to increase sales. The use of 'marketing public relations' – the publicizing of news and events related to the launching and promotion of products or services that thus effectively involves the use of public relations techniques for marketing purposes – has ever since been widely used by organizations. Marketing public relations was found not only to be a cost-effective tool for generating awareness and imagery, but also to imbue the communications of the organization's brands with credibility.[14] Table 2.2 mentions some classic examples where public relations techniques have been effectively used to bring products to the market.

A further blow to the view of public relations and marketing as two separate functions came with the criticism of many theorists and practitioners alike that all forms of communications including public relations are essentially asymmetrical in nature: every form of communication is a value-laden activity employed by an organization with the purpose of exerting symbolic control over its environment. The Dutch theorist Van der Meiden, for instance, has argued in this respect that the classical views that emphasize the exclusive position of public relations relative to marketing on the basis of the mentioned distinction between symmetrical dialogue and asymmetrical persuasion need fundamental opposition. Viewing public relations as an inherently symmetrical form of communications, and setting it aside from marketing on that basis, is, according to Van der Meiden, in fact a form of false 'puritanism', which, in the face of the reality of how communications actually works, is 'old-fashioned and unrealistic'. However, he added that, despite the recognition that all forms of communications share asymmetrical roots, there is 'no need for complete amalgamation or fusion'[15] between marketing and public relations. In other words, marketing and public relations are both asymmetrical in nature, but, as Van der Meiden stresses, based on the apparent differences (in their objectives, groups addressed and techniques used) each still largely stands as a function on its own.

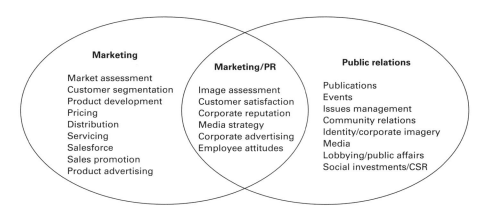

Figure 2.2 Public relations and marketing activities and their overlap

From the perspective of such overlap and similarities between the marketing and public relations functions, the separatist attitude of the past has since come to be considered as a 'hide-bound' approach, and the motives that had guided it have also been criticized by theorists and practitioners alike. The criticism levelled at it was that the motive for strictly marking the two functions off from one another was merely partisan with concerns about 'imperialism' and 'turf' lying not far beneath the surface. And because of such concerns of 'imperialism', 'turf', and indeed 'encroachment', theorists and practitioners realized, little consideration had gone in the past into 'questions of organizational strategy and the organizational basis for bringing public relations, marketing and other related functions into closer alignment with one another'.[16] What is more, many practitioners had already dismissed the separatist attempts to clearly delineate the two functions from one another as political posturing and as rather philosophical, figuring in the scholarly world, whereas, in practice, companies had, particularly since the 1980s, shown an increased interaction and complementary relationships between the two.[17] A more fruitful perspective on the relationship between marketing and public relations was therefore, as academics and practitioners came to realize, to consider them both as full-blown and largely separate functions, but at the same time as sharing some common terrain. Philip Kitchen, a public relations academic, calls this view the 'middle-of-the-road' approach where the public relations and marketing functions are seen as distinct, but where they share important similarities and complementary relationships.[18] Similarities, first of all, exist in the common asymmetrical nature of public relations and marketing; the related understanding that both marketing and public relations cultivate communications with targeted groups; and the sharing of research techniques and communications tools. Figure 2.2 displays a number of core activities of both the public relations and marketing functions, and outlines a set of activities (including specific tools and techniques) that are shared, indicating the overlap between the two functions.

Besides the direct sharing of activities such as image measurement tools (the middle of Figure 2.2), there are also a number of ways in which marketing and public relations activities can complement one another. For example, there is ample evidence that corporate imagery, created through public relations programmes, can positively reflect upon the product brands of a company, thereby increasing the awareness of the product brand as well as adding an additional attribute that enhances consumers' favourability of the brand.[19] Another complementary relationship that exists is the guarding role of public relations as a 'watchdog' or 'corrective' for marketing in bringing other strategic viewpoints to bear besides the need to create customer exchanges.[20]

Integration in marketing and public relations functions

As a result of this overlap and complementarity – suggesting that it is useful for organizations to more closely align marketing and public relations or at least manage both functions in a more integrated manner – since the 1980s and 1990s a lot of discussion and debate has been around integration in communications management. This notion of 'integration', or an integrated approach to communications management, shines through in a number of concepts that have since emerged as an outcome of these debates, including integrated marketing communications (IMC), integrated communications (IC), and corporate communications.[21] The idea of integration that underlies each of these concepts, while at times having been dismissed as a buzz word or as mere rhetoric,[22] has been advanced in response to a number of highly significant changes in the practice of communications management. Understanding these changes is quintessential for attaining a greater understanding of the emergence of corporate communications and the relevance of this management function for contemporary organizations. The following section details these changes, and outlines why the notion of integration in communications management has become so pertinent today.

2.3   Communications management comes of age

The different concepts of IMC, IC and corporate communications that have emerged in recent years and that all proclaim some form of integration – at the message, media, process or organizational levels – obviously differ somewhat from one another in their positions and in their perspectives of the practice of communications management. All of them, however, agree on the idea that in any case there should be some alignment or coordination (integration) of marketing and public relations activities in order to achieve the best possible communications impact for an organization and its products with external audiences. This does not mean that both the marketing and public relations functions are actually merged or reduced to one and the same function – as this is hardly if at all feasible in practice given the still apparent differences in activities and audiences addressed by each (see Figure 2.2) – but that both functions, while still existing as such, are balanced and managed together from within an overarching framework (which is then termed as IC, IMC or corporate communications). Such a framework suggests a holistic way of viewing and practising communications management that cuts across the marketing and public relations functions (and disciplines such as advertising and media relations within them) and as such recognizes, as Anders Gronstedt puts it, that communications management 'is too complex and interactive to be fractionalized into insular disciplines'.

Table 2.3   Drivers for integration

Market and environment-based drivers
Stakeholder roles – needs and overlap
Societal and market demands
Increased competition – need for differentiation
Greater levels of audience communications literacy
Greater amounts of message clutter
Media and audience fragmentation

Organizational drivers
Improved efficiency (increasing profits)
Increased accountability
Provision of strategic direction and purpose through consolidation
Corporate/organizational positioning
Streamlining of activities in complex organizations (global, multinational and/or multidivisional businesses)

Communication-based drivers
Increased message effectiveness through consistency and reinforcement of core messages
Need to build corporate and/or brand reputations and to provide clear identity cues
Complementarity of communications techniques and media cost inflation
Media multiplication requires control of communication channels

A managerial framework is thus needed, Gronstedt suggests, that 'inserts the various communications disciplines into a holistic perspective, drawing from the concepts, methodologies, crafts, experiences, and artistries of marketing communications and public relations'.[23] This need for some form of integration has now been widely accepted by many communications practitioners across the globe, and the corporate communications concept has, as will be shown below, made considerable inroads since the 1990s as a result. Organizations, it seems, are now increasingly working from the framework of corporate communications, but what were the conditions and factors that triggered it? In other words, it is important that, before the chapter defines some of the key changes that corporate communications has brought to the practice of communications management, the factors that lie behind the need for integration in communications management and the adoption of corporate communications as a management function are revisited.

The explosion of interest in integration, and the emergence of corporate communications in its slipstream, has resulted from a variety of factors or 'drivers' as these can be more aptly called. Generally, these drivers can be grouped into three main categories: those drivers that are market and environment based, those that arise from the communications mix and communication technologies, and those that are driven by opportunities, changes and needs from within the organization itself. All of these drivers are set out in Table 2.3.

Market and environment-based drivers

The environment in which organizations operate has changed considerably over the past two decades. Not only has the environment become more complex for many organizations, greater public scepticism and government interference has, together with increased competition in many markets, created a situation where organizations now need to *meet the demands of multiple and diverse stakeholder groups*, while at the same time expressing a coherent image of themselves. In 1994, Robert Heath, a communications scholar, formulated this challenge as follows:

> Some companies and other organizations are well known for their ability to conduct a truly integrated communications campaign designed to get the message across even though it is tailored to various stakeholders. Not only is the matter one of providing a coherent and consistent message that fosters an understanding of the company as its management and employees want it to be understood, but it also means that key audiences are addressed in terms of the stake each of them holds with regard to the organization.[24]

The guiding idea here is that ever since the early 1990s organizations have needed to communicate with a whole range of stakeholder groups; not only with stakeholder groups that they depend upon in economic or market terms (e.g. suppliers, investors and stockholders, employees, customers), but also with groups that are of moral or social importance (e.g. government, communities, NGOs), so that the organization and its operations are found to be 'legitimate' by all of society. Meeting such dual *market and social demands*, while at the same time providing a clear and credible image of oneself, has ever since forced organizations to put considerable effort into integrating all their public relations and marketing communications efforts. This integration of 'public' and 'marketing' communications is even more important in consideration of the multiple stakeholder roles that any one individual may have, and the potential pitfalls that may occur when conflicting messages are sent out.[25] Box 2.1 illustrates this problem, and emphasizes the importance of managing and coordinating all public relations and marketing messages that may originate from very different parts of the organization.

Box 2.1 Case study: Barclays Bank (UK)

Early in 2003, Barclays, a UK-based financial services group engaged primarily in retail banking, investment banking and investment management, appointed a new advertising agency Bartle Bogle Hegarty (BBH). BBH was hired to spearhead a 'more humane' campaign, after the bank was lambasted for its 'Big Bank' adverts in 2002 that featured the slogan 'a big world needs a big bank'. Barclays had spent £15 million (US$ 24.6 million)/(21.5 million €) on its 'Big Bank' campaign, which featured celebrities such as Sir Anthony Hopkins and Tim Roth. The adverts were slick and had received good pre-publicity, but they turned into a communications disaster when they coincided with the news that Barclays was closing about 170 branches in the UK, many in rural areas.

One of the earlier adverts featured Welsh-born Sir Anthony Hopkins talking from the comfort of a palatial home about the importance of chasing 'big' ideas and ambitions. The adverts provoked a national debate in the UK when junior minister Chris Mullin said that Barclays' customers should revolt and 'vote with their feet'. Barclays' image crisis worsened when it was revealed that the new Chief Executive Matthew Barrett had been paid £1.3 million (US$ 2.1 million)/(1.8 million €) for just three months' work. Competitor NatWest has since capitalized on the fall-out from the 'Big Bank' campaign. It has been running adverts that triumph the fact that it has abolished branch closures.

Barclays has since extended opening hours at 84 per cent of its branches and recruited an extra 2,000 staff to service the extra hours. Together with the new adverts that will be 'more humane and more tangible and based on actual products rather than the brand', Barclays hopes that the stains from the 'Big Bank' campaign will finally start to wear off.

Questions for reflection

1. What was the exact cause or event that led to this communications crisis for Barclays?
2. What could Barclays have done better to avoid this crisis? And what do you suggest the bank needs to do now to repair the damage done to its reputation?

A further trigger for an integrated approach to communications management involved the *heightened competition* in many markets, which emphasized the importance of differentiated product offerings and corporate image, and thus also of an integrated management of communications. Equally, the greater *audience fragmentation* that came to characterize many markets as consumption had become more individualized also meant that organizations needed to go to greater lengths than before to find ways in which messages could be effectively channelled to their target markets. Both factors again underline the need for coordinated communications campaigns and consistent messages, a point that is further supported by the *communications clutter* ruling many markets. Industry commentators reckon that on average a person is hit by 13,000 commercial messages a day, and suggest that integrated communications strategies, rather than fragmented or ill-coordinated attempts, are more likely to break through this clutter and make the company name or product brand heard.[26]

Organizational drivers

The opportunities offered to organizations internally to move to an integration of their communications were considerable. One of the main organizational drivers for integration was the need to *become more efficient*. By using management time more productively and by driving down the cost base – for instance, as research and promotional materials are more widely shared and used for more than one communications campaign – organizations could substantially improve the productivity of their communications practitioners. With the powerful restructuring trend in the 1980s where every function was examined on its *accountability*, an internal realignment of communications disciplines such as media relations, advertising, sales promotions and product publicity was an obvious path for many organizations. Such a realignment of communications, basically consisting of bringing various communications disciplines together into departments or specific working practices, also proved productive in that it offered new organizational and managerial benefits that were non-existent before. For one, the consolidation of communications activities, besides leading to new interactions and complementary relationships between various communications disciplines, enabled organizations to provide *strategic direction* to their communications and to guide communications efforts from the strategic interests of the organization as a whole. In other words, organizations increasingly started to recognize that the fragmentation and spreading out of the communications responsibilities across the organization, which had characterized many organizations in the past, proved counterproductive. Such fragmentation, as Anders Gronstedt points out, is likely to lead to a situation where 'each department sub-optimizes its own performance, instead of working for the organization as a whole'.[27] Many organizations, as Chapter 5 outlines in more detail, have therefore since developed innovative procedures (e.g. communication guidelines, house style manuals) and implemented coordination mechanisms (e.g. council meetings, networking platforms) to overcome fragmentation and integrate their communications on an organization–wide scale.

The 'corporate' perspective upon communications management, which involves looking at all communications in a holistic manner and linking the communications strategy to the corporate strategy (and thus to overall corporate objectives), was often also taken as organizations realized that *investing in their corporate profile or corporate identity* instead of their product brands alone is of great value.[28] With brand choices expanding and product homogeneity increasing, consumers were seeking out the company behind the brand even more as an extra point of difference and reassurance. This marked an extension from a customer-to-brand bond to an additional customer- to-company bond. The corporate identity thus often became a filter for overwhelming product multiplicity and a critical difference in a 'sea of sameness' for consumers. But investing in corporate identity, and in the profiling of the organization as a whole, delivers more benefits for the organization than customer preferences alone, as a strong and well-crafted identity also leads to members of the community appreciating the organization in its environs, investors granting financial resources, (prospective) employees wanting to work for the organization, and so on.

Communications-based drivers

In contemporary market environments, in which it is increasingly difficult to be heard and stand out from one's competitors, organizations are, as already mentioned, well served by integrated communications strategies. Through *consistent messages*, and by having all communications 'sing from the same hymn sheet', an organization is more likely to be known and looked upon favourably by key audiences. This means that considerable effort needs to be put into choosing the corporate profile and/or product brand profile(s) that an organization wants to communicate to its key stakeholders, followed by a consideration of all communications campaigns and other contact points with stakeholders that need to be managed in order to achieve this in a consistent manner.

The insight that *messages in various media can complement one another*, leading to a greater communications impact than any one single message can achieve, also made organizations look upon their media choices in a much broader sense. Particularly with advertising increasingly being under fire, as according to some commentators it had far too long been 'highly visible in its appearance and highly invisible in its effects',[29] and with the explosion of media options available, many organizations re-examined their *media presence and how to control it*. In the light of these media developments, many industry commentators, practitioners and academics have argued that organizations and practitioners should now move away from rigid classifications of media in 'above-the-line' advertising and 'below-the-line' promotions or publicity, and towards a notion of *through-the-line* or *zero-based* communications, where rather than pre-fixed choices for particular communications media, the most appropriate medium given a particular communications objective is chosen.[30]

Taken together, these drivers explain the preoccupation with integration in communications management that has characterized the latter two decades of the twentieth century and that is still with us through the adoption and entrenchment of corporate communications as the guiding framework for how communications is managed today. From the historical sketch that has been presented in this chapter, the following section outlines the key changes that the corporate communications philosophy has already brought to the practice of communications management.

2.4 Corporate communications and communications management

Research materials and anecdotal evidence have in recent years been stacking up supporting the view that organizations now increasingly approach their communications from an integrated perspective, and, what is more, primarily through the lens of corporate communications instead of IC or IMC. This is evident in a number of organizational changes and initiatives that emphasize the adoption of corporate communications, including the following:

1. A greater consolidation of communications disciplines.   Instead of being dispersed over an organization or delegated to other functions (such as Finance and Human Resources), communications disciplines have increasingly been brought together and consolidated into departments or as the responsibility of a single communications manager (see also Chapter 5 for a more detailed look at the subject of organizing communications). Many organizations in the US, UK, continental Europe and elsewhere have consolidated communications disciplines as media relations, government relations, employee communications, community relations, investor relations, corporate design and issues management into 'corporate affairs', 'public relations' or 'communications' departments, while disciplines such as branding, advertising, promotions and direct marketing are put under the marketing department. This greater consolidation of communications disciplines, yet still in separate corporate affairs or public relations and marketing departments, not only emphasizes the expanded scope and breadth of disciplines and expertise that is now available, but also the more holistic view of communications that most organizations are now taking.

2. Increased coordination from a corporate perspective. While communications disciplines are still often organized into separate departments, organizations have also increasingly recognized that fragmentation needs to be tackled by having a managerial framework from where both public relations and marketing communications disciplines are guided and coordinated. The widespread existence of coordinating bodies and the increasing use of a consensus approach to decision making (where the heads of various communications disciplines work together to develop communications strategies) attest to this integrated approach to communications that is now taken in many organizations in the US, UK and elsewhere. Importantly, such coordination and decision making takes place between practitioners from various public relations (or corporate affairs) and marketing communications disciplines, underlining the fact that organizations undertake the management and integration of their communications activities from a total organizational or corporate perspective, and not just from a marketing perspective as the concept of IMC would suggest. In other words, IMC has lost ground to corporate communications as the guiding managerial framework for communications management.

3. More input of communications into management decision making. Communications departments and practitioners now also increasingly enjoy a high position in the organization's hierarchical structure; in some organizations senior communications practitioners are even members of their organization's management team (or support this management team in a direct reporting or advisory capacity). Companies such as Marks & Spencer and Sony have recently promoted their most senior communications director to a seat on the executive board. Such moves, of which there are now plenty across the business world, affirm and formalize the strategic involvement of communications at the corporate level and credit corporate communications as a strategic management function charged with strategically guiding and managing relationships with an organization's stakeholders (rather than as a technical support function for other managerial functions and as largely concerned with putting communications to work to effectuate management decisions).

4. The rise of the corporate communications manager. Not only are communications disciplines to a greater extent consolidated and coordinated than before, but the last 15 years or so have also seen the rise of the corporate communications manager. This is a 'new style' manager who is able to take a more strategic and holistic perspective on communications, and is also more business savvy than his/her predecessors – the old-style public relations tactician and advertising man. A survey of Fortune 500 companies regarding the status of communications managers in 1985 indicated that the position of the corporate communications manager existed in 84 per cent of the sample[31] and that on average the position had existed for a period of 11 years! More recent analyses in the Netherlands in 1995 and France in 1998 provide further support for this new style corporate communications manager. Corporate communications managers working across the Netherlands and France in companies such as ABN-AMRO, BNP, Air France, Philips and Renault were found to embody the holistic perspective that is needed 'to take on responsibility for the communications strategy' and 'have bridged the traditional gaps between public relations and marketing communication'. The closing of these gaps, both studies suggest, is due to the fact

that these corporate communications managers in the Netherlands and France work 'from the position that the total communications effort must serve the corporate strategy, the importance of which is paramount' and that they therefore 'found it natural to link the two disciplines'.[32]

5. Adoption of the vocabulary and concepts of corporate communications. The term 'corporate communications' has made a steady inroad into professionals' vocabulary, as well as in job and departmental titles. This adoption of the term and its associated vocabulary is in part political as it underlines the decline of public relations as the field's guiding descriptive term. Olasky,[33] among many others, has noted that practitioners of public relations have become associated with a litany of derogatory terms such as 'tools of the top brass', 'hucksters', 'parrots', 'low-life liars' and 'impotent, evasive, egomaniacal, and lying'; and that corporate communications seems a politically better alternative. But the change is also more than just political or nominal, as corporate communications' central concepts of stakeholder, identity and reputation are on top of the professional agenda and have in fact become central to the current practice of communications management. A survey of Fortune 500 companies in 2001 found that managing reputation was considered the lead philosophy among communications departments.[34] And identity, the question of what the company is and stands for, is considered by many senior managers and communications practitioners as one of the cornerstones of stakeholder engagement and communications programmes.

The adoption of the vocabulary and tools of corporate communications is, as Chapter 3 outlines, linked to the rise of the stakeholder model of strategic management, which required a broader, strategic and management oriented communications function in comparison with the craft and tactical communications approaches of before. Freeman, one of the intellectual leaders of stakeholder theory, suggested in 1984 that 'the stakeholder approach requires a redefinition of the public relations function which builds on the communications skills of PR professionals, yet is responsive to the real business environment of today'. Freeman acknowledged the need for savvy communications professionals who can build and maintain relationships with key stakeholders, but maintained that 'in the current business environment the concepts and tools that have evolved for PR managers to use are increasingly ineffective'. Speaking in 1984, he even went on to suggest that because of these traditional concepts and tools such as 'the vitriolic press release, the annual report, a slick videotape, corporate philanthropy, etc. today's PR manager is a sacrificial lamb on the altar of multiple stakeholder dissatisfaction with corporate performance'.[35] Freeman's analysis, albeit somewhat charged, did point to the crux of the matter at that time. New concepts and tools were effectively needed for managing communications with stakeholders and for understanding how communications could be strategically employed to meet organizational objectives. Corporate communications is the strategic management function that has since arisen to this end. Within the corporate communications framework communications to stakeholders is approached and managed in a strategic manner through the central concepts of identity and reputation, and communications programmes are more clearly linked to the corporate strategy and corporate objectives. To illustrate the adoption of the stakeholder model of strategic management within the world of business, Box 2.2 presents a case study of how the stakeholder concept has become the dominant strategic orientation for Shell and BP in the petroleum industry.

Box 2.2   Case study: stakeholder management in the petroleum industry[36]

In terms of economic and geopolitical importance, drama and controversy, the petroleum industry has no counterpart in the 20th century. Great explorations and technological innovations went hand in hand with public scorn and outrage. Nowhere is this characterization more true than among the select group of firms operating at the apex of the petroleum industry, including the industry giants Royal Dutch Shell and British Petroleum. Both companies have gone through tumultuous periods at one time or another in the 1990s, and have realized the value of a broader stakeholder orientation (instead of a narrower production or shareholder orientation) as a result.

Royal Dutch Shell

Shell was one of the first truly international corporations and has been one of the ten largest companies in the world for nearly a century. Historically, its regional operating units were the dominant elements in a decentralized management structure. The company is now somewhat more centrally controlled through a committee of managing directors and is organized globally into five lines of business: exploration and production, chemicals, gas and coal, international renewables and oil products. Shell had, historically, a strong technical and engineering orientation in all of its strategies and operations, and placed a strong emphasis on long-range planning based on the construction of competing 'scenarios' about major long-term market trends that would affect its economic status and market operations.

In the 1990s, Shell executives came to believe that its corporate identity and reputation were at stake in both the marketplace and the policy arena. One reason for this, executives believed, was Shell's weak organizational structure, which was clearly inadequate for effective control of a global enterprise and stymied them in their desire to build a strong reputation in the marketplace. In March 1995, the CEO of the Dutch parent company announced that partly for this reason the group wished to drastically change its organizational structure. The old matrix structure, with regions, sectors and functional responsibilities, would disappear. The proposed new structure consisted of separate business organizations, each led by a business committee with worldwide responsibility. A newly created strategy and business services unit would control strategy, finance, personnel and corporate communications ('public affairs') at the group level. Corporate communications activities would thus become more centralized after these changes, with the aim of controlling communications better and channelling messages more effectively to Shell's audiences.

At the height of this restructuring exercise, of which one of the aims was to strengthen its corporate communications, Shell, ironically, got enmeshed in two communications crises. In June 1995, Royal Dutch Shell found itself in heated debates with a whole range of critics (including The Movement for the Survival of the Ogoni

People, Greenpeace, the Sierra Club, Amnesty International and the media) over the environment and associated human rights issues that were played out in a variety of public forums. These crises resulted from the public dismay around Shell UK's proposed action to dispose of Brent Spar, an enormous oil storage and loading platform, in the waters of the North Atlantic, and Shell's failure to take a high profile public stance against the Nigerian government, Shell Nigeria's local business partner, when it executed nine Ogoni environmentalists including Ken Saro-Wiwa, an internationally acclaimed journalist and writer who had spearheaded protest against Shell.

These crises, ensuing in public debates about Shell's environmental and societal stance, have also led to corporate reflexivity and questions of identity for the company and effectively challenged its modernist, technical and rational way of approaching its operations. In one sense, these crises have moved the company from a taken-for-granted discourse of economic development towards a cautious adoption of the language of sustainable development, with attempts to balance interests of economic development with environmental well-being. This move is well expressed in the position of former Shell Group Chairman Cor Herkströter, who initially defined Shell's role as strictly economic and commercial, arguing that the company 'lacked "license" to interfere in politics, society or the sovereign mandate of government', but has now become one of the most fervent promoters of corporate social responsibility. As Herkströter said:

> Most of us at Royal Dutch/Shell come from a scientific, technological background. That type of education, along with our corporate culture, teaches us that we must identify a problem, isolate it and then fix it. That sort of approach works well with a physical problem – but it is not so useful when we are faced with, say, a human rights issue. For most engineering problems there is a correct answer. For most social and political dilemmas there is a range of possible answers – almost all compromises.

The corresponding move to a stakeholder orientation in its business principles and modes of operation, seen by some as a U-turn in managerial priorities, is evident in a number of initiatives including platforms for stakeholder engagement and dialogue, Shell's Society Report, and the recent 'Profits and Principles' campaign where the company explains its new-found credo. Shell now claims to 'listen' to all of its stakeholders, who have explicitly told the company that 'a commitment to sustainable development is key to a company's reputation'.

British Petroleum

British Petroleum is one of the world's largest petroleum and petrochemicals groups, with business operations including the exploration and production of crude oil and natural gas; refining, marketing, supply and transportation; and the manufacturing and marketing of petrochemicals. After a period of diversification (including a move into the nutrition business) in the 1970s and 1980s, BP rationalized its operations in the 1990s and is now focusing again on its core activities in petroleum and chemicals. In 1989, the company launched a campaign to introduce a stronger corporate identity, featuring a restyled BP shield and an emphasis on the colour green. And in a complementary programme BP started to reimage its global network of service stations in a new design and livery.

To equip itself for the challenges of the 1990s and beyond, the company introduced, in a programme called Project 1990, major changes in its organization and way of working to improve efficiency and flexibility. The key turning point for this came with the 1992 recession. 'We suffered a down turn like many companies in '92', said one BP executive, 'and it became a crisis for us. Our '92 financials were dramatically bad and that triggered a sea change in how BP viewed its operations. We took a lot of steps to refocus and became a much flatter organization. Browne [the CEO of BP] was crucial in this organization'.

One of the outcomes of this change at BP was a greater emphasis on partnering and strategic alliances. BP became organized around small business units that were free to get what they needed from the best sources. This decentralization of business operations went hand in hand with group-wide consultation meetings that gathered feedback from environmental NGOs and experts on health, safety and the environment as an input for BP's overall strategy as well as its communications. These meetings presented the company with a report card on its environmental performance, from which it took specific recommendations and guidance.

One outcome of these meetings, a point taken on in its strategy ever since, is that BP could be the first of the pack, taking an overall proactive stance on climate change and demonstrating a long-term strategic awareness that competitive advantage comes from proactively creating policy, rather than attempting to slow the course of change. In May 1997, BP's CEO, John Browne, announced to the world both BP's decision to accept that climate change is occurring and its intention to reduce its contributions to the process. This action attracted attention from President Clinton, environmentalists and the business press, and raised expectations regarding the actions of its direct competitors. Browne's speech was a breakthrough, as BP was the first multinational corporation other than reinsurance companies to join the emerging consensus on climate change, and committed itself to reduce greenhouse emissions from all of its own business operations. 'It transformed the global climate issue because there was no one in the corporate world who, in such a public way, came out and said, this is a problem and we have a responsibility to do something about it', says Eileen Claussen, president of the Pew Center on Global Climate Change.

The Environmental Defense Fund (EDF) called BP's action an 'historic acceptance of responsibility for the overriding environmental problem of our time'. The executive director of the EDF, Fred Krupp, said that it 'puts real pressure on the other oil companies to act like responsible adults, and I think it puts substantial pressure on the Clinton White House to advance a meaningful reduction target'. In a second address in Berlin, in late September, Browne re-emphasized BP's commitment to reducing the greenhouse effect and reflected upon the widespread support that existed for this strategy within his own organization: 'I've been struck since I first spoke on this subject ... by the degree of support there is within our company for a constructive approach – an approach which doesn't start with a denial of the problem, but rather with a determination to treat this as another challenge which we can help to resolve'.

BP's strategy of stakeholder engagement has subsequently been targeted at environmental policies and environmental consultation, rather than social or community initiatives. Concrete initiatives include an environmental and social report (audited by third parties to ensure that views of stakeholders truly have an impact upon BP's operations), interactive policy-making and environmental forums in relation to sensitive projects (e.g. operations in China), and consultations of investment houses and pension funds in the US and UK regarding their expectations and interest in socially responsible investment (SRI). With each and every one of these initiatives, BP aims to position itself in a market that is demanding more responsible behaviour of the company. As John Mogford, acting president and CEO of BP Solar, remarked: 'the industry is going to change, and we need to be positioned to take advantage of this and not be on the outside'.

Questions for reflection

1. Is it necessary for every organization to shift to a stakeholder orientation; to attend to all of its stakeholders and to accommodate them? In other words, what does an organization risk if it ignores or fails to act upon the claims and concerns of important stakeholder groups?
2. Is a stakeholder orientation necessary for organizations in every type of business sector? In other words, is there a greater need for companies such as Shell and BP in the petroleum industry to abide by a stakeholder orientation than, for instance, banks and insurance companies in the financial sector?
3. How can an organization develop and institutionalize a comprehensive stakeholder orientation? And what sort of results will this deliver?

Taken together, these five changes to the practice of communications management provide evidence of the adoption of the management function and vocabulary of corporate communications. The full scope of these strategic and organizational changes is reflected in the subjects of each of the remaining chapters in Part 2 of this book. The next chapter further specifies the key theoretical concepts of corporate communications – stakeholder, identity and reputation – so that the theoretical groundwork is sufficiently covered before the book continues with the more concrete strategic and organizational issues around corporate communications in practice.

2.5   Chapter summary

The chapter has spent a substantial amount of space discussing the historical development of communications management, and the rise of corporate communications in particular. Such an historical overview is essential for an understanding of the characteristics of corporate communications management and its relevance to the communications practitioner of today. The variety of factors or drivers that have led to the emergence of corporate communications, and effectively continue to drive its widespread use with companies around the globe, were outlined, followed by a consideration of the key changes that corporate communications has brought with it. The rest of the book expands on these changes in communications management and other issues, but it is worthwhile emphasizing them again. First of all, the diverse communications disciplines (e.g. advertising, media relations, lobbying and public affairs, branding, direct marketing, corporate design) that exist within an organization are to a greater extent brought together and consolidated in one or two separate departments, instead of being wholly dispersed over the organization or brought under departments with different responsibilities (e.g. human resource, finance). A second change, and in line with the greater consolidation of communications disciplines, has been that many organizations now notably use coordination mechanisms to guide and integrate all of the work coming out of the different communications disciplines for the strategic interests of the organization at large. A third observation is that many organizations now place communications at a higher position within the organization's hierarchy and appreciate communications practitioners for their input and strategic involvement in decision making concerning the overall corporate strategy of the organization. A fourth change that corporate communications has brought is that it has led to a new style corporate communications manager, who in contrast with the old-style public relations tacticians and advertising executives, is a strategic generalist and is more business savvy in his/her view of communications and in what it can do for the organization at large. The fifth and final change is that corporate communications has introduced new vocabulary and concepts to the practice of communications management. The concepts of stakeholder, identity and reputation are of particular significance, and these are discussed more fully in the next chapter.

Key terms

Accountability	Marketing public relations
Asymmetrical communication	Market orientation
Audience fragmentation	Press agentry
Clutter	Production orientation
Corporate communications	Public
Corporate identity	Public information
Corporate reputation	Public relations
Integrated communications (IC)	Sales orientation
Integrated marketing communications (IMC)	Stake holder
Integration	Strategic management function
Market	Symmetrical communication
Marketing	Through-the-line/zero-based

Notes

[1]Lippmann, W. (1922), *Public Opinion*. New York: Macmillan, p. 345.

[2]Grunig, J.E., and Hunt, T. (1984) *Managing Public Relations*. New York: Holt, Rinehart & Winston.

[3]See for instance Ewen, S. (1996), *PR! A Social History of Spin*. New York: Basic Books; Marchand, R. (1998), *Creating the Corporate Soul: The Rise of Public Relations and Corporate Imagery*. Berkeley: University of California Press; Grunig and Hunt (1984); Cutlip, S.M., Center, A.H., and Broom, G.H. (2000), *Effective Public Relations*. London: Prentice Hall, seventh edition.

[4]Kotler, P. (1989), in Grunig, J.E., and Grunig, L.A. (1991), 'Conceptual differences in public relations and marketing: the case of health-care organizations', *Public Relations Review*, 17 (3), 257–278, p. 261.

[5]Olasky, M.N. (1987), *Corporate Public Relations: A New Historical Perspective*. Hillsdale, NJ: Lawrence Erlbaum Associates.

[6]Broom, G.M., Lauzen, M.M., and Tucker, K. (1991), 'Public relations and marketing: dividing the conceptual domain and operational turf', *Public Relations Review*, 17 (3), 219–225, p. 220.

[7]Broom et al. (1991), p. 220; see also Tedlow, R.S. (1990), *New and Improved: The Story of Mass Marketing in America*. New York: Basic Books.

[8]For more information on marketing's historical development, see the excellent Fullerton, R.A. (1988), 'How modern is modern marketing? Marketing's evolution and the myth of the "production era"', *Journal of Marketing*, 52, 108–125.

[9]Duncan, T., and Moriarty, S.E. (1998), 'A communications-based marketing model for managing relationships', *Journal of Marketing*, 62 (April), pp. 1–13.

[10]Kotler, P., and Mindak, W. (1978), 'Marketing and public relations, should they be partners or rivals?', *Journal of Marketing*, 42 (10), 13–20, p. 20.

[11]See Ehling, W.P., White, J., and Grunig, J.E. (1992), 'Public relations and marketing practices', in Grunig, J.E. (ed.), *Excellence in Public Relations and Communications Management*. Hillsdale, NJ: Lawrence Erlbaum Associates, pp. 357–383; Ehling, W.P. (1989), 'Public relations management and marketing management: different paradigms and different missions', paper presented at the meeting of the Public Relations Colloquium, San Diego.

[12]Kotler and Mindak (1978), p. 17.

[13]Ehling et al. (1992).

[14]Harris, T.L. (1991), *The Marketers Guide to Public Relations: How Today's Top Companies Are Using the New PR to Gain a Competitive Edge*. New York: John Wiley & Sons; Harris, T.L. (1997), 'Integrated marketing public relations', in Caywood, C. (ed.), *The Handbook of Strategic Public Relations & Integrated Communications*. New York: McGraw-Hill, pp. 90–105.

[15]Van der Meiden, A. (1993), 'Public relations and "other" modalities of professional communications: asymmetric presuppositions for a new theoretical discussion', *International Public Relations Review*, 16 (3), 8–11, p. 11; see also Miller, G.R. (1989), 'Persuasion and public relations: two P's in a pod', in Botan, C.H., and Hazleton, V. (eds), *Public Relations Theory*. Hillsdale, NJ: Lawrence Erlbaum Associates, pp. 45–66.

[16]Van Leuven, J. (1991), 'Corporate organizing strategies and the scope of public relations departments', *Public Relations Review*, 17 (3), 279–291, p. 283.

[17]Hart, N.A. (1988), *Practical Advertising and Publicity: Effective Promotion of Products and Services to Industry and Commerce*. London: McGraw-Hill, p. 3.

[18]Kitchen, P.J. (1993), 'The developing use of public relations in fast-moving consumer goods firms', doctoral dissertation, Keele University.

[19]Brown, T.J., and Dacin, A. (1997), 'The company and the product: corporate associations and consumer product responses', *Journal of Marketing*, 61 (January), 68–84; Biehal, G.J., and Sheinin, D.A. (1998), 'Managing the brand in a corporate advertising environment: a decision-making framework for brand managers', *Journal of Advertising*, 27 (2), 99–111.

[20]White, J. (1991), *How to Understand and Manage Public Relations: A Jargon-free Guide to Public Relations Management*. London: Business Books.

[21]See Schultz, D.E., Tannenbaum, S.I., and Lauterborn, R.F. (1993) *The New Marketing Paradigm: Integrated Marketing Communications*. Lincolnwood: NTC Publishing; Wightman, B. (1999), 'Integrated communications: organization and education', *Public Relations Quarterly*, 44 (2), 18–22; Marion, G. (1998), 'Corporate communications managers in large firms: new challenges', *European Management Journal*, 16 (6), 660–671.

[22]Cornelissen, J.P., and Lock, A.R. (2000), 'Theoretical concept or management fashion: examining the significance of integrated marketing communications', *Journal of Advertising Research*, 40 (5), 7–15.

[23]Gronstedt, A. (1996), 'Integrating marketing communications and public relations: a stakeholder relations model', in Thorson, E., and Moore, J. (eds), *Integrated Communications: Synergy of Persuasive Voices*. Mahwah, NJ: Lawrence Erlbaum Associates, pp. 287–304, p. 302.

[24]Heath, R.L. (1994), *Management of Corporate Communications: From Interpersonal Contacts to External Affairs*. Hillsdale, NJ: Lawrence Erlbaum Associates, p. 55.

[25]Scholes, E., and Clutterbuck, D. (1998), 'Communication with stakeholders: an integrated approach', *Long Range Planning*, 31 (2), 227–238.

[26]Clarke, S. (1996), 'Brand-building through integration', *Marketing,* 17 October.

[27]Gronstedt, A. (1996), 'Integrated communications at America's leading total quality management corporations', *Public Relations Review*, 22 (1), 25–42, p. 26.

[28]Hatch, M.J., and Schultz, M. (2001), 'Are the strategic stars aligned for your corporate brand?', *Harvard Business Review*, February, 128.

[29]Poiesz, T.B.C., and Robben, H.S.J. (1994), 'Individual reactions to advertising: theoretical and methodological developments', *International Journal of Advertising*, 13, 25–53, p. 27.

[30]See for instance Schultz et al. (1993).

[31]Harris, T.E., and Bryant, J. (1986), 'The corporate communication manager', *Journal of Business Communications*, 23, 19–29.

[32]Van Riel (1995), p. 141; [Marion, G. (1998).]

[33]Olasky, M.N. (1984), 'The aborted debate within public relations: an approach through Kuhn's paradigm', paper presented to the Qualitative Studies Division of the Association for Education in Journalism and Mass Communication, Gainesville, Florida.

[34]Hutton, J.G., Goodman, M.B., Alexander, J.B., and Genest, C.M. (2001), 'Reputation management: the new face of corporate public relations?, *Public Relations Review*, 27, 247–261.

[35]Freeman (1984), pp. 219, 220, 221.

[36]Herkströter, C. (1996), 'Dealing with contradictory expectations – the dilemmas facing multinationals' (speech). p. 59. Available at www.shell.com/library/speech/0.1525, 2424, 00.html.

Shell (2001), 'People, planet and profits – a summary of the Shell report', p. 21. Available at www.shell.com.

BP executive, Claussen Environmental Defense Fund and Browne quotes at www.indigodev.com/BPclim.html (initially published in Ernest A. Lowe and Robert J. Harris (1998), 'Taking climate change seriously: British Petroleum's Business Strategy', *Corporate Environmental Strategy*, 5 (2), 22–31, now accessible at www.indigodev.com/BPclim.html.

Mogford quoted in Warren, C. (2003), 'A green giant: can being green help BP stay in the black?', *Continental*, May, 35–37, p. 37.

Chapter 3
Corporate Communications in Theoretical Perspective: Stakeholders, Identity and Reputation

Central themes

- Three concepts form the cornerstones of corporate communications: stakeholders, identity and reputation.

- Understanding stakeholder management facilitates the ability of organizations to manage within the current business environment.

- An organization needs to attend to a rich variety of claims and interests of stakeholder groups in the environment, yet at all times needs to profile a coherent corporate identity of itself to each and every one of these groups.

- Corporate identity involves the self-representation of an organization through communications, products and services, and employee behaviour. It is based on the basic, distinct and enduring values of an organization that guide its operations and that, when figuring in communications, set it apart from rival organizations in the eyes of important stakeholder groups.

- The ways in which stakeholder groups regard and value the organization is defined as corporate reputation. Ideally, from a corporate perspective, such a corporate reputation is in line with the communicated corporate identity and thus broadly consistent with the way in which the organization wants itself to be understood.

3.1 Introduction

The previous two chapters have circumscribed the field of corporate communications, its historical antecedents and its uptake in the contemporary world of organizations. The present chapter follows on from these chapters and provides a theoretical extension of the strategic management perspective on corporate communications that was introduced in these first two chapters. Three theoretical cornerstones are presented in this chapter – the concepts of stakeholder, identity and reputation – that together provide the groundwork for the strategic management view of corporate communications. Each of these concepts is central to the theory and practice of corporate communications. The theoretical overview presented in this chapter is therefore also a necessary hurdle that needs to be overcome before the reader is able to delve into the more detailed discussions of strategic and organizational issues around corporate communications practice in the remainder of the book.

Stakeholders and strategic management

The chapter starts by outlining how stakeholder management is now central to the corporate strategies, operations and communications of many, if not all, contemporary organizations. Organizations, it seems, have increasingly realized that now more than ever they need to attend to a whole range of stakeholder groups successfully for their own as well as for society's sake, and in order to avoid certain stakeholder groups causing a stir or raising issues that are potentially damaging to their reputations. This chapter is about this centrality of stakeholder management to the strategic management of the organization, and the role of corporate communications within it. The nature of stakeholder management is outlined together with its impact on the ways in which organizations are run.

A stakeholder model of strategic management, as was already suggested in Chapter 2, requires a broader and management oriented communications function in comparison to the craft and tactical approaches that have gone before. Corporate communications has arisen as this strategic management function and is equipped with the relevant concepts and tools for gaining acceptance of the organization and its operations with important stakeholder groups. The central concepts of corporate identity and reputation management are presented as one important way in which corporate communications, and the practitioners working within it, can guide organizations in their dealings with various stakeholders and harness the strategic interests of the organization at large.

3.2   Understanding stakeholder management and corporate communications

The previous chapter briefly mentioned how a broader stakeholder conception of the environment permeated the business world in the early 1990s. This stakeholder perspective is the result of a powerful restructuring trend that swayed through the business world in the 1980s and 1990s, and effectively established the view that every organization is dependent upon a number of stake-holding constituents instead of just a rather select group of financial investors or customers alone.[1] Heightened competition, greater societal claims for 'corporate citizenship', and pressures from the side of governments and the international community continue to suggest to corporations that the stakeholder perspective is the preferred option, if not the standard, for doing business in the first decade of the new millennium and beyond. A raft of stakeholder initiatives and schemes at the industry, national and transnational levels has arisen to this effect – including Green Papers of the European Union (Promoting a European Framework for Corporate Social Responsibility 2001, Partnership for a New Organization of Work 1997), UK Business and Society Report 2002 (Department of Trade and Industry 2002), UN World Summit for Sustainable Development (Johannesburg 2002), UN Global Compact (2004), the Global

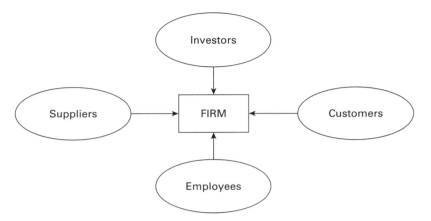

Figure 3.1   Input–output model of strategic management

Reporting Initiative (1997), the World Bank's Business Partners for Development, and the OECD Guidelines for Multinational Companies (2003) – all emphasizing the wider responsibilities of organizations to *all* of their stakeholders, and indeed society at large, that stretches beyond financial performance alone. The Social Economic Council, a government think-tank and advisory body in the Netherlands, illustrates this 'wider' responsibility by stating that an organization 'has a visible role in society that extends beyond the core business and legal requirements, and that leads to added value to the organization as well as the society at large'.[2]

The stakeholder model of strategic management

Conceptually, the widespread adoption of the stakeholder perspective in business marks a move away from the *neo-classical economic theory* of the firm to a *socio-economic theory*, within which the stakeholder perspective is embedded. A neo-classical economic theory of the firm prescribes that the purpose of organizations is to make profits in their accountability to themselves and shareholders, and that only in doing so can business contribute to wealth for itself as well as society at large.[3] The socio-economic theory suggests in contrast that the notion of accountability in fact looms larger: to other groups outside shareholders, for the continuity of the organization and the welfare of society. This distinction between a conventional neo-classical 'input–output' perspective and a stakeholder conception of strategic management is highlighted by the contrasting models displayed in Figures 3.1 and 3.2.[4] In Figure 3.1, the firm is the spill of the economy, where investors, suppliers and employees are depicted as contributing inputs, which the 'black box' of the firm transforms into outputs for the benefit of customers. Each contributor of inputs is rewarded with appropriate compensation and, as a result of competition throughout the system, the bulk of the benefits will go to the customers. It is important to note that within the input–output model power lies with the firm, upon which the other parties are dependent, and that the interest of these other groups and their relationship to the

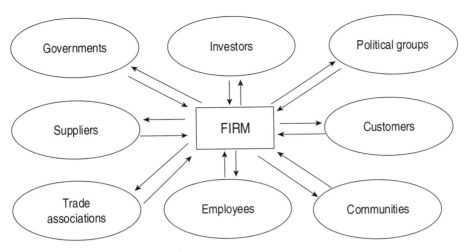

Figure 3.2   Stakeholder model of strategic management

firm is merely financial. The stakeholder model (Figure 3.2) contrasts explicitly with the input–output model in all its variations. Stakeholder management assumes that all persons or groups with legitimate interests participating in an enterprise do so to obtain benefits and there is no prima facie priority of one set of interests and benefits over another. Hence, the arrows between the firm and its stakeholder constituents run in both directions. All those groups which have a legitimate stake in the organization, whether purely financial, market-based or otherwise are recognized, and the relationship of the organization with these groups is not linear but one of interdependency. In other words, instead of considering organizations as immune to government or public opinion, the stakeholder management model recognizes the mutual dependencies between organizations and various *stake-holding* groups – groups that are themselves affected by the operations of the organization, but can equally affect the organization, its operations and performance.

The picture that emerges from all this is a far more complex and dynamic one than the input–output model of strategic management that preceded it. More persons and groups with legitimate interests in the organization are recognized and accounted for, and these individuals and groups all need to be considered, addressed and/or accommodated by the organization to bolster its financial performance and secure continued acceptance of its operations. One further significant feat of the stakeholder model of strategic management is that it suggests that an organization needs to be found 'legitimate' by both 'market' and 'non-market' stake-holding groups, the notion of legitimacy stretching further than financial accountability to include accountability for the firm's performance in social (social responsibility, community involvement, labour relations record, etc.) and ecological (e.g. the reduction of harmful waste and residues, the development of ecologically friendly production processes, etc.) terms.

True, organizations have always, even before the widespread adoption of the stakeholder philosophy in the early 1990s, dealt with so-called 'non-market' groups or publics (see also Chapter 2). However, before stakeholder management, such non-market groups were seen as necessary to communicate with only because of their indirect or more direct capacity to block markets within the context of the input–output model,[5] or their ability to condition or affect customer relationships and sales. Igor Ansoff, an eminent strategy professor, illustrated this feat of the input–output model, in his 1960 *Corporate Strategy* book in which he made a distinction between economic or market objectives and social or non-market objectives; with the latter objectives being a secondary, modifying and constraining influence on the former.[6] The stakeholder concept, in contrast, provides a drastically different view of the nature of the relationship of an organization with such non-market parties as governments, communities and special interest groups. These non-market groups are first of all credited as forces that need to be reckoned with; and the relationship of the organization with these non-market groups, as well as with market groups, is characterized by institutional meaning. In this institutional or socio-economic view, an organization is seen as being part of a larger social system that includes market and non-market parties, and as dependent upon that system's support for its continued existence. Organizational goals and activities must in this sense be found *legitimate* and valued by all parties in the larger social system, where every market or non-market stakeholder has to be treated by the organization 'as an end in itself, and not as a means to some other end'.[7]

Accountability of the organization towards all stake-holding groups stretches, as mentioned, further than financial performance alone into the social and ecological realms, and is captured with the roomier concept of *legitimacy*. This notion of legitimacy derives from norms and values of each of the stakeholder groups depicted in Figure 3.2 about what each deems acceptable and favoured of an organization. Having a *reputation* as a financially solid organization with a proven social and ecological track record (particularly in such areas as labour conditions, environmental performance and promotion of human rights) normally provides sufficient ground to be found legitimate by most, if not all, stakeholder groups. Framing accountability through the concept of legitimacy also means that organizations engage with stakeholders not just for *instrumental* reasons where it leads to increases in revenues and reductions in costs and risks (as transactions are triggered from stakeholders or as a reputational buffer is created for crises or potentially damaging litigation) but also for *normative* reasons. Instrumental justification points to evidence of the connection between stakeholder management and corporate performance. Normative justification appeals to underlying concepts such as individual or group 'rights', 'social contracts', morality, and so on.[8] From this normative perspective, stakeholders are persons or groups with legitimate interests in aspects of corporate activity; and they are identified by this interest, whether the corporation has any direct economic interest in them or not. The interests of all stakeholders are in effect seen as of some intrinsic value in this view. That is, each group of stakeholders merits consideration for its own sake and not merely because of its ability to further the interests of some other group, such as the shareowners.

Instrumental or normative motives for engaging with stakeholders, however, often converge in practice, as social and economic objectives are not mutually exclusive[9] and as 'doing good' with one stakeholder group delivers reputational returns and easily carries over and impacts on the views of other stakeholder groups. So, while certain initiatives and communications towards stakeholder groups may have been started for normative, even altruistic reasons – to be a 'good corporate citizen' as an end in itself, so to speak – the gains that this delivers in terms of employee morale, reputation, and so on, are often considerable and clearly of instrumental value to the organization. Kotter and Heskett specifically observed that such highly successful companies as Hewlett-Packard (HP) and Wal-Mart, although very diverse in other ways, share a stakeholder perspective: 'almost all [their] managers care strongly about people who have a stake in the business – customers, employees, stockholders, suppliers, etc.'[10] As HP's former chairman and CEO Lewis Platt once noted, many companies consider their shareholders to be far more important than their customers and employees, but he suggested that by doing so they loose their employee's support and the quality of their customer service also declines. Kotter and Heskett also observed that although HP and Wal-Mart had originally adopted a stakeholder philosophy for both instrumental and normative reasons, this philosophy has turned out instrumental and successful overall.

The nature of stakes and stake-holding

Having sketched some of the background to stakeholder management, it is helpful to devote a bit more space to discussing the concepts of 'stake' and 'stake-holding'. The standard definition of a stakeholder is the one provided by Freeman, where *a stakeholder is any group or individual who can affect or is affected by the achievement of the organization's purpose and objectives.*[11] A stake, which is central to this definition and to the notion of stake-holding in general, can be described as 'an interest or a share in an undertaking, [that] can range from simply an interest in an undertaking at one extreme to a legal claim of ownership at the other extreme'.[12] The content of stakes that are held by different persons and groups is varied, and depends on the specific interests of these individuals or groups in the organization. Special interest groups and NGOs which demand ever higher levels of 'corporate social responsibility' from an organization, for example, in such instances exercise their societal stake in the organization, which at any one time may coincide with investors who for their part apply relentless pressure on that same organization to maximize short-term profits. Stakes of different individuals and groups may thus be at odds with one another, putting pressure on the organization and demanding it to balance stakeholder interests.

Understanding the stakes of stakeholders and their priority thus offers strategic advantages to organizations in the current business climate over conceiving of an organization's environment as being composed of innumerable individuals and institutions, or as consisting of markets alone. Freeman was among the first to offer a classification for coming to terms with all those groups which hold a stake in the organization. In his classic 1984 book *Strategic Management: A Stakeholder Approach*, Freeman considered three groups of stakes: equity stakes, economic or market stakes, and influencer stakes. Equity stakes, in Freeman's terminology, are held by those who have some direct 'ownership' of the organization, such as stockholders, directors or minority interest owners. Economic or market stakes are held by those who have an economic interest, but not an ownership interest, in the organization, such as employees, customers, suppliers and

Table 3.1   Contractual and community stakeholders

Contractual stakeholders	Community stakeholders
Customers	Consumers
Employees	Regulators
Distributors	Government
Suppliers	Media
Shareholders	Local communities
Lenders	Pressure groups

competitors. And lastly influencer stakes are held by those who do not have either an ownership or economic interest in the actions of the organization, but who have interests as consumer advocates, environmental groups, trade organizations and government agencies. By considering these groups of stakes, Freeman specified the nature of stakes in terms of the interest of various groups in the organization – whether this interest was primarily economic or moral in nature – and whether this interest was bound in some form through a contract or (moral) obligation.

One way of looking at stakes is thus whether the interest of a person or group in an organization is primarily economic or moral in nature. Clarkson suggests in this respect to think of primary and secondary groups of stakeholders, with primary groups being those groups that are important for financial transactions and necessary for an organization to survive.[13] In short, in Clarkson's view, a primary stakeholder group is one without whose continuing participation the corporation cannot survive as a going concern. Secondary stakeholder groups are defined as those which generally influence or affect, or are influenced or affected by, the corporation, but are not engaged in financial transactions with the corporation and are not essential for its survival in strict economic terms. Media and a wide range of special interest groups fall within the secondary group of stakeholders. They do, however, have a moral or normative interest in the organization and have the capacity to mobilize public opinion in favour of, or in opposition to, a corporation's performance, as demonstrated in the cases of the recall of Tylenol by Johnson & Johnson (favourable) and the Exxon Valdez oil spill (unfavourable).

A second way of viewing stakes is to consider whether or not stakeholder ties with an organization are established through some form of contract or formal agreement. Charkham talked about two broad classes of stakeholders in this respect: contractual and community stakeholders.[14] Contractual stakeholders are those groups which have some form of legal relationship with the firm. Community stakeholders involve those groups whose relationship with the firm is more diffuse but nonetheless real in terms of its impact. Put differently, while community stakeholders are not contractually bound to an organization, such groups as the government, regulatory agencies, trade associations, professional societies and the media are important in providing the authority for an organization to function, setting the general rules and regulations by which activities are carried out, and monitoring and publicly evaluating the conduct of business operations. Contractual groups, including customers, employees and suppliers, are formally and more directly tied to an organization, and the nature of their interest is often economic in providing or extracting resources from the firm (Table 3.1).

In sum, the notion of having a true and legitimate stake in an organization is rather 'inclusive' and ranges from economic to moral interests, and from formal, binding relationships as the basis of stake-holding to more diffuse and loose ties with the organization. This inclusiveness implies that organizations attend to all of their stakeholders, and communicate with them; a point that once again emphasizes the need for organizations to project a favourable image to all stakeholder groups in a coordinated manner through all of their public relations and marketing activities. One further way in which this inclusive nature of the stakeholder concept is shown is in corporate social responsibility (CSR) initiatives that have been adopted by many organizations in recent years. CSR can be defined as the adoption by an organization of 'the responsibilities for actions which do not have purely financial implications and which are demanded of an organization under some (implicit or explicit) identifiable contract'.[15] CSR includes philanthropy, community involvement, and ethical and environmentally friendly business practices. CSR falls neatly within the stakeholder philosophy of strategic management, and underlines that for the majority of organizations today the input–output model of strategic management has indeed become a relic of the past.

Stakeholder management and corporate social responsibility

The impetus for CSR came with a recognition of the need for business to deliver wider societal value beyond shareholder and market value alone, and has in recent years become more pertinent through expectations voiced by the international community, NGOs, pressure groups, as well as many market parties. At the European Summit in Lisbon (March 2000), the European Council made a special appeal to companies' sense of responsibility, and linked CSR closely to the Lisbon 2010 strategic goal for a knowledge-based and highly competitive, as well as socially inclusive, Europe. Internationally, the UN World Summit for Sustainable Development in Johannesburg in 2002 voiced the need for businesses to contribute to the building of equitable and sustainable societies, wherever they work. Recognizing the urgency of this responsibility, many CSR schemes and standards have in recent years been developed and suggested by major international agencies. These schemes and standards should not merely be seen as an effort to support or judge companies' licence to operate in countries all over the world; rather they mark the priority that is now given to finding new ways to take up larger development and societal goals and towards establishing a new role for business in the new millennium.

On top of the momentum that has gathered around CSR in the international community and public policy arenas, organizations often also consider CSR in an effort to boost their own reputations. With the media constantly reporting on their affairs, and because of the greater product homogeneity and competition in many markets, many organizations realized that doing business in a responsible and just manner offers strategic and reputational advantages. As with stakeholder engagement, CSR initiatives may in the first instance be started for either moral or instrumental reputational reasons, which is nonetheless very hard to clearly establish or infer given the 'significant difficulties in distinguishing whether business behavior is truly moral conduct or instrumental adoption of an appearance of moral conduct as reputational strategy'.[16] Yet, despite the motives for engaging in it, CSR initiatives are nonetheless of instrumental value to the firm in that research has over and again found that these initiatives are related to reputational returns and an overall better financial performance.[17] Box 3.1 presents a case study of the Co-operative Bank in the United Kingdom, an organization that places CSR at the heart of its business operations and market strategy.

Box 3.1   Case study: the Co-operative Bank and corporate social responsibility

The Co-operative Bank PLC is a mid-size clearing bank operating in the United Kingdom. By the mid-1980s the enviroment and context of the Co-operative Bank had changed dramatically because of the financial service revolution where deregulation had removed barriers to entry (e.g. building societies), new technology had become the basis of competition and the consumer had become more sophisticated. In short, there was at that time an increase in competition both between the banks and within the financial sector as a whole within the UK. As a result, the major banks (including Barclays, NatWest and the Bank of Scotland) turned to a more selective positioning strategy, placing the Co-operative Bank PLC at a major competitive disadvantage because of the high awareness that these other banks enjoyed through size, high street presence and advertising expenditure. Hence, the Co-operative Bank PLC needed to find itself a niche or secure a long-term positioning strategy.

The Bank started a soul-searching exercise and reinterpreted the Co-operative philosophy that lies at its foundation. The Bank asked itself whether it can 'conduct its business in a socially and environmentally responsible manner while being consistently profitable at the same time' and concluded that it could. As the Bank's website now states: 'In fact we believe that, in the years to come, the only truly successful businesses will be those that achieve a sustainable balance between their own interests, and those of society and the natural world … The Co-operative Bank is seeking to achieve this balance'.

The Co-operative Bank PLC is indeed now well known within the financial and banking industry for its unique ethical positioning and CSR reporting that distinguishes it from its competitors. This ethical positioning strategy, according to some academic commentators, is not so much a moral affair but needs rather to 'be seen as a pragmatic response to the Bank's conundrum relating to its positioning strategy', where 'the Bank could promote itself as a proponent of people's capitalism, an ethical bank, in contrast to the images of the big banks tainted by association with Third World debt, South African involvement, city scandals and huge profits'.[18]

Whether its ethical policy is indeed based on more pragmatic and economic rather than purely moral reasons, the Bank's strategy has nevertheless been successful on many accounts. Since launching its ethical positioning in May 1992, the Bank has attracted large numbers of customers who do not wish their money to be used in ways that they object to ethically, as the Bank will not do business with certain organizations deemed 'unethical'. The Bank also generally believes that it has sharply positioned itself within an increasingly homogeneous financial services industry and estimates that around 15 to 18 per cent of annual profits is directly due to its responsible stance and behaviour. And Sustainability, a consultancy that evaluates CSR reporting of organizations worldwide, ranked the Co-operative Bank as the absolute number one in 2002: as a true 'expert' in stakeholder engagement. The Bank was judged as an industry leader in setting CSR targets and being clear about how it has performed against previous ones; in having its social report independently verified; and in its discussion of financial exclusion that was seen as 'a good example of economic impacts well beyond the traditional understanding'.

Questions for reflection

1. What were, do you think, the motives for the Co-operative Bank to adopt its ethical positioning strategy and place it at the heart of all its business operations? Were these motives economic or rather moral in nature?
2. What aspects of the CSR strategy followed by the Co-operative Bank have led to its success and acclaim in the business world? And what, in general, are sound and just tactics in CSR behaviour and reporting?

For the above-mentioned reasons, many organizations have now started talking about the 'triple bottom line': people, planet and profits.[19] John Elkington introduced the term and suggested that firms need to develop and report on CSR activities, activities that include social (people) and ecological (planet) initiatives (see Box 3.2), to meet their responsibilities beyond the generation of profits and healthy financial accounts. 'People' stands for all social and labour issues both inside and outside the organization, including employee support and compensation, gender and ethnic balance of the workforce, reduction of corruption and fraud, and more general *codes de sanitaire*. 'Planet' refers to the responsibility of organizations to integrate ecological care into its business operations, such as the reduction of harmful waste and residues and the development of ecologically friendly production processes. 'Profit' involves the conventional bottom-line of manufacturing and selling products so as to generate financial returns for the organization and its shareholders. This latter category of responsibilities is often considered as a baseline or requisite before an organization can even start considering meeting its social (people) and ecological (planet) responsibilities. That is, these other responsibilities cannot be achieved in the absence of economic performance (i.e. goods and services, jobs and profitability) — a bankrupt firm will cease to operate.[20]

Box 3.2 Management brief: corporate social responsibility reporting[21]

The founders of Ben & Jerry's, the funky ice cream manufacturers now part of the Unilever group, believe that business should give something back to the community that supports it. But what makes Ben & Jerry's unique and from a CSR perspective interesting is that the company was one of the first organizations to acknowledge its shortcomings publicly, going so far as to print them as part of the social assessment in its annual report to shareholders. A growing number of organizations have since followed suit, and are among the elite that now publish rather frank society or social reports that appear alongside financial reports and in which they systematically report upon their social and ecological performance over the past year.

Yet, at the same time, most of the large organizations around the world still report little, if anything, about their impact upon society. And, what is worse, many who have pledged to take CSR reporting on board often put out glossy reports that are more about style than substance, according to Sustainability, the consultancy that evaluates CSR reporting of organizations worldwide. A recent report from think-tank Demos strengthens these observations through its comments that companies view social responsibility as a PR exercise instead of a refocusing and reshuffling of their business operations. The Institute of Public Policy Research in the UK equally controversially revealed that only four out of ten company boards discuss social and environmental issues, routinely or occasionally, and that only a third of organizations have a board member with an environmental remit or with an interest in social issues.

So what appears to be at stake is that despite paying lip service to CSR, many organizations have not yet come round to developing and implementing fully fledged CSR initiatives within their business operations. This may be due to the fact that it is still early days, and that transparent standards and benchmarks of what constitutes social and ecological performance are lacking. As a result, many organizations fence with CSR, but take it rather easy and loosely when it comes down to implementing it in a substantial and comprehensive manner. In a recent article in the *Financial Times*, Schrage, an expert on social auditing, warned that these days may soon be over. On a worldwide scale, the public is demanding ever greater scrutiny and more evidence of CSR activities, and also governments are toughening their stance on what they endorse as good CSR reporting. Schrage writes: 'the message to multinational business – and to global regulators – is that social accountability demands the same kind of independent scrutiny as financial auditing'.

There are, however, difficulties with setting clear, unequivocal standards and with enforcing them, also because (transnational) authorities and institutions that would develop and guard such standards have not come forward yet. This of course plays into the hand of the current CSR malpractice and the 'anything goes' strategy. Schrage acknowledges these difficulties, yet advocates that 'just as the Securities and Exchange Commission and Financial Accounting Standards Board establish a framework in the US for public accountants to evaluate corporate financial performance, a new reporting system is needed for independent review of corporate social performance'. Such a system, when governments and industries are ready for it, will at least need clear social standards (in such areas as labour conditions, environmental performance and promotion of human rights), a professional corps of social auditors (independent of corporate control and accountable to the public), and safe harbours that limit legal liability (so as to encourage companies to open their businesses to social audits).

Until that day comes, and in order to be ahead of the pack, here are five guidelines for CSR reporting that according to Sustainability and others have proven successful:

1.   An organization needs to show that it is serious about CSR by setting clear objectives for social and ecological performance annually, and by systematically reporting on the results achieved afterwards.

2. Targets should include issues that are relevant to stakeholders, and should be linked to benchmarks and standards (at the industry and policy levels) wherever possible.
3. Targets need to be progressive in bringing new aspirations and standards to bear upon business operations instead of a regurgitating of existing practices that may be seen as socially and ecologically viable.
4. Reporting needs to be an honest, transparent and full-scale self-assessment instead of a polishing of performance data.
5. Performance data need to be rigorously assessed and verified by credible auditors (accountants or consultants) wherever possible.

Up to this point, the discussion has been around the more general aspects of the stakeholder management model. The concept of stake-holding was outlined, and the discussion emphasized the interdependency between an organization and its stakeholders and in particular the need for an organization to be found *legitimate* by all of them. This stakeholder model provides the context within which organizations, and particularly the senior managers and communications practitioners who work within them, now work and manoeuvre. Important implications that follow from this model are that:

- A corporate image needs to be actively projected to all stakeholder groups, so that these groups upon which the organization is dependent accept and value the organization and its operations as *legitimate*. The input–output model (Figure 3.1), in comparison, never demanded organizations to readily profile themselves and stand out on both financial and societal issues; nor did it require the approval of parties other than customers and investors. Stakeholder management thus requires organizations to think about their business and the profile that they want to have with important stakeholder groups, and whether this profile is sufficient to be accepted and favoured. The conceptual machinery that organizations have at their disposal to address this issue involves the concepts of identity and reputation, to which the chapter turns next.
- Stakeholder management emphasizes the need for both marketing and public relations as 'equal management partners' for communicating with and building relationships with *all* the stakeholders of an organization, and for a managerial framework from where communication efforts can be balanced and coordinated.[22]

3.3   Understanding identity and corporate communications

The stakeholder model posits that the various stakeholders of the organization need to be identified and they must be addressed for the stake that they hold. In practice, this comes down to providing stakeholders with the type of information about the company's operations that they have an interest in. Financial investors and shareholders, for instance, will need to be served with financial information or cues concerning the organization's strategy and operations (e.g. via annual reports, shareholder meetings, etc.), while existing and prospective customers need to be supplied with information about products and services (e.g. advertising, sales promotions, in-store communications). Each of these stakeholder groups, on the basis of the stake(s) that an individual holds in an organization, looks for and is interested in certain aspects of the company's operations. While the interests of stakeholders are intricately varied, and at times even at odds with one another (e.g. staff redundancies are a blow to the workforce, but may be favoured by shareholders and investors who have an interest in the financial strength and continuity of the firm), it is important that an organization provides each stakeholder group with specific information, yet at the same time projects a unified, clear and single corporate identity to all of them.

Stakeholder management and identity

The issue of identity takes shape and becomes salient in the context of a stakeholder management model of strategic management. An input–output model (Figure 3.1) of strategic management, where a corporation's strategies are wholly geared towards shareholder or customer capitalism, in comparison, obviously does not force an organization to think about itself, about the business it is in, and about what it wants to be known and appreciated for by all of its stakeholder groups beyond the financial community or customers alone. The notion of identity, in other words, is central to stakeholder management, as the following points from research and practice suggest:

- An individual may have more than one stakeholder role in relation to an organization, and ensuring that a consistent picture of the organization is sent out avoids potential pitfalls that may occur when conflicting messages are sent out. Employees, for instance, are often also consumers in the marketplace for the products of the company that they themselves work for. When companies fail to send out a consistent identity (and thus fail to match all their internal and external communications), it threatens employees' perceptions of the company's integrity: they are told one thing by management, but observe that a different message is being sent to the marketplace.
- A sense of identity, and the core values that underpin it, provide an anchor around which all activities and communications can be structured and carried out. Everything a company says, makes or does leaves an impression with stakeholders, or, put differently, 'communicates' in the broad sense of the word. Identity, when permeating all of the diverse behaviours, communications campaigns and products and services issued by the organization, facilitates the process of ensuring that consistent messages are being sent out.
- As a result of the distinctiveness that an identity gives, it also helps stakeholders find or recognize an organization. Identity, when consistently communicated, creates awareness, triggers recognition, and may also instil confidence among stakeholder groups, because these groups will have a clearer picture of the organization.[23]
- Inside the organization a strong identity can help raise motivation and morale among employees by establishing and perpetuating a 'we' feeling, and by allowing people to identify with their organizations.

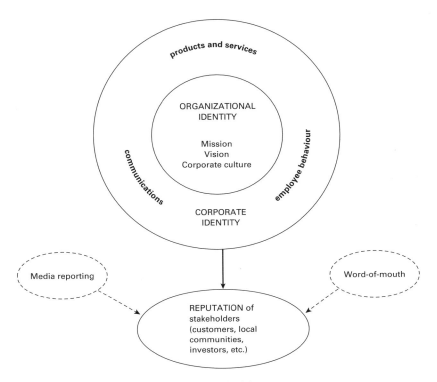

Figure 3.3   Identity, reputation and stakeholder management

The above-mentioned points underline that the concept of identity is paramount to organizations, the scope of their strategies, and how communications with stakeholders are managed. The spectrum of identity involves at one end deep-seated questions concerning what the organization is and what it stands for, often referred to as the organization's identity or *organizational identity*. At the other end, identity involves the act of expressing an image of the organization to stakeholders through all communications campaigns, employee behaviour and products and services. The management of all such communications and expressions towards stakeholders is conceptually referred to as *corporate identity*. Christensen and Cheney, two communications scholars, suggest that because of these two sides to identity – organizational identity and corporate identity – it 'includes under its head both the strict sense of an organization's name or identifying emblems (e.g. logos) and the much broader sense of a system's representations by/to itself and by/to others'.[24] Figure 3.3 displays these two concepts and their relationship to another central concept within corporate communications: the *reputation* that stakeholders have of an organization.

Figure 3.3 spells out that organizations need to be conscious of the corporate identity that they project to external stakeholders in order to achieve strong and favoured reputations, and that this corporate identity needs to be managed, as well as informed and guided, by the organizational identity: the organization's core values. Of course, reputations that stakeholders form of the organization are not only based on the information and cues that are received from the organization itself, as other sources including word-of-mouth and media reporting have an impact as well. Figure 3.3 suggests nonetheless that successful companies realize and work from the position that their own communications, products and behaviour have a key impact on the reputations that stakeholders hold, and that their own corporate identity mix needs to be managed accordingly. In this process, organizations need to link the corporate identity – the picture of the organization that is presented to external stakeholders – to the organizational identity – the values that members of the organization themselves associate with the organization and ascribe to it. This idea is present in many academic and practitioner writings, where corporate identity is considered as the self-presentation or outward manifestation of an organization that is based on the company philosophy, strategy, culture and vision; in short, its organizational identity.[25] Making sure that the corporate identity is rooted in the organizational identity then not only offers a distinctive edge in the marketplace, but also ensures that the image that is projected is not cosmetic but authentic and actually carried and shared by members of the organization.

Organizational identity and corporate identity

Conceptually, corporate identity can thus be defined as the picture of the organization in terms of how this is presented to various audiences. Originally, corporate identity was associated with logos and the company house style (stationary etc.) of an organization, but has gradually been broadened to include all communications (e.g. advertising, events, sponsorship, press/publicity and promotions), and all the ways – including products and services and employee behaviour – through which a picture of the organization is communicated. Corporate identity is thus quite encompassing, and as a consequence, spirals out into different functional areas within the organization. Communications practitioners (including marketing communications professionals), while involved with senior management in the overall formulation of the corporate identity, often bear the direct responsibility only for corporate symbolism and communications, while product and brand managers are responsible for the positioning of products and services, and human resource staff and middle managers for the guidance to and monitoring of employee behaviour.

Organizational identity relates to how an organization's members perceive and understand the organization.[26] Organizational identity is often defined with the central questions of 'who we are' and 'what we stand for' that managers put to themselves and other members of the organization. This then results in a number of values, beliefs and aspirations that are commonly captured in the mission, strategic vision and the more general corporate culture of an organization. The mission and vision represent the basic who and what of an organization: what business the organization is in and what it wants to be known and appreciated for. The mission often already includes a statement on the beliefs that constitute the organization's culture and underpin its management style and strategy, and also suggests how it wants to be known by groups outside the organization. Design guru Wally Olins phrased the difference between organizational identity (a concept that he initially labelled as corporate personality) and corporate identity rather vividly within the following quote:

Corporate personality [i.e. organizational identity] embraces the subject at its most profound level. It is the soul, the persona, the spirit, the culture of the organization manifested in some way. A corporate personality is not necessarily something tangible that you can see, feel or touch — although it may be. The tangible manifestation of a corporate personality is a corporate identity. It is the identity that projects and reflects the reality of the corporate personality.[27]

In sum, *corporate identity is thus concerned with the construction of identity to differentiate a company's position and offerings in the eyes of important stakeholder groups. Organizational identity, on the other hand, is founded in deeper patterns of meaning and sense-making of people within the organization and leads to shared values, identification and belonging.* While these two concepts can be analytically separated (as I have just done), corporate identity and organizational identity should rather be seen as two sides of a coin within organizational practice. Developing corporate identity must start with a thorough analysis and understanding of the underlying mission and culture, the existing organizational identity, rather than rushing into communicating what might be thought to be the company's core values in a superficial manner. Equally, whatever picture is projected to external stakeholders has an effect upon the beliefs and values of employees, and thus on the organizational identity, as employees mirror themselves in whatever messages are being sent out to external stakeholder groups.[28] The two sides to identity in organizations, organizational identity and corporate identity, therefore cannot and should not be seen as separate. This point is also affirmed and strengthened by studies into 'excellent' companies carried out over the past two decades. Writers such as Hamel and Prahalad, Peters and Waterman, and Collins and Porras, have all found that what truly sets an 'excellent' company apart from its competitors in the marketplace in terms of the power of its images and products can be traced back to a set of values and related competencies that are authentic and unique to that organization and therefore difficult to imitate. Collins and Porras, in their analysis of companies that are industry leaders in the US, argue that 'a visionary company almost religiously preserves its core ideology — changing it seldom, if ever'.[29] From this adherence to a fundamental set of beliefs or a deeply held sense of self-identity, as Collins and Porras point out, comes the discipline and drive that enables a company to succeed in the rapidly changing, volatile environments that characterize many contemporary markets.

So, what constitutes an organizational identity, and in what way, when informing and leading into a corporate identity, does it set an organization apart from other companies in the same sector? Albert and Whetten, who were among the first in 1985 to come to terms with the notion of organizational identity, talked about specific characteristics or 'traits' of an organization in all of its strategies, values and practices that give the company its specificity, stability and coherence. They argued that just as individual human beings express a sense of personal distinctness, a sense of personal continuity, and a sense of personal autonomy, organizations equally have their own individuality and uniqueness. And just as the identity of individuals may come to be anchored in some combination of gender, nationality, profession, social group, life style, educational achievements or skills, so an organization's identity may be anchored in some combination of geographical place, nationality, strategy, founding, core business, technology, knowledge base, operating philosophy or organization design.

Table 3.2   Identity structures

Identity structure	Definition	Example
Monolithic	Single all embracing identity (products all carry the same corporate name)	Sony, BMW, Virgin, Philips
Endorsed	Businesses and product brands are endorsed or badged with the parent company name	General Motors, Kellogg, Nestlé, Cadbury
Branded	Individual businesses or product brands each carry their own name (and are seemingly unrelated to each other)	Procter & Gamble (Ariel, Ola), Electrolux (Zanussi), Unilever (Dove)

For each organization, according to Albert and Whetten, its particular combination of identity anchors imbues it with a set of distinctive attributes and values that are core, distinctive and enduring to it.[30] For example, many people would argue that Sony's differentiation in the marketplace is quality consumer products, and it certainly has ability in that area. But what makes Sony truly unique is its core ideology of 'miniaturization', of producing ever smaller technology. This feature of miniaturization, which is grounded in a drive for technological innovation, is at the heart of Sony's organizational identity, and having been carried through in all products, services and communications (i.e. Sony's corporate identity) it has set the company apart from its direct rivals, and is likely to continue doing so. Equally, Virgin, a company that is active in very different markets – airlines, mega-stores, cola and mobile phones – has meticulously cultivated the value of 'challenge' with all of its employees. Headed by its flamboyant CEO Richard Branson, Virgin has carried its core identity of challenge through in its distinctive market positioning of David versus Goliath: 'we are on your side against the fat cats'. This projected corporate identity has led to the widespread perception that Virgin is a company with a distinctive personality: innovative, challenging, but fun.

Corporate versus brand identities

The Sony and Virgin examples illustrate the point that a company's organizational identity or core ideology can give it a distinctive edge in its positioning within the marketplace and in its reputation with stakeholders. But, importantly, core values or a company's ideology do not always play a part in the identity that an organization crafts and puts out in the marketplace. Companies such as Unilever and Procter & Gamble follow a so-called branded identity structure where neither the company's name nor its core values figure in the positioning and communications of its products (see Table 3.2). This is a *strategic* decision to position and bring products to market each with their own distinct name and values, instead of badging all products with one and the same corporate name. This strategy is preferred for organizations where a tightly defined organizational identity is missing, where the parent company therefore also lacks a strong corporate identity (and reputation!), and where an organization is addressing very different market segments through the different products in its product portfolio.

The choice of a branded identity structure has served certain companies well, and will continue to do so. But more companies, it appears, are now moving to endorsed and monolithic identity structures, and thus towards a strategy that puts the corporate identity and badge on all of their products. Companies that were branded giants before, such as Procter & Gamble, SmithKlineBeecham and Kingfisher, are moving in the direction of Disney, Microsoft and Sony in having a single umbrella identity that casts one glow over a panoply of products. In recent years, corporate identities have become enormously valuable assets – companies with strong corporate identities, and the reputations associated with this, can have market values that are more than twice their book values[31] – and can save money as marketing and communications campaigns can be leveraged across the company.

Perhaps because of these reasons, the above-mentioned companies as well as others around the world have realized the value of having a strong and distinctive corporate identity, and have recognized that they need to look inside the company for values and ideologies of the organizational identity that provide the basis for it and truly set the company apart. Unfortunately, this recognition and interest has not always been matched with action. Many companies, both large and small, often have not given enough care to articulating their unique and distinctive values, and have easily fashioned value statements for convenience or because of short-term thinking. British Airways, for instance, tried to make cosmopolitanism part of its identity, expressing the diversity of routes and communities it serves in the decoration of its planes' tail fins. British Airways obviously did not live the touchy-feely, eclectic, multi-cultural ethos communicated in the designs, as it was not carried and appreciated by staff, let alone its customers.

Drawing out the organizational identity and corporate identity

As a result of this sluggishness, as in the case of British Airways, many values statements that are meant to capture the organizational identity of the company in question end up being bland, toothless or just plain dishonest. This happens when companies view a values initiative in the same way they view a marketing launch: a one-time event measured by the initial attention it receives, not the authenticity of its content. The empty or too generic values statements that this produces may create cynical and dispirited employees, alienate customers, undermine managerial credibility and, most importantly, do not set the company apart from its nearest rivals in the eyes of important stakeholder groups.[32] In fact, 55 per cent of all Fortune 500 companies claim integrity is a core value, 49 per cent espouse customer satisfaction and 40 per cent tout teamwork. While these are inarguably good qualities, such terms hardly provide a distinct blueprint for employee behaviour; nor is it likely to set a company apart. Box 3.3 takes a closer look at corporate identities of banks, and discusses what values banks express in their quest for customers and the general appreciation of stakeholders.

Managers need to open the dialogue about values and attributes of the organization with staff and discuss them systematically and concretely.[33] Generic professional values *do* matter, and form the bedrock of every professional organization. Generic values like technological innovation, customer care and ethical conduct are in fact essential for conveying an image of the organization to all stakeholders, including employees, that the organization is financially solid, socially engaging, ecologically sound in its business practices, and so on. But over and above such generic values, the more authentic and deeper values that uniquely define the company need to be elicited and drawn out as they truly are the icing on the cake. This often comes down to a soul-searching exercise that senior managers and communications professionals should engage in (see Table 3.3) aimed at producing and triggering the attributes and values of the organization that are perceived as authentic, characterize it, are unique to it and set it apart from other companies in its sector. Wal-Mart is a case in point. Its vision of 'giving working people the opportunity to buy the same things previously available only to wealthier people' is wonderful, but is just a generic aspect of its positioning and pricing strategy, and is not the one specific feature that is differentiating or hard to imitate by rival firms. What is unique to Wal-Mart, however, is its core values of 'community' and 'partnership' that lie at the root of its founding and has propelled its success. Community and partnership are values that are meticulously carried through in its stores, advertising campaigns, employee ownership schemes and supply chain management. Wal-Mart has, for instance, changed the role of their suppliers into partners with them in their stores, thereby cunningly shifting inventory responsibilities back to the suppliers.

Box 3.3   Case study: corporate identity in the financial sector

Banks and the financial services industry as a whole have traditionally been characterized by generic and monolithic identities, where the image of the industry and the generic identities of banks (with perceptions of integrity and professionalism) were generally seen as imparting more value to the products and services than any brand could possibly achieve.[34] Historically, such a choice for a generic and monolithic corporate identity reflected the conjunction of historical forces, product characteristics (product differentiation is difficult in the financial service industry as services are easily copied) and environmental influences to which financial organizations are subject. However, because of the problems facing the banking industry as a whole in the 1980s (e.g. staff redundancies, poor customer service and lending decisions of dubious integrity), banks around the globe claim to have since put greater effort into redefining their individual corporate identities and brands as part of a search for differentiation in the marketplace.

Yet, when taking a closer look at corporate identities in the banking sector, it seems that banks have made little progress in developing truly *differentiating* corporate identities in terms of the values that they proclaim and the images projected. With the exception of niche players such as the Co-operative Bank (United Kingdom) and Triodos Bank (the Netherlands), which follow their own distinctive ethical positioning strategies, all the major banks still maintain monolithic identities and communicate a range of values that are not distinct but are commonly proclaimed by every professional firm.

Citigroup, for instance, the global industry leader that is based in the US, has recently decided to realign all business units and products under its monolithic Citigroup umbrella. In May 2001, Sanford Weill, CEO of Citigroup, announced that as the brand name 'Citigroup' has become strongly established in the corporate and institutional marketplace and that many of their clients now use 'Citigroup', regardless of the business with which they may work, greater efforts were being put into having a 'more unified brand'. Such a unified Citigroup brand, it is believed, strengthens the 'common culture' within the group, clarifies its image in the marketplace, and will deliver economies of scale as 'marketing and advertising campaigns can be leveraged across the company'.

The values that the Citigroup organization projects under the Citigroup heading are that it aspires and claims to be 'the leader in global financial services' and 'one of the great companies in the world' that is known for 'the highest standards of moral and ethical conduct', its great staff, and its customer orientation and excellent service.

While Citigroup in fact enjoys a solid reputation for its strategy and business (coming in at number six in the 2003 Fortune 500 ranking of the world's largest firms), it is questionable whether it enjoys this high distinction for the values that it extols (and this might in fact rather be the result of smooth marketing and the market capitalization of its business). Other banks such as BNP-Paribas profess exactly the same values, and equally claim that these are unique, distinct in comparison to other banks and inspiring. BNP-Paribas, based in Paris, defines itself as a 'bank for a changing world' (with 'change' and 'global' being incorporated in its logo of stars circling around the name BNP-Paribas) and communicates the values of 'customer orientation', 'service and value creation', and 'technological and financial innovation'.

The picture is repeated across the banking sector all over the world. ABN-Amro, a global market player headquartered in Amsterdam, frames its identity with the central corporate values of 'integrity', 'teamwork', 'professionalism' and 'respect', and aims to instil an image with its employees and external stakeholders of a bank that is professional, caring, accountable and strives for excellence in value creation and service. The Bank's logo designed by Landor Associates (London) consists of a symbol (shield) plus the logotype ABN-Amro and is meant to represent this professionalism, reliability and service excellence.

An interesting twist is that ABN-Amro decided to frame its corporate identity by using these generic professional values a couple of years ago when the new bank emerged from a merger between Algemene Bank Nederland (ABN) and the Amsterdam-Rotterdam Bank (Amro Bank). The Dutch government was very supportive of the merger at the time, as it was keen to have a world-class bank to compete on the world stage with the likes of Deutsche Bank. The government owned the rights to the name 'Holland Bank' and had offered the directors of the newly merged Bank the opportunity to call their new company by this name. With this name, the new Bank would be unequivocally Dutch, and would have an identity (relating to Dutch history and Dutch values) that would give it a distinctive edge in the financial marketplace. Yet, the directors of ABN and Amro considered the offer but declined in favour of the ABN-Amro acronym and decided to infuse the newly merged Bank with a set of generic professional values for framing and communicating their identity instead.

Questions for reflection

1. What can you say about the projected corporate identity of each of these banks? Is each corporate identity authentic, distinct and truly differentiating? And are corporate values sufficiently carried through in business principles, as well as logos, communications, employee behaviour and products and services?
2. What would be the added value if banks would really distinguish themselves from one another by positioning themselves with their own distinctive identity? And is it at all possible within the banking sector for organizations to have their own distinctive values stand out when the market appreciates general professional values and service excellence?
3. To what extent does the situation of the banking sector transfer to other business sectors (e.g. consumer goods, oils, manufacturing, retail, etc.)?

Table 3.3   Organizational identity research methods

Method	Participants	Data collection	Ease of analysis	Expert analysts needed	Costs
Cob-web method	Group of senior managers	Brainstorming session	High	No	Low
Focus group	Groups of senior managers and employees	Brainstorming session	High	No; but group facilitator (consultant)	Low–moderate
Projective tests	Groups of senior managers and employees	Interviews with use of visual aids	Low	Yes; trained psychologist/ researcher	Low–moderate
Laddering/ critical incident	Groups of senior managers and employees	Open interviews	Low	Yes; trained researcher	Low–moderate
Audit/survey	Groups of senior managers and employees	Questionnaire	High	Yes; trained researcher	Low–moderate

Without doubt, the values that an organization stands for through its members to be true, authentic and differentiating stretch beyond communications and the remit of communications practitioners alone. The CEO and the senior management team are the most obvious patrons of organization–wide identity questions, and the way in which these become translated into mission and vision documents and become spread throughout the organization. When Carlos Ghosn for instance took the helm at Nissan in 1999 he personally led the restoration and strengthening of Nissan's identity, which had become sloppy, weak and insufficiently exploited.[35] Alongside a restructuring and cost-cutting programme to boost productivity and profitability (for which he took a lot of flak), Ghosn revamped Nissan's identity of quality engineering and the uniquely Japanese combination of keen competitiveness and sense of community. He ensured that through his own performance and commitment as well as through internal communications these values trickled down through the ranks to embrace all employees.

As the example of Nissan shows, it is important that a sense of organizational identity becomes internalized by members of the organization, so that they can live and enact the company's values in their day-to-day work. In particular, those members of the organization who personally represent the organization in the eyes of stakeholders such as the CEO, front-office personnel and shopkeepers, and those who are responsible for marketing and communications, need to have a fine grasp of the company's core ideologies and values. Senior managers with the help of senior communications practitioners, as experts on stakeholder management, can facilitate this understanding by articulating and actively communicating the company's values to all staff within the organization through policy documents and internal communications.

A number of analytical tools are available to senior managers and senior communications professionals for drawing out and articulating the organizational identity (Table 3.3). These different tools, ranging from management exercises to more psychological projective tests, can all be used to elicit the values within the organizational identity of the corporation, but vary in measurement (open versus closed measurement) and in pragmatic considerations, such as the ease of analysis and the costs involved in their use.

1. Cob-web method.   This method consists of a group of senior managers coming together and sharing their views on the organization's key characteristics in a management session. At the beginning of the session, these managers are asked to name those attributes that, in their opinion, characterize and define the organization best. This part of the session is a brainstorming exercise, so there are no true or false answers regarding the attributes that are mentioned. After this brainstorming, managers have to choose eight attributes that they consider to be most relevant and to have most value in describing the organization. These eight attributes can then be displayed visually in the form of a wheel with eight scaled dimensions upon which, for further definition, the organization can be rated (and which can be further compared with stakeholder views of those attributes). The method is very easily carried out, but has obvious limitations in that it only captures the views of managers regarding the key characteristics of the organization.

2. Focus group.   This method has the advantage over the cob-web method that a broader group of representatives from the organization can be selected, and that their views of the key characteristics of the organization can be captured in a more detailed manner. A focus group starts with a brainstorming session in which all participants are asked to write down (on oval cards) and share their views on the identity of the organization. After each participant has articulated his or her views, these ovals are grouped and structured into a map on a blackboard, providing a synthesis of each participant's views upon the identity of the organization. Further analysis and groups discussions then follow to select the key characteristics that define the organization best.

3. Projective techniques.   These techniques (including cognitive mapping and repertory grids) stem from psychotherapy and aim to generate rich ideas and to involve individual members of the organization in a discussion of a subject such as organizational identity, which may be difficult to verbalize in discrete terms. Visual aids such as pictures, cards, diagrams or drawn out metaphors may be used to elicit responses. These visual aids are usually designed to be ambiguous so that respondents will 'project' their own meaning and significance on to the visuals. By doing so, they will declare aspects of their deeper values, beliefs and feelings concerning the organization, and this can be used for a further discussion of the key aspects of the organization. A common form of projective technique is the thematic apperception test (TAT). This approach asks individuals simply to write a story about an image that depicts a work situation; the researcher's task is then to find themes in what people say about their organization.[36]

4. Laddering/critical incident.   This widely used management technique can also be applied to organizational identity, where it is used to infer the basic values that guide people's work in an organization. The method involves open interviews, where

employees are asked to describe what they do on a daily basis, and how they look upon their work. Such descriptions of critical work incidents can then be further analysed to decipher the underlying values. The method can, when aggregated, give important insights into the general values that people working within an organiza-tion seem to share.[37]

5. Audit or survey.   A more structured research method involves an audit or survey that asks members of the organization to select from lists of attributes those charac-teristics that define the organization best. The selected characteristics can then be further screened by asking respondents in the same survey to evaluate the impor-tance and value of each of the selected characteristics for describing the organiza-tion. Surveys are easy to administer, but may not be able to capture the richness and detail of organizational identity that more open methods can.

   Once the value and attributes that make up an organizational identity are drawn out and made explicit, senior managers and communications practitioners need to consider whether the identified values are inspiring and stand out, whether they offer potential for differentiation in the marketplace, and whether they are likely to be appreciated by stakeholders of the organization. In other words, it needs to be decided whether the elicited core values are to play a role in the corporate identity mix and are to be made public through products and services, communications and employee behaviour. Some of the values expressed through the corporate identity mix will in fact derive from the organizational identity; other values may be included because of the sector in which the organization is operating or because of the expectations of its stakeholder groups. Surveying the opinions of stakeholders regarding the organization is therefore essential to capture their views of the organization and its relative standing in the sector in which it is operating, and to offset a strict view of the company's orga-nizational identity alone. Organizations cannot myopically focus internally on their identities alone and trust that on the back of their identity's strength they will achieve glowing reputations. Equally, organizations should not be led solely by stakeholder opinions (and opportunistically manufacture and fashion a corporate identity for it), as such opinions may be changing and sometimes short-lived. An internal orientation on organizational identity, which may be a source of inspiration and differentiation, needs to be balanced with an external stakeholder orientation, so that a company avoids myopically focusing on either one.[38] Polaroid, for example, is a case in point. The com-pany had from its beginning created a strong and distinctive identity around its business model and core competence of instant photography. In line with this identity, the focus was originally on self-developing film technology, garnering healthy profits on the film while earning relatively little on the cameras. This worked well until the advent of dig-ital photography, which offered instant photographs but made film unnecessary. Digital photography altered investors' and consumers' expectations, and as Polaroid was rather slow in following suit (and redefining itself as an imaging company and moving into digital photography), it had to file for Chapter 11 bankruptcy protection in October 2001. Surveying and being attuned to the reputation that an organization has with its stakeholders provides an important strategic indication as to whether the company's identity is at all valued and whether it has been successfully communicated. The concept of corporate reputation is therefore the subject that the chapter turns to next.

3.4   Understanding reputation and corporate communications

As we have seen, the purpose of corporate identity is to project a consistent and distinctive image of the organization, which, it is hoped, leads to favourable images and reputations with stakeholders. Having a reputation as a financially healthy organization with quality products and a solid social and ecological track record is essential in order to be found *legitimate* by important stakeholder groups and to ensure that sufficient financial transactions are generated. Stronger bottom–line performance in fact comes about because better-regarded companies achieve 'first-choice' status with investors, customers, employees and other stakeholder groups. For customers, for instance, a reputation serves as a signal of the underlying quality of an organization's products and services, and they therefore value associations and transactions with high reputation firms. Equally, employees prefer to work for high reputation organizations, and will therefore work harder, or for lower remuneration.

In other words, a good corporate reputation has a strategic value for the organization that possesses it. It ensures acceptance and legitimacy from stakeholder groups, generates returns and may offer a competitive advantage as it forms an asset that is also difficult to imitate. A good corporate reputation, or rather the corporate identity upon which it is based, is exactly an intangible asset of the organization because of its potential for value creation, but also because its intangible character makes replication by competing firms more difficult.[39] Not surprisingly therefore, managers continue to rate reputation as the most important intangible resource of a firm, and a survey of Fortune 500 companies in 2001 found that managing reputation was considered the lead philosophy among communications departments.[40]

Identity and reputation

Recent research firmly suggests that organizations with stronger identities have more positive reputations. That is, a strong identity is more visible to stakeholders outside the organization and serves as a differentiation signal. When a reputation is indeed broadly consistent with that organization's corporate identity, it also ensures that the organization is respected and understood in the way in which it wants and aims to be understood.[41] Alternatively, when there is a discrepancy between the identity of an organization and the way in which it is regarded, an organization is not standing out on its own turf and may not have a strong enough reputation as a result. Its reputation is then based, rather, upon more general associations with the industry in which the organization is based or is informed by reports from the media. Shell, for instance, in the wake of the Brent Spar crisis, realized that its lousy reputation in the 1990s had more often than not been based upon media reports and the tainted image of the oil industry than its own identity and the values that are at the heart of its business and operations. Shell has since put considerable effort into a rethinking of its identity and values, redesigning systems for stakeholder management, and running a global identity campaign to close the gap between its identity and reputation. Fombrun and Rindova refer to this alignment of identity and reputation as transparency, which they consider as an ideal situation (in comparison with a discrepancy between identity and reputation and the pitfalls that this brings). Transparency, according to Fombrun and Rindova is 'a state in which the internal identity of the firm reflects positively the expectations of key stakeholders and the beliefs of these stakeholders about the firm reflect accurately the internally held identity'.[42] Box 3.4 provides a case study of Starbucks, a company that is known for its efforts in achieving distinctiveness and transparency by aligning its identity and reputation.

Such transparency will be achieved when an organization is serious about its corporate identity; that is, when it frames values that are not only expected (as a socially responsible firm) but also authentic and distinctive, and has put organizational structures, processes and incentives in place to ensure that a consistent corporate identity is carried over to important stakeholder groups. As I have indicated above, there are certain values that an organization in any case needs to endorse (or at least needs to be seen to endorse) as a fully responsible and professional firm. These values include general attributes such as proficient management and leadership, social responsibility and community involvement, market performance, quality of products and services, workforce and labour conditions, and so on. Such attributes also provide the input for the general categories that companies are normally ranked on in such reputation indices as the Fortune 'Most Admired Corporations', the Reputation Quotient, and the Financial Times (FT) 'Most Respected Companies'. Table 3.4 provides a summary of these three publicly syndicated reputation measures. Each of these measures enjoys popularity with managers but all have obvious limitations in that they fail to account for the views of multiple stakeholder groups, and appear to be primarily tapping a firm's financial performance and assets. The Fortune measure, for instance, is known for its financial bias and the high correlation between all of the measure's nine (previously eight) attributes (> 0.60). This means that these nine attributes produce when factor analysed one factor, so that a company tends to rate high, average or low on all nine attributes.[43]

Box 3.4   Starbucks Coffee Company: an exercise in aligning identity and reputation

Starbucks, generally considered to be the most famous speciality coffee shop chain in the world, today has over 6,000 stores in more than 30 countries, with three more stores opening every day (Fortune, 2003). Many analysts have credited Starbucks with having turned coffee from a commodity into an experience to savour.

Starbucks' objective has always been to emerge as one of the most recognized and respected brands in the world. Since it made its IPO (initial public offering) in 1992, Starbucks had been growing at a rate of 20 per cent per annum and generating profits at a rate of 30 per cent per annum. Starbucks has always felt that the key to its growth and its business success lies in a rounded corporate identity, a better understanding of customers and a store experience that would generate a pull effect through word-of-mouth. Howard Schultz, Starbucks' founder and chairman, had early on in the company's history envisioned a retail experience that revolved around high quality coffee, personalized, knowledgeable services and sociability. So, Starbucks put in place various measures to make this experience appealing to millions of people and to create a unique identity for Starbucks' products and stores.

Schultz felt that the equity of the Starbucks brand depended less on advertising and promotion and more on personal communications and word-of-mouth. As Schultz put it: 'If we want to exceed the trust of our customers, then we first have to build trust with our people. A brand has to start with the [internal] culture and naturally extend to our customers … Our brand is based on the experience that we control in our stores. When a company can create a relevant, emotional and intimate experience, it builds trust with the customer … we have benefited by the fact that our stores are reliable, safe and consistent where people can take a break' (*Business Week Online*, August 6, 2001). Schultz regarded the baristas, the coffee makers in the stores, as his brand ambassadors.

Starbucks looked upon each of its stores as a billboard for the company and as a contributor to building the company's brand and reputation. Each detail was scrutinized to enhance the mood and ambience of the store, to make sure everything signalled 'best of class' and that it reflected the personality of the community and the neighbourhood. The company went to great lengths to make sure the store fixtures, the merchandise displays, the colours, the artwork, the banners, the music and the aromas all blended to create a consistent, inviting, stimulating environment that evoked the romance of coffee, and signalled the company's passion for coffee.

By the late 1990s, consumers associated the Starbucks brand with coffee, accessible elegance, community, individual expression and 'a place away from home'. And in 2001, brand management consultancy Interbrand named Starbucks as one of the 75 true global brands of the twenty-first century. Starbucks' identity and positioning as 'a socially responsible purveyor of the highest quality coffee [that is] offered in a unique retail environment' has thus led to a respected and strong reputation with customers, industry analysts, communities and other stakeholder groups.

Starbucks has always been concerned about its image and reputation, and rightly so. One of the possible ways of growing for Starbucks was to distribute its coffee through supermarkets, airlines (United Airlines) or fast food chains such as McDonalds and Burger King. But such alliances and alternative distribution chains carry significant risks for the brand and its reputation. Starbucks has built its distinctive reputation around a unique retail experience in company-owned stores. And customers could perceive the brand differently when, for instance, they encountered it in a grocery store aisle – an environment and channel that Starbucks did not control.

Questions for reflection

1. Consider the risks for Starbucks in forming product alliances with other companies or in adding alternative distribution chains. What rules-of-thumb can you suggest particularly from the viewpoint of Starbucks' corporate identity and the strong reputation that the company enjoys?
2. Reflect upon the corporate identity of Starbucks in the coffee shop market. To what extent do you feel that this identity is unique, authentic and competitive in this marketplace?

Reputation Rankings

Publicly syndicated rankings converge on a number of areas including financial performance, product quality, employee treatment, community involvement, environmental

Table 3.4 Overview of the Fortune, Reputation Quotient and Financial Times reputation surveys

	Fortune 'Most Admired Corporations'	Reputation Quotient (US)	Financial Times 'Most Respected Companies'
Method and sample	Annual survey of over 10,000 senior executives, outside directors and financial analysts.	A large sample of respondents (approx. 8,000) is interviewed to nominate companies. Nominated companies are subsequently rated by an even larger sample (over 20,000).	Annual questionnaire to 1,000 CEOs/senior executives in over 20 countries and 22 business sectors, complemented with a selected cross-section of fund managers, NGOs and media commentators.
Measure	Ranking is based upon the compilation of assessments given by respondents of the ten largest companies in their own industry on nine criteria of 'excellence'.	Ranking is based on the sum of attribute ratings, with each attribute contributing equally to the calculation of the overall RQ, and weighted to be representative of the US adult population on factors including age, sex, education, race, ethnicity, household income, as well as other non-demographic variables.	Simple ranking on the basis of nomination by CEOs, and weighted by GDP of the respondent's country.
Attributes included	Quality of management, quality of products and services, innovativeness, long-term investment value, financial soundness, ability to attract, develop and keep talented people, responsibility to the community and the environment, wise use of corporate assets, global acumen.	20 attributes within 6 dimensions: products and services, financial performance, workplace environment, social responsibility, vision and leadership, and emotional appeal.	Most important unprompted reasons given behind nominations are business performance (growth and long-term profitability) clear leadership and people management, effective strategy of market capitalization, high quality products and services, policies and procedures to assess businesses' environmental impact.
Top 10 companies (2002/2003)	Wal-Mart General Motors Exxon-Mobile Ford Motor General Electric Citigroup Chevron Texaco IBM American Internat. Group Verizon Communications	Johnson & Johnson Harley Davidson Coca Cola UPS General Mills Maytag Eastman Kodak Home Depot Dell 3M	General Electric Microsoft IBM Coca-Cola Toyota Sony General Motors Wal-Mart 3M Dell

performance and a range of organizational issues (such as supporting equality of opportunity and diversity, good environmental performance, improved ethical behaviour, and so on).[44] But these rankings do not take into account that stakeholder opinions vary and that stakeholder groups attend to very different cues when forming an opinion of an organization. Some stakeholder groups would not be at all interested in some of these areas, or would in any case not rate them in their evaluation of the company. What is more, the authentic and distinctive values that a company may project, and that are extracted from its organizational identity, come on top of the general professional values that it must endorse, and stakeholder appreciation of such core values does not always shine through and is not fully captured in publicly syndicated measures.

A reputation thus varies by stakeholder groups. In fact, it may be better to conceive of different reputations that various stakeholder groups hold of an organization. Taking into account the point made earlier that stakeholders have very different interests in the organization, different measures of reputations that include the very different attributes upon which organizations are valued may also be needed. In fact, according to some academic commentators, because of the recognition that there are multiple stakeholders 'no across-the-board measure of reputation is or can be valid for *all* stakeholders'.[45]

The nature of reputation

Before the chapter tackles the problem of how organizations can account for the various reputations of stakeholders in the design of reputation research, it is necessary to come to terms with the concept of reputation first. This is also important as there has been a lot of confusion and debate over the nature of corporate reputation in recent years.[46] Various definitions exist, but by far the most widely cited and used definition is the one provided by Charles Fombrun. According to Fombrun, reputation is 'a perceptual representation of a company's past actions and future prospects that describe the firm's overall appeal to all of its key constituents when compared to other leading rivals'.[47] A few elements stand out in this definition. Reputation is a *perceptual construct* and it involves *multiple stakeholder groups* who *evaluate multiple characteristics* of the firm. Each of these elements is key to reputation, and for developing a valid measurement instrument of it, so it is worth devoting a little bit of space to discussing each of them further.

First of all, reputation is a perceptual construct. This may be plain obvious, but when looking at the extensive literature on corporate reputations this does not appear so. In the literature on the subject, reputation is not only seen as a collective perception of a firm in the minds of stakeholders, but the concept is often extended and associated with organizational behaviour, assets and balance sheets of firms as well. This link is often made as organizational assets (e.g. distinctive capabilities, brand equity) are seen to be directly related to perceptions and evaluations of the firm by stakeholders. The motive for doing so is the assumption that perceptions of stakeholders in the aggregate are often relatively stable (e.g. customer evaluations of brands like Coca-Cola), and that the associated market value (e.g. when customers actually purchase Coca-Cola) therefore can be treated as a company's intangible asset (brand equity or reputation) and be put on the balance sheet.[48] This, by all accounts, is a form of circular reasoning, where perceptions and assets are intimately linked, yet equalled (assets = perceptions),[49] and this brings the danger that firms are not fully conscious of the dynamic nature of reputation and the variation that may occur as a result (e.g. when favourable perceptions of brands do not lead to purchase-related behaviour, resulting in a lower market value and a consequently lower value being placed upon the intangible asset associated with a company's reputation). The first important element of the reputation construct is thus: that it refers to the perceptions of individuals and stakeholders with regard to an organization, while the corporate profile (and the asset and market value arising from it) is denoted as an organization's corporate identity.

A second important element is that a reputation is formed by multiple stakeholder groups. This, again, is a common misperception in the literature and in the views of many managers, as reputation is often imbued with a single, corporeal and monolithic quality as if there would be one single reputation of an organization or only one way in which it is known. Such a view of course fails to account for the diffuse ways in which an organization and its assets come to be valued by various stakeholder groups over time. Rather than presuming a monolithic reputation, different stakeholder groups of an organization are exposed to and look for different signals or messages, and as a result form a reputation, which in its properties or attributes is likely to be distinct from views and impressions held by other stakeholder groups. An organization's characteristics and assets, however broadly defined, thus represent different values to different stakeholder groups, in turn guarding us from the hasty conclusion that the Fortune or FT rankings, for instance, which are based only on executives' evaluations of an organization, unequivocally represent *the* reputation of a particular organization.

The third and final element of reputation that needs to be clarified is that it involves not just a general impression but also an evaluation of the firm by stakeholders. This nuance is crucial, and pinpoints the difference between the corporate image and corporate reputation constructs. While both are the products of a multiple-variable impression formation process that includes cues from the organization's projected identity, as well as word-of-mouth and reports from the media (see Figure 3.4), the image and reputation constructs differ in one theoretically important respect. Images concern the immediate impressions of individuals when confronted by a signal or message that comes from an organization, while reputations are more enduring general estimations established over time. Conceptually, image may be defined as the immediate set of meanings inferred by a subject in response to one or more signals from or about a particular organization. Put simply, it is the net result of the interaction of a subject's beliefs, ideas, feelings and impressions about an organization at a single point in time. Reputation can be defined as a subject's collective representation of past images of an organization (induced through either communication or past experiences) that is established over time. Images might vary in time due to differing perceptions, but reputations are more likely to be relatively inert or constant, as individuals and stakeholders retain their assessment of an organization built over time.[50] Gray and Balmer, two academics, illustrate this distinction between the image and reputation constructs:

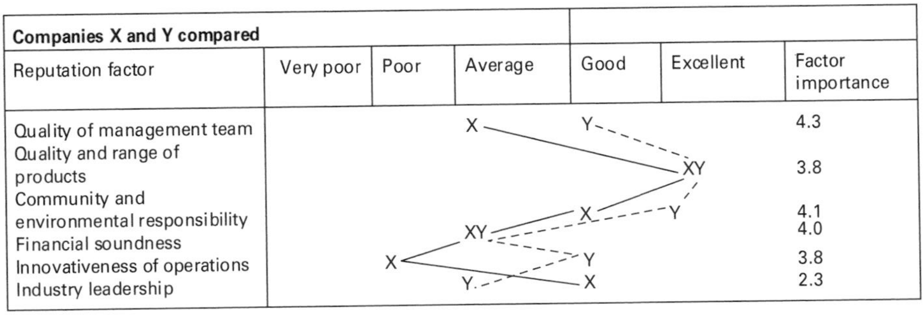

Companies X and Y compared						
Reputation factor	Very poor	Poor	Average	Good	Excellent	Factor importance
Quality of management team			X	Y		4.3
Quality and range of products					XY	3.8
Community and environmental responsibility				X	Y	4.1
Financial soundness		XY				4.0
Innovativeness of operations		X		Y		3.8
Industry leadership			Y	X		2.3

Figure 3.4 The corporate reputation of two companies compared

corporate image is the immediate mental picture that audiences have of an organization. Corporate reputations, on the other hand, typically evolve over time as a result of consistent performance, reinforced by effective communication, whereas corporate images can be fashioned more quickly through well-conceived communication programs.[51]

Corporate reputations can in this light also be seen as the focal effect that organizations should be interested in and focus on, rather than corporate image alone, which concerns more fleeting or ephemeral perceptions.

Measuring reputation

In all, the above-mentioned properties of the reputation construct (i.e. a subject's collective representation of past images of an organization established over time) provide the groundwork for researchers and managers with an interest in reputation, for developing operational measures and for surveying opinions of important stakeholder groups. For one, the time dimension (as reputation is an established perception over time) needs to be factored into the measurement process by having respondents evaluate a company (*vis-à-vis* its nearest rivals) *generally* instead of having them reflect upon a single instant (e.g. a crisis) or image (e.g. a campaign) in relation to that company. Second, reputation is a perceptual construct, so simple proxy measures of the assets, performance or output of a particular organization simply won't do, as these fail to account for the subjective, perceptual nature of reputation and the longer period involved in its formation. And third, measurement and also the sampling of respondents need to account for the various attributes upon which an organization is rated by various stakeholder groups.

Different types of research techniques may be used to gather these reputational data. These techniques exclude the publicly syndicated measures such as the Fortune 'Most Admired Companies' and FT's 'Most Respected Companies', which are a secondary source of research information that managers and communications practitioners can tap into to gain some information about the standing of their companies (when these are included in the rankings). Better still is for a company to set up

Table 3.5   Corporate reputation research methods

Methodology	Techniques	Data collection	Number of respondents	Ease of analysis	Costs
Qualitative	Unstructured interview	Oral interview: each respondent is asked to reflect upon his/her views of an organization and explain why (with or without use of visual aids)	10–40	Moderate/ low	Moderate
	Focus group	Group discussion: in a group, respondents discuss their views of the organization and explain why (with or without use of visual aids)	5–10 (each group)	High	Moderate
	Repertory grid	Oral interview: each respondent is asked to pick two out of three statements which match the organization best or worst and explain why	10–40	Moderate	Low
	Laddering	Oral interview: each respondent is asked to reflect upon beliefs about the organization aimed at discovering means–ends relations	10–25	Low	High
Quantitative	Attitude scales/attribute rating	Questionnaire: respondent ratings of attributes on Likert scales	50 or more	Moderate/ high	Moderate
	Q-sort	Oral interview: each respondent is asked to rate and rank statements about the organization written on cards	30–50	Low	Moderate

and conduct reputation research of its own using applied research techniques and its own stakeholder groups. In doing so, a company will be able to account for the diversity of opinions of its stakeholder groups, and will have a clearer view of the attributes that these different groups actually find important and on which they specifically rate the organization. Table 3.5 displays the two broad classes of research techniques, qualitative and quantitative, that may be used either separately or in combination for reputation research.[52]

Qualitative research such as in-depth interviews with individual stakeholders or focus group sessions with selected groups of stakeholders are one option. These qualitative techniques are more open in nature, allowing selected stakeholders to delve into their associations with the company as they see them. This usually provides very rich and anecdotal data of stakeholder views of the company. Quantitative research where stakeholders are asked to rate the company (and its nearest rivals) on a number of pre-selected attributes is another option. Quantitative research leads to more discrete data that can be statistically manipulated, but is less rich and may also be less insightful (i.e. it reflects to a lesser extent the particular lens of the individual stakeholder). The choice for either qualitative or quantitative research techniques is based on content issues as well as pragmatic and political considerations. Qualitative techniques are chosen when the attributes upon which an organization is rated are simply not yet known, or when there is a need for a comprehensive, detailed and rich account of stakeholders' perceptions and associations with the firm. Quantitative surveys are preferred when the attributes upon which an organization is rated are to a large extent known, allowing for a structured measurement across large sections of stakeholder groups. Many companies also opt for quantitative surveys as these are relatively easy to administer and process, and as it provides them with a 'tangible' indication (that is, a number). Figure 3.4 illustrates the reputations of two companies through an attribute rating that produces such numerical values. A tangible indication is also one of the motives for companies to buy into panel studies such as the Reputation Quotient, which provides them with a score that they can fence and work with, and sets a benchmark for future years.

Continuously measuring reputation is essential in order to understand how stakeholders think of an organization, whether this is in line with the projected corporate identity of the organization, and whether the organization is accepted and valued. Managers and communications practitioners will be particularly interested in what values the company is respected for and whether the core and projected values are actually salient in the minds of stakeholders. This will provide them with an important strategic indication as to whether the company's identity is at all valued and whether the company's identity has been successfully communicated. In the first scenario, when a company's identity is in itself not valued enough, managers may want to redefine their organization, strategies and operations with values that *do* matter to stakeholders and make a difference in the marketplace. Corporate giants such as BP and Shell in the oil sector (see Chapter 2) in the restyling of their identities into responsible businesses are a good example of this. When an identity is not effectively communicated or understood, the second scenario, management needs to rethink the company's stakeholder engagement programmes and the visibility and effectiveness of the communications tools that it has previously used. Gathering feedback from reputation research is an important step in the process of developing and refining corporate identity strategies including stakeholder engagement and communications programmes.

3.5   Chapter summary

In this chapter three theoretical cornerstones were presented. The stakeholder model of strategic management was outlined, together with the concepts of identity and reputation that take shape within it. Each of these concepts – stakeholder, identity, reputation – are central to the corporate communications function and the strategic management of the organization. This centrality will become clearer in the following chapters, which discuss the strategic and organizational issues around the practice of corporate communications in more detail. One important observation that was made in this chapter is that managers would be wise to look inside their organizations for core values that define their business and that can give them a competitive edge in contacts with their stakeholders. While the evidence for this is so far restricted to case studies it does appear to make sense. In fact, companies that have not thought seriously about their corporate identity and whether their profile is appreciated by stakeholder groups, often appear to hire and fire outside agencies with regularity, trying to find the one with the ability to 'sell' a message that people do not seem to be 'buying'. In other words, such companies have not given enough care to craft an identity that is authentic and distinctive, and also meaningful to stakeholders. The following chapter goes beyond the observations and theoretical overview presented here, and considers the actual process of developing communications strategies in practice. Based on research and materials from practice, Chapter 4 outlines in detail how communications practitioners can map and analyse an organization's stakeholders and the reputations that they hold before choosing a strategic corporate identity profile and running and managing stakeholder engagement and communications programmes.

Key Terms

Brand(ed) identity	Legitimacy
Cob-web method	Neo-classical economic theory
Corporate identity	Organizational identity
Corporate image	Projective technique
Corporate reputation	Publicly syndicated rankings
Corporate social responsibility	Q-sort
Economic/market stake	Repertory grid
Equity stakes	Socio-economic theory
Focus group	Stakeholder
Influencer stake	Transparency
Laddering	Triple bottom line

Notes

[1]Preston, L.E., and Sapienza, H.T. (1990), 'Stakeholder management and corporate performance', *Journal of Behavioral Economics*, 19, 361–375.

[2]Social Economische Raad (2000), *De winst van waarden: Ontwerpadvies over maatschappelijk ondernemen*. Den Haag: SER, p. 3.

[3]Friedman, M. (1970), 'The social responsibility of business is to increase its profits', *The New York Times Magazine*, 13 September.

[4]See Donaldson, T., and L.E. Preston (1995), 'The stakeholder theory of the corporation: concepts, evidence, and implications', *Academy of Management Review*, 20 (1), 65–91.

[5]Freeman, R.E. (1984), *Strategic Management: A Stakeholder Approach*. Boston: Pitman; Kotler, P. (1986), 'Megamarketing', *Harvard Business Review*, March–April, 117–124; Baron, D.P. (1995), 'Integrated strategy: market and nonmarket components', *California Management Review*, 37 (23), 47–65.

[6]Ansoff, I.A. (1960), *Corporate Strategy*. New York: Free Press.

[7]Evan, W.M., and R.E. Freeman (1988), 'A stakeholder theory of the modern corporation: Kantian capitalism', in Beauchamp, T. and Bowie, N. (eds), *Ethical Theory and Business*. Englewood Cliffs, NJ: Prentice Hall, pp. 75–93, p. 97; see also Drucker, P.F. (1980), *Managing in Turbulent Times*. New York: Harper & Row.

[8]Berman, S.L., Wicks, A.C., Kotha, S., and Johnes, T.M. (1999), 'Does stakeholder orientation matter? The relationship between stakeholder management models and firm financial performance', *Academy of Management Journal*, 42 (5), 488–506; Jones, T., and Wicks, A. (1999), 'Convergent stakeholder theory', *Academy of Management Review*, 20, p. 206–221, 206.

[9]Jones and Wicks (1999), p. 206; Porter, M.E., and Kramer, M.R. (2002), 'The competitive advantage of corporate philanthropy', *Harvard Business Review*, December, 5–16.

[10]Kotter, J., and Heskett, J. (1992), *Corporate Culture and Performance*. New York: Free Press, p. 59.

[11]Freeman (1984), p. 6.

[12]Carroll, A.B. (1996), *Business and Society: Ethics and Stakeholder Management*. Cincinati, OH: South-Western College Publishing, p. 73.

[13]Clarkson, B.E. (1995), 'A stakeholder framework for analyzing and evaluating corporate social performance', *Academy of Management Review*, 20 (1), 92–117.

[14]Charkham. J.P. (1992), *Keeping Good Company: A Study of Corporate Governance in Five Countries*. Oxford: Oxford University Press.

[15]Gray, R., Owen, D., and Maunders, K. (1987), *Corporate Social Reporting: Accounting and Accountability*. Hemel Hempstead: Prentice Hall, p. 4.

[16]Windsor, D. (2001), 'The future of corporate social responsibility', *The International Journal of Organizational Analysis*, 9 (3), 225–256, p. 226.

[17]Berman et al. (1999).

[18]Wilkinson, A., and Balmer, J.M.T. (1996), 'Corporate and generic identities: Lessons from the Co-operative Bank', *International Journal of Bank Marketing*, 14 (4), 22–35, p. 29.

[19]Elkington, J. (1997), *Cannibals with Forks. The Triple Bottom Line of the 21st Century Business*. London: Capstone Publishing Limited.

[20]Carroll, A.B. (1991), 'The pyramid of corporate social responsibility: toward the moral management of organizational stakeholders', *Business Horizons*, 34 (4), 39–48.

[21]This management brief is based upon Ben & Jerry's (1994), *The inside scoop: how two guys built a business with a social conscience and a sense of humor*. New York: Random House, *Financial Times* (2002), 'Corporate social responsibility: truants, nerds and supersonics', 18 November *The Observer* (2002), Special report on corporate social responsibility, 17 November p. 23, and Schrage, E.J. (2001), 'A new model for social auditing', *Financial Times* 27 May, p. 10.

[22]Scholes, E., and Clutterbuck, D. (1998), 'Communication with stakeholders: an integrated approach', *Long Range Planning*, 31 (2), 227–238; Grunig, J.E., and Grunig, L.A. (1998), 'The relationship between public relations and marketing in excellent organizations: evidence from the IABC study', *Journal of Marketing Communications*, 4 (3), 41–162.

[23]Dowling, G.R. (2001), *Creating Corporate Reputations*. Oxford: Oxford University Press.

[24]Christensen, L.T., and Cheney, G. (1994), 'Articulating identity in an organizational age', in S.A. Deetz (ed.), *Communication Yearbook,* volume 17. Thousand Oaks: Sage, pp. 222–235, pp. 223–224.

[25]Ind, N. (1992), *The Corporate Image. Strategies for Effective Identity Programs*. London: Kogan Page, revised edition; Olins, W. (1978), *The Corporate Personality: An Inquiry into the*

Nature of Corporate Identity. London: Design Council; Olins, W. (1989), *Corporate Identity: Making Strategy Visible Through Design*. London: Thames and Hudson.

[26]Hatch, M.J., and Schultz, M. (2000), 'Scaling the tower of Babel: relational differences between identity, image and culture in organizations', in Schultz, M., Hatch, M.J., and Larsen, M.H. (eds), *The Expressive Organization*. Oxford: Oxford University Press.

[27]Olins (1978), p. 212.

[28]Dutton, J.E., and Dukerich, J.M. (1991), 'Keeping an eye on the mirror: image and identity in organizational adaptation', *Academy of Management Journal*, 34, 517–554.

[29]Hamel, G., and Prahalad, C.K. (1994), *Competing for the Future*. Harvard: Harvard Business School Press; Peters, T.J., and Waterman, R.H. (1982), *In Search of Excellence: Lessons from America's Best Run Companies*. New York: Harper & Row; Collins, J.C., and Porras, J.I. (1997), *Built to Last: Successful Habits of Visionary Companies*. New York: Harper Business, p. 8.

[30]Albert, S., and Whetten, D.A. (1985), 'Organizational identity', in Cummings L.L., and Staw B.M. (eds), *Research in Organizational Behavior*. Greenwich, CT: JAI Press, pp. 263–295.

[31]Hatch, M., and Schultz, M. (2001), 'Are the strategic stars aligned for your brand?', *Harvard Business Review*, February, 129–134.

[32]Lencioni, P.M. (2002), 'Make your values mean something', *Harvard Business Review*, July, 113–117.

[33]Edmonson, A.C., and Cha, S.E. (2002), 'When company values backfire', *Harvard Business Review*, November, 2–3.

[34]Van Riel, C.B.M. (1992), 'Corporate communication in European financial institutions', *Public Relations Review*, 18 (2), 161–175; Morison, I. (1997), 'Breaking the monolithic mould', *International Journal of Bank Marketing*, 15 (4/5), 153–162.

[35]Ghosn, C. (2002), 'Saving the business without losing the company', *Harvard Business Review*, January, 37–45.

[36]Thorpe, R., and Cornelissen, J.P. (2002), 'Visual media and the construction of meaning', in Holman, D., and Thorpe, R. (eds), *Management and Language: The Manager as a Practical Author*. London: Sage, pp. 67–81.

[37]Van Rekom, J. (1997), 'Deriving an operational measure of corporate identity', *European Journal of Marketing*, 31 (5/6), 410–422.

[38]Bouchikhi, H., and Kimberly, J.R. (2003), 'Escaping the identity trap', *Sloan Management Review*, spring, 20–26.

[39]Weigelt, K., and Camerer, C. (1988), 'Reputation and corporate strategy: a review of recent theory and applications', *Strategic Management Journal*, 9, 443–454.

[40]Hall, R. (1993), 'A framework linking intangible resources and capabilities to sustainable competitive advantage', *Strategic Management Journal*, 14 (8), 607–618; Hutton, J.G., Goodman, M.B., Alexander, J.B., and Genest, C.M. (2001), 'Reputation management: the new face of corporate public relations?', *Public Relations Review*, 247–261.

[41]Peteraf, M., and Shanley, M. (1997), 'Getting to know you: a theory of strategic group identity', *Strategic Management Journal*, 18, 165–186; Whetten, D.A., Lewis, D., and Mischel, L.J. (1992), 'Towards an integrated model of organizational identity and member commitment', paper presented at the Academy of Management Annual Meeting, Las Vegas NV.

[42]Fombrun, C.J., and Rindova, V.P. (2000), 'The road to transparency: reputation management at Royal Dutch/Shell', in Schultz, M., Hatch, M.J., and Larsen, M.H. (eds), *The Expressive Organization*. Oxford: Oxford University Press, pp. 76–96.

[43]Fryxell, G.E., and Wang, J. (1994), 'The Fortune Corporate Reputation Index: reputation for what?', *Journal of Management*, 20, 1–14.

[44]Fombrun, C. (1998), 'Indices of corporate reputation: an analysis of media rankings and social monitors ratings', *Corporate Reputation Review*, 1 (4), 327–340.

[45]Hutton et al. (2001).

[46]Fombrun, C., and Van Riel, C.B.M. (1997), 'The reputational landscape', *Corporate Reputation Review*, 1 (1/2), 5–13.

[47]Fombrun, C. (1996*), Reputation: Realizing Value from the Corporate Image*. Boston, MA: Harvard Business School Press, p. 72.

[48]Barney, J. (1991), 'Firm resources and sustained competitive advantage', *Journal of Management*, 17, 99–120.

[49]Cramer, S., and Ruefli, T. (1994), 'Corporate reputation dynamics: reputation inertia, reputation risk, and reputation prospect', paper presented at the National Academy of Management Meeting, Dallas.

[50]Wartick, S.L. (1992), 'The relationship between intense media exposure and change in corporate reputation', *Business and Society*, 31, 33–49; Fombrun and Van Riel (1997); Cramer and Ruefli (1994).

[51]Gray, E.R., and Balmer, J.M.T. (1998), 'Managing image and corporate reputation', *Long Range Planning*, 31 (5), 685–692, p. 687.

[52]Dowling, G.R. (1988), 'Measuring corporate images: a review of alternative approaches', *Journal of Business Research*, 17, 27–34; Van Riel, C.B.M., Stroeker, N.E., and Maathuis, O.M. (1998), 'Measuring corporate images', *Corporate Reputation Review*, 1 (4), 313–326.

PART 2
CORPORATE COMMUNICATIONS IN PRACTICE

The first three chapters in Part 1 of the book circumscribed theory and practice perspectives on corporate communications and introduced the strategic management approach that is central to this book. Key theoretical concepts such as *stakeholder*, *identity* and *reputation* were discussed, the purpose of which is to help readers *think* about corporate communications and the strategic problems and complexities involved. It is important to understand, however, that understanding these theoretical concepts alone does not really indicate or describe how corporate communications is *actually* practised in organizations, in terms of how communications strategies are developed, how communication disciplines (advertising, direct marketing, employee communications, media relations, etc.) are organized, and the types of roles carried out by communications practitioners.

Part 2 of the book departs from this point and includes separate chapters on three topics within the practice of corporate communications: strategy, structure and people. Themes addressed in the strategy chapter are the nature and process of communications strategy development, and the link between corporate, market and communications strategies. The chapter on the structuring, or rather organization, of communications discusses the various ways in which communications disciplines and the staff involved can be organized to secure the strategic input of communications into corporate decision making and to enable the integration of their work. The final chapter on people discusses the competencies and skills of communications practitioners, and the trajectories of professional development involved.

After reading Part 2, the reader should have an intimate understanding of the practice and practicalities concerning corporate communications, and be able to put that understanding into use.

Chapter 4
Communications Strategy: Theory and Practice

Central themes

- Strategy is essentially concerned with general manoeuvres taken by managers for managing the interaction between an organization and its external environment.

- Corporate communications operates at the interface between the organization and its environment, to help gather, relay and interpret information from the environment as well as representing the organization to the outside world.

- Corporate communications strategy needs to be linked to the general corporate and market strategies of the organization, to which it must contribute if it is to be seen to have a genuine strategic role.

- The process of strategy making in corporate communications can be seen to consist of a number of stages: strategic analysis, strategic intent, strategic action and evaluation.

- There are a number of challenges for corporate communications strategy if it is to have a genuine involvement in managerial decision making and the overall strategic management of the organization.

4.1   Introduction

In the first three chapters of the book the strategic management perspective on corporate communications was introduced, as were the key concepts that define this area of practice: stakeholder, identity and reputation. These concepts combine to create a model (Figure 3.3), the purpose of which is to help readers *think* about strategic problems in corporate communications and formulate strategies for it. It is important to understand, however, that this model does not really describe how corporate communications strategies *actually* come about. The present chapter elaborates on this point and provides an account of communications strategies in practice. The chapter has three parts.

The first part introduces different schools of thought on the subject of strategy in general and corporate communications strategy in particular. The second and main part of the chapter discusses the process and practice of strategy making in corporate communications, taking the reader through the strategic analysis, strategic intent, strategic action and evaluation stages. Each of these stages is discussed in some detail as, figuratively speaking, they are the grist for the mill in strategy, and as they are important when it comes to considering how, in practice, managers might develop and implement a corporate communications strategy. Such an understanding of the full process of strategy is also important, as still in many organizations managers pay lip service to the notion of corporate communications as a strategy and rather view it as a tactical plan. The final part of this chapter builds on from this review of strategy practices to raise some challenges and issues concerning strategy development in corporate communications. Among other things, it discusses the need for executive support and for savvy professionals with an understanding of strategic management as critical factors for effective corporate communications strategies.

4.2   Perspectives on strategy in corporate communications

Over the last 30 years or so, strategy has become established as a legitimate field of research and managerial practice.[1] On the practice side, the massive interest in strategy in a sense reflects the complexity of managing contemporary organizations, which forces managers to think about strategic courses of action for their organization in interactions with markets, publics or stakeholders in the environment (see Chapter 2). In the subsequent evolution of research and thinking on strategy, a diversity of paradigms or schools of thought has since emerged.[2] Mintzberg[3] has forcefully argued that the concept of strategy itself has variously been defined as a plan (i.e. a specific guide or course of action in the future), a ploy (i.e. a specific manoeuvre to outwit an opponent or competitor), a pattern (i.e. consistency in behaviour over time), a position (i.e. the location of products in certain markets), or a perspective (i.e. an organization's fundamental way of doing things). Also, the *process* of strategy formation within organizations has become variously depicted in these different paradigms as following a rational planning mode, in which objectives are set out and methodically worked out into comprehensive action plans, as a more flexible intuitive or visionary process, or as rather incremental or emergent in nature, with the process of strategy formation being rather continuous and iterative. Each of these paradigms thus varies in whether the process of strategy formation is characterized and described as top-down or bottom-up, as deliberate and planned or ad-hoc and spontaneous, as analytical versus visionary, and whether it assumes perfect rationality versus bounded rationality. And, of course, processes of strategy formation may vary across organizations, emphasizing one or more of these elements from strategy theorizing.

General perspectives of strategy

Moving beyond the diversity and the distinct views presented by each of these different schools of thought, there is also a large consensus and some general patterns in thinking about strategy concerning the following three points.

1. Combination of planned and emergent processes of strategy formation.   First of all, it is recognized that, within practice, strategy formation often involves a combination of a logical rational process in which visions and objectives are articulated and systematically worked out into programmes and actions, as well as a more emergent processes in which behaviours and actions simply arise (emerge) yet fall within the strategic scope of the organization. Johnson has pointed out that within strategy theorizing there are accordingly two main thrusts in thinking about the process of strategy formation that reflect this combination. On the one hand, Johnson suggests, strategy formation can be seen to involve logical, rational processes conducted through either a planning mode or an adaptive, logical incremental mode whereby a direction and strategic objectives for the organization are articulated. On the other hand, strategy formation can involve what Johnson termed an 'organizational action' approach in which strategy is confined to manifest behavioural actions and considered as 'the product of the political, programmatic, cognitive or symbolic aspects of management within the organization'.[4]

The same combination of planned and emergent processes of strategy formation can also be observed at the level of communications strategy. In practice, communications strategy typically consists of pre-structured and annually planned for programmes, campaigns and actions, as well as more ad-hoc, reactive responses that emerge in response to issues (crises!) and stakeholder concerns in the environment. In the following quote from an interview with the vice president of corporate affairs at Kingfisher, a large retail group in the UK, this is aptly illustrated:

> The area [of corporate communications] that we work in is not like finance, and, of course, I have this discussion all the time with [managers in] finance, because it means that for instance managing our budget is much more difficult as we are constantly responding to both the external and internal environment ... Your environment is changing all the time, which means that your tactical approach is probably adjusting all the time. So, what is a priority one day is no longer a priority the next day. It requires continuous flexibility.[5]

2. Strategy involves a general direction, and not simply plans or tactics.   The term strategy is itself derived from the Greek 'strategos' meaning a *general* set of manoeuvres carried out to overcome an enemy. What is notable here is the emphasis on *general*, not *specific*, sets of manouvres. Specific sets of manouvres are seen as within the remit of those concerned with translating the strategy into operations or tactics. In other words, strategy embodies more than plans and tactics, which often have a more immediate and short-term focus, and rather concerns the organization's direction and positioning in relation to its environment for a longer period of time.

3. Strategy is about the organization and its environment.   Related to the previous point, the strategy literature is permeated with the concepts of 'mission' and 'environment'. Together, they suggest that organizations must make long-term, strategic choices that are feasible in their environments. According to Steiner and his colleagues strategic management can be distinguished from operational management (or input–output management, see also Chapters 1 and 3) by 'the growing significance of environmental impacts on organizations and the need for top managers to react appropriately to them'.[6] Managers who manage strategically do so by balancing the

mission of the organization – what it is, what it wants to be, and what it wants to do – with what the environment will allow or encourage it to do. Often therefore, strategy is characterized as continuous and adaptive in that it needs to be responsive to external opportunities and threats that may confront an organization. A broad consensus thus exists in the strategy literature that strategy is essentially concerned with a process of managing the interaction between an organization and its external environment so as to ensure the best 'fit' between the two.

Perspectives of corporate communications strategy

Given that the central concern of strategy is with matching or aligning the organization's mission, and its resources and capabilities, with the opportunities and challenges in the environment, one would perhaps have expected lengthy discussions in the strategy literature about the stakeholders that constitute the environment. But this, unfortunately, has not been the case. Although the concept of environment pervades the literature on strategic management, until recently it has been conceptualized in 'general, even rather vague' terms.[7] Environments were and often still are just characterized, as Chapter 3 already outlined, in terms of markets or operating domains, which ignores the whole range of other stakeholder groups that nowadays have a profound impact upon an organization's strategic scope and operations. What is more, one would expect acknowledgement on the part of strategy scholars for the role of corporate communications as a 'boundary-spanning' function, where the function's key concepts and tools for mapping stakeholders and stakeholder reputations could easily fill the 'environmental void' in theories of strategic management.[8] Here it is suggested that boundary-spanning functions can play a key role in the process of managing such environmental interaction. As a boundary-spanning function, corporate communications operates at the interface between the organization and its environment; to help gather, relay and interpret information from the environment as well as representing the organization to the outside world. The academics White and Dozier, for instance, argue in this respect that 'when organizations make decisions, they do so based on a representation of both the organization itself and its environment', and they go on to suggest that communications practitioners should therefore play an important role in shaping perceptions of the environment and the organization itself among decision-makers.[9]

However, this role of corporate communications is not reflected in most strategic management theories. In these strategy theories, communications is often still seen as a largely tactical or 'functionary' activity, in which professionals are considered 'communications technicians'. In such a view, communications is concerned primarily with sending out messages and publicizing a favourable image for an organization with little, if any, involvement in more strategically important activities such as environmental scanning, analysis or management counselling. Moving beyond these strategy theories, White and Dozier argue that this picture is also repeated in practice with their suggestion that for the vast majority of organizations, the strategic potential of corporate communications in its boundary-spanning role appears to go largely unrealized. This is the case, White and Dozier argue,[10] as senior management equally tends to treat communications largely as a tactical function, concerned primarily with the technical gathering of information and with carrying out publicity and promotion campaigns to external audiences.

Seeing corporate communications as a strategic function, in contrast, requires the strategic involvement of communications practitioners in managerial decision making. Such a strategic view of communications, which in part has already been realized within the business world but in part is also still aspirational, means that communications strategy is not just seen as a set of goals and tactics at the functional level – at the level of the communications function – but that its scope and involvement in fact stretches to the corporate and business unit levels as well. At the corporate level, where strategy is concerned with the corporate mission and vision as well as corporate positioning through the corporate identity mix, communications practitioners can aid managers in developing strategies for interaction with the environment. In this sense, communications practitioners are directly involved or support strategic decision making through their 'environmental scanning' activities, which may assist corporate strategy-makers in analysing the organization's position and identifying emerging issues that may have significant implications for the organization and for future strategy development. Communications practitioners can at this corporate level also bring identity questions and a stakeholder perspective into the strategic management process, representing the likely reaction of stakeholders to alternative strategy options, and thereby giving senior management a more balanced consideration of the attractiveness and feasibility of the strategic options open to them. Lastly, communications practitioners of course may also implement the corporate strategy by helping to communicate the organization's strategic intentions to both internal and external stakeholders, which may help avoid misunderstandings that might otherwise get in the way of the smooth implementation of the organization's strategy. With such intricate involvement in the corporate and business unit levels, corporate communications strategy is also more substantial – in being linked to the corporate vision and objectives – instead of being just a tactical ploy, and can be neatly built around the analysis of stakeholder relationships and key issues that are identified at the corporate and business unit or market levels and which form the basis for formulating specific communications programmes.[11] In other words, in an era of stakeholder management, corporate communications strategy cannot be divorced from the organization's corporate and business unit strategies, to which it must contribute if it is to have a genuine strategic role.[12] As one practitioner put it, communications 'must pass one basic test: at minimum; everything done must be aligned with the corporate vision or mission ... and must substantially contribute to achieving the organization's objectives'.[13]

This nested model of strategy and strategy formation, in which corporate, business unit and functional communications strategies are seen as interrelated layers in the total strategy-making structure of the organization, depends on a number of conditions. First of all, a conventional view of strategy formation where strategy is seen to cascade down from the corporate to the business unit and ultimately to the functional level, with each level of strategy providing the immediate context for the next, 'lower' level of strategy making, needs to be aborted. As scholars such as Mintzberg and Whittington[14] have suggested, strategy making fares better when it does not strictly follow such a rigid, hierarchical top-down process, but when it is more flexible and at least in part decentralized, so that business units or functional teams are

Figure 4.1 A traditional process of developing communications campaigns

encouraged to initiate ideas that are then passed upward for approval at the appropriate senior management level. From such a perspective, business units and functional management teams may be responsible not only for developing strategic responses to the problems or opportunities encountered at their own level, but may sometimes initiate ideas that then become the catalyst for changes in strategy throughout the organization. Communications practitioners, for instance, may relay their understanding and mapping of stakeholder relationships at the functional level to the senior management level and may as such initiate a revision of corporate strategy in terms of how the organization needs to build and maintain relationships with those organizational stakeholders who may have the power to influence the successful realization of its goals.

The layers between the corporate, business unit and corporate communications levels thus need to be permeable and relaxed, allowing decentralized initiatives and input from the lower level corporate communications function to the higher senior management echelon. For this to happen communications practitioners need to meet management expectations in terms of understanding and responding to the needs and concerns of the corporation or its separate business units – i.e. in terms of demonstrating how corporate communications can contribute to the bottom-line or provide invaluable counsel on the organization's environment. A different view of communications, and what it can do, follows from this. Instead of seeing communications 'strategy' as campaign planning or a set of programmed tactics, as has often been the case in the past[15] (see Figure 4.1 above), communications becomes a strategic management function that is charged with counselling senior management, and guiding and managing the reputations and relationships with important stakeholder groups that may impact upon the organization's operations. An illustration of this view of corporate communications – as a critical management function and as linked to corporate strategy – is provided in Box 4.1.

Box 4.1   Case study: the launch of Orange in the UK – clarifying the link between corporate strategy and communications strategy

The story of Orange tells one of the most exciting corporate brand-building successes in recent years with the company's market value having gone from nothing in 1994 to £28 billion ($46.6 billion, (39.7 billion €) in the year 2000. Apart from great deal making, shrewd distribution building, service innovations and technological development, the lion's share of this achievement can be attributed to the power of the Orange brand and its communications that enabled the company to achieve the corporate objectives that it had set at its launch.

The enormity of the task facing Orange at its launch is perhaps difficult to grasp and appreciate today, given the current popularity of mobile phones. In 1994, the UK mobile phone market was a confusing place for customers. Digital networks had just been introduced, but few people yet understood the benefits. On top of this, Orange also faced an uphill task in differentiating itself in this market as the last entrant in a field of four. Cellnet and Vodafone, two of its competitors, already had ten years of market dominance at that time, with full national coverage for their mobile phones and millions of captive subscribers on their analogue networks. Both Cellnet and Vodafone had also successfully developed low-user tariffs as part of a pre-emptive strategy to block entry into the consumer market and had assiduously strengthened their dominance of the business market through the development of their digital (GSM) networks.

Orange faced a daunting task in 1994 to reach the ambitious corporate objective that it had set 'to become the first choice in mobile communications'. Before the Orange name was launched in 1994, the company's trading name was Microtel; and executives of Hutchison group, Microtel's parent corporation, met at that time to discuss strategies for overcoming, or minimizing, the huge disadvantage of being last in the market. They soon realized that communications would be an integral part of this and instrumental for achieving the ambitious aim of market leadership. In May 1993 a team of senior managers and communications specialists from Microtel, corporate identity specialist Wolff Olins and advertising agency WCRS was set up and charged with developing a clear and strong communications strategy and positioning. This team quickly realized that the new brand could not be built around a low cost strategy, emphasizing price benefits, as this would have pitched the brand directly against one of Cellnet and Vodafone's greatest strengths, namely exceptionally low entry costs. Instead, there was room to develop a fully rounded brand identity built upon the market high ground, which had been left conspicuously unoccupied by the competition and would be a better alternative for capturing market share.

The team brainstormed names and propositions and finally arrived at the word Orange as best representing their ideas, with its connotations of hope, fun and freedom. Market research indicated that people found the name Orange distinctive and friendly, extrovert, modern and powerful. The name Orange, along with the term 'wirefree' (as one of the communicable values), were subsequently registered as trademarks. Advertising and corporate identity followed and were based around the positioning for Orange as formulated by the team:

> There will come a time when all people will have their own personal number that goes with them wherever they are so that there are no barriers to

communication; a wire-free future in which you call people, not places, and where everyone will benefit from the advances of technology. 'The Future is Bright. The Future is Orange'.

The team also realized that given the doubts that surrounded Orange as a late entrant at its launch, the most important task for the media strategy was to imbue the brand with as much confidence as possible. A multimedia schedule was therefore adopted: a dominating presence for the Orange brand with posters heralding each new campaign theme, TV communicating core brand benefits and press providing detailed messages in the information-led environment of newspapers. Since its launch, the branding and communications strategy chosen has delivered on its corporate targets. Although Orange has not become the market leader in the UK, a position still firmly in the hands of Vodafone, it quickly gained market share and a market capitalization that enabled it to expand into other international markets. In 1996, hardly two years after its launch, Orange Plc underwent its first public offering with the shares being listed on the London and Nasdaq markets on 2 April 1996. With a valuation of £2.4 billion, Orange Plc became the youngest company to enter the FTSE-100.

In October 1999, Orange was acquired by Mannesmann AG, which itself was bought in February 2000 by Vodafone, a deal approved by the European Commission subject to an undertaking from Vodafone to divest Orange Plc. In August 2000, France Télécom acquired Orange Plc from Vodafone. Despite the changes in ownership, Orange has continued to concentrate on its brand-led communications strategy, rather than on hard-hitting competitive strategies including price cuts and distribution growths, as this strategy has propelled the company to the corporate success and position that it now enjoys.

Questions for reflection

1. What does the launch of Orange tell you about the link between corporate strategy and communications strategy?
2. Is communications strategy therefore vital to the achievement of corporate objectives for every kind of organization (in other business sectors)?

4.3   Making strategy: the process and practice of communications strategy

The preceding section has indicated that for most organizations the central purpose of strategy revolves around attempts to match the organization to its environment. And, as mentioned, although writers on strategic management discuss the environment, only a few of these writers have traditionally recognized or described the role of corporate communications in identifying the most important components of its environment, and in using communications to build relationships with them.[16] This is unfortunate as for many organizations the question of how particular strategies may affect key stakeholder relationships has *now* become an increasingly important concern shaping the thinking of strategy makers.

The process of strategy making that is outlined in this section meets this concern. The process describes how communications strategies are built from the corporate level and are not just seen as functional level strategies or campaign tactics used to implement and effectuate decisions made at a more senior level. Communications issues and stakeholder groups become themselves identified at the corporate level in relation to corporate objectives and business operations; and corporate communications strategies are subsequently developed for addressing them.

Another characteristic of the strategy process described below is that it recognizes that the process of strategy formation may be conducted predominantly through a combination of planning approaches and emergent behaviour and activities. In other words, strategy making is outlined below as a stage-by-stage and planned process of working from analysis and objectives to programmes and evaluation, which may seem rather linear and prescriptive. But it is recognized that in practice this process is rather more flexible, cyclical and iterative, allowing for strategy makers to cycle backwards and forwards through the various elements of the programme (to ensure the feasibility and consistency of the developed strategy), as well as for strategic behaviour and actions to simply emerge in response to issues, crises or other environmental opportunities.[17] The process of communications strategy that is outlined below may therefore best be seen as a route map that guides senior managers as well as communications staff (public relations, marketing, etc.) in their work.

Developing communications strategy

It is important to stress that the model presented in this book is a useful device or means by which managers and students of corporate communications can *think through* strategic issues and explore the domain of communications strategy – it is not, to be fair, an exact empirical description of how the process of strategy making in communications necessarily takes place within each and every organization. Put differently, and as mentioned above, communications strategy in many organizations does not always involve a logical sequence of steps in which strategies are the outcome of careful analysis, objective setting and planning. Although many organizations, it needs to be said, do have formal planning systems and find that they contribute usefully to the development of the strategy of their organizations, others do not. Managers in such organizations may still think about the strategic position of their organization, or the choices it faces, but may then do so through a process of crafting instead of in a highly formalized way. Here strategy making is seen not as a formal planning process, but rather in terms of processes by which strategies develop in organizations on the basis of managers' experience, their sensitivity to changes in their environments and what they have learned from the past. Nonetheless, even though some organizations are thus characterized by such a crafting approach to strategy, the model outlined below still gives them some reference points for thinking through the process of developing communications strategy.

The whole process or cycle of strategy making in communications can be divided into four phases – strategic analysis, strategic intent, strategic action and evaluation[18] – with each of these phases incorporating a number of activities. The process is graphically depicted in Figure 4.2 with the communications strategy model. Each of the

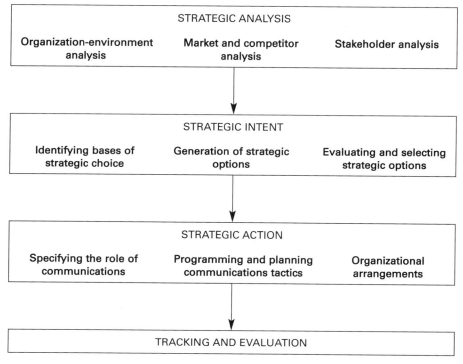

Figure 4.2   The communications strategy model

phases and the activities that come with it are described in detail and illustrated below with a case study of Wal-Mart.

Phase 1: Strategic analysis

Strategic analysis is concerned with understanding the strategic position of the organization. What changes are going on in the environment, and how will they affect the organization and its activities? What are the resources, values and competencies of the organization and can these provide special advantages or new opportunities? What is it that those stakeholder groups associated with the organization aspire to, and how do these groups affect what is expected for the future development of the organization?

The case study of Orange (Box 4.1) suggests that a great deal of care was taken by those planning the launch of the brand and the development of the business in analysing different strategic moves. First of all, the decision to enter the UK mobile telecommunications market required careful consideration by the parent company of the current and future demand in the market for telecommunications, the historical and likely future activities of competitors, and so on. An equally important issue in the case of Orange was how the new brand could overcome its weakness of being last in the UK market and then be launched to become one of the market leaders.

This was done by re-conceiving how value might be provided to customers; an inspiring and differentiated brand was developed that appealed to customer's demand for 'upstream' value.

The aim of strategic analysis is, then, to form a view of the key influences on the present and future well-being of the organization, and what opportunities are afforded by the environment and the competencies of the organization. In other words, the objective with strategic analysis is to analyse and draw out what the current position of the organization is with all stakeholders in its environment, and what this means for the organization's corporate, business unit or market and communications strategies. Such strategic analysis is rather broad-based, and may range from analyses of the organization and its environment, to competitor and market analyses, to stakeholder analysis. A range of analytical tools can be used here to make sense of the organization's position in the environment and the factors affecting its position. With the use of these tools, strategic analysis should seek to arrive at (a) a clear understanding of the external environment, particularly stakeholders and market forces affecting the organization; and (b) a clear understanding of the organization's internal strengths, weaknesses, values and capabilities. In this way, strategic analysis indicates in what way the organization should respond to its external environment, and as such provides the input for the next phase of strategy making: strategic intent. The different elements of strategic analysis and the analytical tools involved are briefly discussed below.

1. Organization-environment analysis.   The organization exists in the context of a complex commercial, economic, political, technological, social and cultural world. This environment changes and is more complex for some organizations than for others: how this affects the organization could include an understanding of historical and environmental effects, as well as expected or potential changes in environmental variables. This is a major task because the range of variables is so great. Many of those variables will give rise to *opportunities* and others will exert *threats* on the organization. Whether environmental forces have such an impact on the organization depends furthermore on how the organization itself, in terms of the *strengths* and *weaknesses* in its values, resources and competencies, can respond to them. A problem that has to be faced is that the range of variables is likely to be so great that it may not be possible or realistic to identify and analyse each one; and therefore there is a need to distil out a view of the main or overarching environmental impacts on the organization. Two analytical tools can be used for this: DESTEP analysis and SWOT analysis.

A *DESTEP analysis* is a broad analysis of the various demographic, economic, social, technological, ecological and political developments and factors that are expected to have an impact upon the organization and its operations. This includes a summation of factors, such as government regulation (political), that affect the industry in which the organization operates, changing societal attitudes towards certain industries and increasing demand for 'corporate citizenship' (social/ecological), and the effects of an economic slump and recession for the organization's supply and pricing strategies (economic). The DESTEP analysis provides a framework for summarizing and prioritizing all of these factors. Through such a guided analysis of the environment, managers are able to describe the most important current environmental changes and to predict future changes.

A *SWOT analysis* stands for an investigation of the strengths, weaknesses, opportunities and threats. The first half of this analysis – strengths and weaknesses – examines the company's position, its capabilities, operations and products *vis-à-vis* stakeholders, competitor activities, environmental trends and company resources. The second half of the SWOT takes this review further to examine the opportunities and threats identified within the environment, including, for instance, market opportunities, political regulation and shareholder activism. The result of the SWOT analysis should be a thorough understanding of the organization's status, of its standing with important groups in its environment and of the factors in the environment that may impinge upon it. A SWOT analysis should be carried out in an objective and detailed manner, with evidence provided to support the points cited.

Together, these two analytical tools will provide managers with an understanding of the organization – its capabilities and operations – and with a general overview of the organization's position within the environment. The whole purpose of organization-environment analysis is not to generate long lists of factors and points, but to provide a concise and to-the-point analysis of the organization and its current position within the environment.

2. Market and competitive analysis.　One part of the overall environment of an organization includes the markets or market environment in which the organization operates. With market and competitive analyses, the aim is to identify what the competitive position of the organization and its products is within the markets in which it operates and whether the organization can target and serve those markets in a way that at least rivals, if not exceeds, its nearest competitors. Analytical tools include market analysis and competitive analysis.

A first step towards understanding the market environment is to analyse the structure and customer requirements within a market or market segment, or market analysis. An analysis of the structure of a market includes identifying the size of the market and trends within it, and whether the market can be further partitioned into different market segments. An analysis of the customers includes gathering data and drawing up a detailed profile of customers within the market or market segments in terms of their buying and consumer behaviour. Such customer analysis should also aim to draw out whether customers appreciate and value the products and services, as well as the entire corporate identity profile of the company behind it.

Most market environments of organizations are furthermore characterized by competition (instead of a monopoly). Within this competitive environment, organizations thus need to understand the nature of the competition they face. Who are the main competitors? At which segments are they targeting their products and services? Answering these questions allows managers to make decisions about the most appropriate segments to target and the kind of competitive advantage to seek. Michael Porter's five-forces model is often used for this type of competitor analysis. The five-forces model is a well-tested model that determines the intrinsic long-run profit attractiveness of a market or market segment to an organization, taking account of the competitive threats posed to it.[19] The five forces – each with a different threat – are industry competitors (threat of intense segment rivalry), potential entrants (threat of new entrants), substitutes (threat of substitute products), buyers (threat of buyers' growing bargaining power), and suppliers (threat of suppliers' growing bargaining power). Identifying the nature of these five forces for a particular market or market segment allows organizations to understand its competitive position and ways of consolidating and/or strengthening it.

3. Stakeholder analysis.   While the above analyses of the organization's environment, position and capabilities provide the essential background context for the development of any corporate, market or communications strategy, from a corporate communications perspective, it is in any case crucial to identify and understand the relationships with the organization's key stakeholders. This analysis should at least provide some answers to the following questions: how will the organization's actions impact on stakeholders? What influence can stakeholders exert on the organization that may affect the realization of its goals? What type of consequences may result from either's actions? What type of behaviours from stakeholders does the organization wish to encourage? What reputation does the organization have with its stakeholders? Two analytical tools can be used to provide answers to these questions: stakeholder mapping and reputation research.

Stakeholder mapping is an analytical tool whereby managers start with identifying all stakeholder groups of an organization and display their relationship to the organization and one another visually in a map. This mapping exercise should enable the primary stakeholder relationships to be identified and the patterns of interdependence to emerge. When all stakeholder groups are identified, the analysis continues with a classification of stakeholders in terms of the nature of the claim and their priority to the organization. Freeman's classification of equity stakes (i.e. those who have some direct 'ownership' of the organization, such as stockholders, directors or minority interest owners), economic or market stakes (i.e. those who have an economic interest, but not an ownership interest, in the organization, such as employees, customers, suppliers and competitors), and influencer stakes (i.e. those who do not have either an ownership or economic interest in the actions of the organization, but who have interests such as consumer advocates, environmental groups, trade organizations and government agencies), which was mentioned in Chapter 3, is one way of classifying stakeholder groups in an understandable and workable manner. Another way of categorizing and analysing stakeholders is the approach advocated by Mitchell and his colleagues.[20] They identify three key attributes of stakeholder groups whose presence or absence can be used to identify, classify and prioritize stakeholder relationships: power (the power of the stakeholder group upon an organization), legitimacy (the legitimacy of the claim laid upon the organization by the stakeholder group) and urgency (the degree to which stakeholder claims call for immediate action). Combining these three attributes and their presence or absence leads to seven different types of stakeholders as shown in Box 4.2 and provides managers with a prioritized list of stakeholder groups as an input for strategy.

A second form of stakeholder analysis is to identify the different reputations that organizations have with various stakeholder groups. Chapter 3 distinguished between qualitative methods such as in-depth interviews and focus group sessions, and quantitative methods of reputation research; the latter including a larger sample of respondents who are then asked to rate the organization on a number of pre-defined dimensions. Both qualitative and quantitative methods can be used but should be attentive to the diversity of stakeholder groups of the organization (as identified by the stakeholder mapping exercise) and the variety of attributes (e.g. financial performance, community involvement, employee treatment, product quality, environmental performance, and so on) by which stakeholders evaluate and rate an organization. The outcomes of such reputation research may be compared to a target or benchmark that the company has set for itself in terms of how it wants to be known and appreciated by key stakeholder groups.

Box 4.2   Management brief: stakeholder mapping

Once stakeholders have been identified and drawn into a stakeholder map, they can be further classified and prioritized according to the presence or absence of three key attributes: power (the power of the stakeholder group upon an organization), legitimacy (the legitimacy of the claim laid upon the organization by the stakeholder group) and urgency (the degree to which stakeholder claims call for immediate action). Together, these three attributes form seven different types of stakeholders, as shown in the figure below.

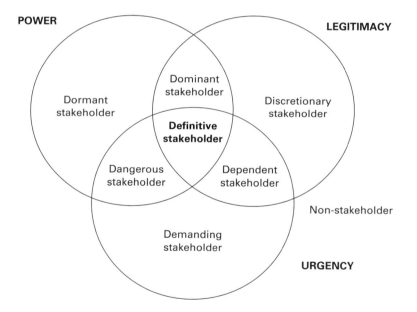

The three stakeholders groups on the outer sides of the figure are classified as *latent* stakeholders groups – as groups possessing only one attribute:

1. *Dormant stakeholders*: those who have the power to impose their will on others, but because they do not have a legitimate relationship or urgent claim, their power remains dormant. Examples of dormant stakeholders are plentiful. For instance, power is held by those who have a loaded gun (coercive), those who

can spend a lot of money (utilitarian), or those who can command the attention of the news media (symbolic). However, dormant stakeholders have little or no interaction with the firm, but because of their potential to acquire a second attribute (urgency or legitimacy), management should remain cognizant of such stakeholders.

2. *Discretionary stakeholders*: those who possess legitimate claims but have no power to influence the firm, and no urgent claims. Recipients of corporate charity, for instance, fall within this group.

3. *Demanding stakeholders*: those who have urgent claims, but neither the power nor legitimacy to enforce them. These groups can therefore be bothersome but do not warrant serious management attention. That is, where stakeholders are unable or unwilling to acquire either the power or the legitimacy necessary to move their claim into a more salient status, the 'noise' of urgency is insufficient to project a stakeholder claim beyond latency. For example, a lone millenarian picketer who marches outside corporate headquarters with a sign that says, 'The end of the world is coming! Acme chemical is the cause!' might be extremely irritating to Acme's managers, but the claims of the picketer remain largely unconsidered.

Three further groups are considered and classified as expectant stakeholders; groups with two attributes present:

4. *Dominant stakeholders*: those who have both powerful and legitimate claims; hence their influence is assured. Examples include the employees, customers, owners and significant creditors of the organization.

5. *Dangerous stakeholders*: those who have power and urgent claims, but lack legitimacy. They are seen as dangerous as they may resort to coercion and even violence. Examples of unlawful, yet common, attempts at using coercive means to advance stakeholder claims (which may or may not be legitimate) include wildcat strikes, employee sabotage and terrorism. Other examples of stakeholders using coercive tactics include environmentalists spiking trees in areas to be logged and religious or political terrorists using bombings, shootings or kidnappings to call attention to their claims.

6. *Dependent stakeholders*: those that lack power, but who have urgent, legitimate claims. They rely on others for the power to carry out their will – perhaps through the advocacy of other stakeholders. Local residents of a community in which a plant of a large corporation is based, for instance, often need to rely on lobby groups or some other form of political representation to have their concerns voiced.

The seventh and final type of stakeholders group that can be identified is:

7. *Definitive stakeholders*: those who have legitimacy, power and urgency. In other words, definitive stakeholders are powerful and legitimate stakeholders who by definition will already be a member of the firm's dominant coalition. When the claim of a definitive stakeholder is urgent, managers have a clear mandate to give priority and attention to it. Stockholders, for example, who are normally classified as dominant stakeholders, can become active when they feel that their legitimate interests are not being served by the managers of the company in which they hold stock and then effectively act as definitive stakeholders. That is, as the

> actions of such powerful stockholders may imply the removal of senior executives, managers of the company urgently need to attend to their concerns.
>
> Together, the three attributes of legitimacy, power and urgency, and the stakeholder typology provided, allows managers to classify the stakeholder groups of an organization, and to determine which stakeholder claims require attention and/or action. In a nutshell, the typology provides an insight into which stakeholder groups hold valid and urgent claims, and have the power to exercise their will, and thus require the organization to respond to their claims or rather refrain from doing so.[21]

Together, a consideration of the organization–environment, market environment, and stakeholders provides a basis for the strategic analysis of an organization. Such an understanding must take the future into account. Is the current strategy capable of dealing with changes taking place in the organization's environment? Is it likely to deliver the expected or desired results? If so, in what respects, and if not, why not? It is unlikely that there will be a complete match between current strategy and the picture emerging from the strategic analysis. The extent to which there is a mismatch here is the extent of the strategic problem facing the organization. It may be that the adjustment that is required is minimal, or it may be that there is a need for a more fundamental realignment of strategy. The strategic problem also indicates whether strategic adjustments concern the corporate, market or operational levels, and the extent to which it is a communications problem.

It is thus important that all of the three types of analyses mentioned above are carried out, so that a comprehensive analysis and overview of the strategic issues faced by the organization in relation to the stakeholders and markets in its environment is provided for, and the strategic problem can be more accurately identified. As such, from this strategic analysis, it should be possible to identify the key strategic actions that need to be taken and the role that communications is to play in the overall strategy of the organization.

Phase 2: Strategic intent

Strategic analysis is concerned with understanding the position of the organization in its environment. Strategic intent proceeds from this analysis and involves the formulation of a strategic vision, around which possible courses of action are formulated, evaluated and eventually chosen. In other words, strategic intent sets the general direction, often articulated in objectives, and defines the general patterns of actions that will be taken to achieve these objectives. As Hamel and Prahalad put it:

> On the one hand, strategic intent envisions a desired leadership position and establishes the criterion the organization will use to chart its progress … At the same time, strategic intent is more than simply unfettered ambition. The concept also encompasses an active management process that includes: focusing the organization's attention on the essence of winning; motivating people by communicating the value of the target; leaving room for individual

and team contributions; sustaining enthusiasm by providing new operational definitions as circumstances change; and using intent consistently to guide resource allocations.[22]

Thus on account of the outcomes of the strategic analysis phase, i.e. the current position of the organization within its environment, strategic intent sets a general direction for the organization and the change or consolidation of that position which it aims for. This aspect of strategic management can be conceived of in the following ways.

1. Identifying bases of strategic choice.   There are a number of fundamental issues, which need to be addressed in generating and considering strategic options open to an organization. Some of these bases of strategic choice arise from an understanding of stakeholder expectations and influence, which may already be reflected in *mission and vision statements* that provide overall guidance about the nature or aspirations of the organization; for example, in terms of product, market or geographical scope or matters as fundamental as ownership of the organization. There are also bases of strategic choice in terms of how the organization seeks to compete at the business unit level. This requires an identification of *bases of competitive advantage* arising from an understanding of both markets and customers, and special competencies that the organization has to offer which contribute to its *generic competitive strategy*: low cost or differentiation. A low cost strategy is a market strategy in which products are produced and sold at the lowest cost, allowing high returns even when competition is intense. Differentiation involves organizations developing a product or service that is unique or superior in some way. Products with this quality, whether in terms of features, image or design, often have higher than average prices, and the organization using this strategy thus seeks to penetrate the market on the basis of differential features rather than price alone. Another important basis of strategic choice is the *identity of the organization* that runs through its culture and operations. Identity, as Chapter 3 suggested, sets boundaries to the strategic options open to the organization in terms of how people within the organization see themselves and the company they work for, and also predetermines how the company should be profiled and positioned with stakeholders and the markets in its environment.

2. Generation of strategic options.   There may be several possible courses of action that an organization could follow. These courses of action emanate from the bases of strategic choice as identified above, and include options concerning which stakeholders and markets to address and target, and what the organization wants to achieve with them. In the 1970s and 1980s, Shell, for example, was a respected multinational in the petroleum industry steeped in a technological and engineering ethos. By the 1990s changing market conditions and public scepticism posed the organization other choices of *strategic direction*. The company had to ask itself what the basis of its business and success was: profitability or public legitimacy, or both? And whether the existing culture and competencies of Shell staff would offer sufficient latitude for introducing and supporting a new corporate identity and a new way of running and promoting the business? Often such questions need to be asked in order to identify the strategic options open to an organization. Besides identifying strategic options at the corporate and business unit level, in terms of carrying out their missions and implementing new market strategies, organizations also need to consider

the strategic options for their communications strategy. Dependent upon the strategic direction taken at the corporate and business unit level, the generic strategic options are that *communications either plays a lead or support role in effectuating the corporate and/or market strategy*. At the corporate level, a lead role is taken when communications is key to gaining legitimacy with important stakeholder groups upon which the organization is dependent. Here, communications may be used to enhance the organization's reputation and perceived legitimacy or to alter the definition of legitimacy with stakeholder groups so that it conforms to the organization's present practices, output and values.[23] At the business unit or market level, a lead role for communications coincides with a differentiated competitive strategy, where communications and imagery are key to a differentiated product or service offering. A support role for communications comes into play when it is employed at the corporate level just to make decisions of the organization and its operations public and inform relevant stakeholder groups (e.g. investors, government officials), and communications thus takes a back seat. This happens when an organization lacks fully developed programmes of engagement with a wide range of its stakeholder groups, or when instead of relying on communications it rather strategically adapts its output, goals and methods of operation to conform to prevailing definitions of legitimacy.[24] At the business unit or market level, communications typically has a support role within a low cost competitive strategy, where it is put to use as a promotional tool at a level-playing field with instruments such as pricing and distribution.

All of these considerations are important to developing a strategic intent and for determining the role of communications within the overall strategy of the organization, and thus need careful consideration. Indeed, in developing strategies, a potential danger may be that managers do not consider any but the most obvious course of action – and the most obvious is not always the best. A helpful step in strategic intent can therefore be to evaluate and limit strategic options.

3. Evaluation and selection of strategic options.   Strategic options can be examined in the context of the strategic analysis to assess their relative merits. In deciding between options open to them, managers may ask themselves a series of questions. First, which of these options builds upon strengths, overcomes weaknesses, and takes advantage of opportunities, while minimizing or circumventing the threats that the business faces? It can be thought of as a 'fit' between the organization, its resource capability and its environment. This fit is an assessment of the *suitability* of the strategic option. The differentiated competitive strategy of Orange discussed above (see Box 4.1), for example, minimized its weakness of being last in the UK market, while taking up the market opportunity for developing a fully rounded brand identity. A second set of questions is also important. To what extent can a strategic option be put into effect? Can the required finance be raised? Is it reasonable to expect that corporate reputations with stakeholders can shift in the direction anticipated by the strategic option? Can staff be recruited and trained to help reflect the sort of image that the company wants to project? These are questions of *feasibility*. A final set of questions over and above the criteria of suitability and feasibility is whether an option would be *acceptable* to stakeholders within and outside the organization. For example, suppose, in reviewing strategic options, management could see logic in diversifying the company into new products and markets. Would this be acceptable to the staff, and

perhaps ultimately to the identity that has become established within the organization over the years?

Useful though such criteria of evaluation are, there is unlikely to be a clear-cut 'right' or 'wrong' choice because any strategy inevitably has some dangers or dis-advantages. So, in the end, choice is likely to be a matter of managerial judgement by the dominant coalition (with or without the direct input of corporate commu-nications practitioners). The process of selecting strategic options cannot always be viewed or understood as a purely objective, logical act. It is strongly influenced by the values of managers and other groups with interest in the organization, and ulti-mately may very much reflect the power structure within the organization (see Section 4.4).

Phase 3: Strategic action

Strategic action is concerned with the translation of the strategic intent or chosen strategic option into action. The ways in which this is done can be thought of as the overall strategic programme of the organization, and successful implementation of strategy is likely to be dependent on the extent to which the various components of the programme work together to effectuate the programme and achieve the strategic intent. Various strategic programmes will emanate from the strategic intent, but the focus here is only on the sort of steps that are important in planning communica-tions strategy implementation. These are the following:

1. Specifying the role of communications and defining communications objectives.   A first fundamental issue that needs to be decided upon before working out the content of the communications strategy, the communications programme, is the role that communications is to play in the overall corporate and market strategies for the orga-nization. The basis of *strategic choice* is, as mentioned, whether communications plays a lead or support role − whether it has a full-scale or more subsidiary role in effectu-ating the corporate and/or market strategies of the organization; what contributions it therefore needs to make; and what stakeholder groups this involves. From this, it will then be possible to determine the *communications objectives* as well as the *commu-nications tactics* that are feasible to use. Communications objectives, for the communi-cations strategy as a whole and relating to each key tactic and stakeholder audience addressed, should be as tightly defined as possible: specific, measurable actionable, realistic and targeted (SMART). Here it is crucial to think through how communi-cations may be used to influence audience attitudes and behaviours and test out the reality of any assumptions. Once objectives have been determined, it is then neces-sary to identify and plan for the key communications tactics: the messages and chan-nels to be used.

2. Planning communications tactics.   After communications objectives have been defined, and the contribution of communications to corporate and/or market strate-gies has been specified, the next step is to determine the elements of the communi-cations programme: the stakeholder audiences to address and the message and channel tactics that will be used. Stakeholder analysis carried out in the earlier strategic

analysis phase represented the first key step in identifying and prioritizing the key audiences that will be the focus of the communications programme. From this initial analysis, it is then possible to further define the *target audiences* as precisely as possible drawing on further data such as media usage, usage of the company's products, geo-demographic characteristics, membership of interest groups, etc. Once the audiences are sufficiently characterized, and against the background of the communications objectives, the *message of the communications programme* can be determined. This involves determining the main themes of the communications message (from which the specific copy can be developed), and the tone and type of response (awareness, attitude/reputation, behaviours) that the message will seek to evoke. The important factor is thus to decide what the message should say in relation to the organization's identity, as it needs to reflect and be in tune with the values of the organization, as well as the stakeholder audience in hand. For programmes where communications plays a support role for corporate strategy, for instance, a message may be to explain the company's position on a certain issue or to motivate a decision to audiences in a way that has credibility and addresses their interests and concerns. Thus for environmental issues-based campaigns, the message strategy should seek to demonstrate the organization's recognition of stakeholder concerns and demonstrate the organization's willingness and commitment to listen and be responsive to interest groups' concerns. This may then be translated into a slogan or strap-line, which encapsulates the organization's position, as shown in Shell's 'profits and principles' campaign where advertising and public relations were used to inform the general public and selected audiences of Shell's environmental work in helping to conserve the natural environment and bio-diversity in locations where it undertakes oil and gas exploration.

When communications plays a lead role in effectuating the market strategy (as in the case of Orange), for instance, the emphasis will often be placed on identifying the key meaning and imagery that a message needs to evoke, around which all other operational and marketing elements (including products and distribution) needs to be based. Such a message then defines the unique selling proposition of a product; the message being the key that makes the product different from its competitors and thus attractive to consumer audiences. Once the message of the communications programme has been identified, it is then key to determine what the appropriate and effective *media channels* are through which it can be delivered to selected audiences. In developing the media or channel-based element of the communications programme, the overriding aim is to identify the most effective and efficient means of reaching the target audiences within the given budgetary constraints. Here such criteria need to be considered as the reach and coverage of the target audience provided by certain media, the creative match of the medium with the message, the degree of control over the message available, competitors' use of the media, and the ability of media to enable dialogue and interaction with the audience.[25] Discussion around media selection has recently centred or the notion of 'zero-based' selection,[26] where the most appropriate medium in the light of the criteria selected is chosen, rather than a pre-fixed and standard choice for a medium that may have worked in the past. That is, rather than heading straight for, say, (corporate) advertising, other media including free publicity, promotions, interactive meetings (with stakeholders), personal communications or sponsoring may be equally feasible means to get the message across. Another area of importance is the need for coordinating or integrating the use of different media, and the messages that they carry, at least throughout the period of the programme, to deliver the message in a consistent and therefore effective manner. This means first of all that the communications programme needs to specify not only which media are chosen (and the budget required), but also how they complement each other towards the achievement of the communications objectives, and when each is effectively put to use within the timeline of the programme. Using a combination of media also requires collaboration between communications specialists, for which organizational arrangements need to be made.

3. Organizational arrangements.   Once the communications programme has been filled in – that is, when the objectives, message, media and audience are all specified – the next step is to consider the organizational arrangements that need to be made to carry out the programme and as such effectuate the communications strategy. What budget is required for the envisaged plan? Who is to be responsible for carrying it out? What changes in organizational structure and design are needed to support and carry out the plan? What will different departments be held responsible for? What are the key tasks to be carried out? Are the practitioners involved up to the task, or is retraining necessary? These sorts of questions are important in working through whether and how the organization is capable of effectuating the communications strategy. One important area of concern is the fact that often practitioners from different functional areas (sales, marketing, public relations) need to work together, and this requires the need for organizational mechanisms that support collaboration and interaction. These mechanisms are likely to be concerned not only with organizational redesign, the subject of Chapter 5, but also with changing day-to-day routines, and overcoming political blockages to collaboration or change. A related point is to take into account whether the proposed communications strategy adapts or builds on existing strategies – an incremental approach – or whether, because of the inadequacy of existing strategies or because management sees the need to change fundamentally the direction of the organization, a completely new communications strategy is suggested. In the case of the latter, it may be that the organization, in terms of the work processes and structures that support communications practitioners in their work, needs to be rethought and, perhaps, transformed.

Stage 4: Tracking and Evaluation

The final element in any communications strategy should be the provision for effective evaluation of the results – in terms of how far the programme has contributed to the achievement of the communications objectives set. Effectiveness of the programme can be evaluated and assessed on the basis of process and communications effects. *Process effects* concern the quality of the communications programme (in terms of intelligence gathered, appropriateness of message content and organization, etc.) and whether the programme has been carried through and implemented in a cost-effective manner. *Communications effects* include the range of cognitive and behavioural effects on stakeholder audiences that a set of communications tactics produces. Here it is important to identify suitable impact measures (i.e. changes in awareness, attitude and reputation, or behaviour) rather than relying on interim measures of communications effects such as media coverage or simple exposure,[27] and to evaluate the effects achieved against the target or benchmark set with the initial objectives of the communications programme. Such evaluation will then also provide important insights as to whether and how the communications programme has worked, whether it has contributed to the achievement of corporate and market strategies, and whether changes or alterations to communications strategy need to be made for the following period(s). As part of a formal evaluation of the communications programme and the period in which it has run, it is often also important to consider how emergent issues or crises were handled through communications. Here, one may look at the effectiveness of the issue handling (e.g. whether the potential for damage to the corporate reputation was minimized) and the operational costs involved; and whether the response and handling of the issue was in line with the general scope and direction of the communications strategy.

Tracking and evaluating for both process and communications results through research, and improving on them, is also politically important within the organization for showing the accountability of communications, and for garnering executive support. While at times it may be difficult, for instance, to measure and pin down communications effects or to single out the effect that communications has had upon stakeholder behaviour amid other factors of influence (such as news media and peer support), continuous efforts at evaluation are nevertheless essential for ensuring that senior managers consider communications as valuable and as being used in a responsible, professional and accountable manner. Being perceived as valuable and accountable is essential for ensuring that communications continues to play an important role alongside other business functions like finance or human resources within the overall strategic management of the organization.

The whole process of communications strategy making is illustrated in Box 4.3 with a case study of Wal-Mart, the US retail group.

Box 4.3   Case study: Wal-Mart and its communications strategy[28]

From the beginning, the Wal-Mart retail firm and its founder, Sam Walton, have been enormously successful. Sam Walton opened his first Wal-Mart discount store in 1962, the company became a public company in 1970, SAM's Clubs were rolled out in the 1980s and became super-centers in the 1990s. Today, Wal-Mart is the largest retailer in the world and easily topped the latest Fortune 500 list of the world largest corporations in 2003.

Wal-Mart's success and its exemplary growth first and foremost within the US market has been attributed to the large size of the US market, founder Sam Walton's inspirational leadership, an associate-focused organizational culture, a capacity for reinvention and innovation, low cost operations, vendor partnering, an efficient logistics system, extensive internal communications, continuous merchandising, a customer service orientation and competitor inattention. But, one important and previously overlooked cause for Wal-Mart's phenomenal growth seems to be its communications strategy, which is linked to its corporate mission and identity of serving customers and the communities in which the company operates, and also enables it to reach its market objectives and to cancel out opposition to its aggressive low cost strategy.

Wal-Mart is exemplary of the low-cost competitive strategy and it has fine-tuned the low margin, high inventory turnover, and volume selling practice that comes with it. Volume buying enables lower costs of goods, and the key, according to Sam Walton, 'is to identify the items that can explode into big volume and big profits if you are smart enough to identify them and take the trouble to promote them'. Wal-Mart demands vendors forgo all other amenities and quote the lowest price. And its retail strategy for capturing market share involves an aggressive carpet bombing campaign in which an area is chosen and competitors are challenged and eventually driven out by its low cost strategy.

The mega-retailer's low cost strategy is, according to Thomas Zaucha, president of the National Grocers Association in the US, alarming enough to call 'saturation bombing'. Zaucha explains that 'they [Wal-Mart] have the ability to come into a market with their super-centers, with their Neighborhood markets, with their traditional Wal-Marts, and with the Clubs. I think there is a growing concern that not only do we have the potential for concentration, we have the real possibility of [monopoly] power'. 'They are re-structuring the industry', according to David Rogers, a market consultant; 'When you put that amount of store space in, you have to take an equivalent amount of floor space, and that is going to happen through store closings, isn't it? That's the brutal truth'. The latest industry surveys in the US indicate that of all recent bankruptcies of supermarket chains, eight out of nine were heavily influenced by Wal-Mart's expansion strategy.

Of course, with such an aggressive low cost market strategy, one would expect the Wal-Mart corporation to run into fierce opposition from citizens, communities, the industry and the US government. But the retail giant has not, because of its sophisticated communications strategy that connects the retailer symbolically to the dominant ideologies of American life. Through the imagery of frugality, family, religion, neighbourhood, community and patriotism, Wal-Mart locates itself centrally on Main Street of a nostalgic hometown. This symbolism and imagery, carried through in all its advertising, in-store promotions and staff communications, not only positively disposes shoppers but it also 'decouples' Wal-Mart from unfavourable outcomes of its low cost strategy and its market success. These consequences include local retailers being forced out of business, small town opposition, accusations of predatory pricing and allegations about products being sourced from overseas sweatshop suppliers. It is noticeable in this regard that Wal-Mart, a hard-hitting low cost firm, has received fairly little public opposition and shuns the limelight in recent anti-globalization demonstrations (that have instead targeted such companies as Starbucks and Shell).

In other words, Wal-Mart is able to couch its low cost market strategy in terms that not only fit with its own customer-focused corporate identity, but also are acceptable to consumers and the general US public – with language such as 'Our aim is to lower the world's cost of living', 'Our pledge … to save you more', 'Our commitment … to satisfy all your shopping needs' – and that appease opposition to it. This is done, as mentioned, by referring to retail symbolism of saving, family, America and patriotism, and community and hometown. Advertising flyers, for instance, present 'plain folks' (as opposed to professional models), apparently ordinary people including Wal-Mart 'associates', spouses, children, parents, pets, suppliers and customers, and devote an inordinate amount of space to community-oriented and patriotic topics, delving in places into philosophical monologues about American enterprise, friendly customer service and other topics. The general public that is exposed to such flyers is, because of its nostalgia and patriotism, likely to be favourably predisposed to them.

Stephen Arnold, a professor at Queens School of Business (Canada) and his colleagues observed that the symbolic presentation of Wal-Mart might be different from the objective reality. That is, Wal-Mart projects an innocent, homespun image of a happy community involving vendor 'partners', associates and customers. The extremely rich weave of cultural-moral symbols upon which this interpretation is based, however, may have as much to do with Wal-Mart's communications strategy and its quest for legitimacy as it does with a true and profound community spirit. For example, in lieu of the 'vendor-partner' persona, aspiring Wal-Mart suppliers wait long periods before meeting a buyer and are then squeezed aggressively for the lowest prices. And many goods, apparel in particular, do not display a 'Made in the USA' label and 'Buy American' signs are found situated embarrassingly on racks of imported products. Furthermore, some have alleged that the goods are sourced at overseas sweatshops and that the low prices are a consequence of child labour. Newsgroups and websites have sprung up for disgruntled former Wal-Mart associates to vent their unhappiness (e.g. http://www.walmartworkerslv.com, http://www.walmartsuck.com). Wal-Mart is regarded by some as a wolf in sheep's clothing, and its communications strategy, which is closely linked to its corporate mission and has also successfully supported its low cost market strategy, may in such a view have been the instrument for constructing and legitimizing the sheep's costume.

Questions for reflection

1. What communications strategy has Wal-Mart followed? Would an alternative strategy have been more successful?
2. Why has Wal-Mart been so successful on this account, while other large firms with aggressive low cost market strategies have been subject to public scrutiny and outrage?

4.4   Challenges and issues in communications strategy

The 1990s were dominated by a realization that the organizations and environments of today's global economy are very different than they were a generation ago. Stakeholders, and not just publics or markets, are now crucial forces in an organization's environment, and appropriate strategies are needed for dealing with them. As in all times of social and organizational change, the 1990s and early 2000s have witnessed a great deal of discussion and debate about what such stakeholder strategies should actually look like, and which professionals or functions within the organization should be responsible for them (and thus effectively guide the strategic efforts of the organization as a whole). In this chapter I have made the case for the corporate communications function to take up such a strategic role and have outlined what communications can contribute to the overall corporate strategy of an organization.

This, of course, is at least in part aspirational and also prescriptive as the strategic role of communications has not yet everywhere, in each and every organization around the globe, come to full gestation. In fact, in some organizations White and Dozier remarks referred to earlier still ring true in the sense that communications practitioners may be found to operate only on the periphery of the dominant coalition, functioning largely as communications technicians and with a limited influence on the decision-making process. In such cases, as well as for other organizations that aim to actively pursue stakeholder management strategies, research suggests that a number of closely related challenges exist and need to be met for the corporate communications function to indeed deliver upon its strategic potential. Some of these challenges may not be entirely new, but they are nonetheless central to securing the strategic involvement of communications.

Challenge 1: Having communications professionals who can think and act strategically. One of the basic problems of why the strategic potential of corporate communications often remains unmet in organizations is the lack of communications practitioners who can enact a strategic role and contribute to strategy making at the corporate and/or business units levels. In many organizations, communications practitioners tend to be cast in the role of communications technicians rather than managers or strategists, and are not included in the dominant coalition responsible for the formulation of organization-wide strategies. This happens when practitioners fail to enact a strategic role, because of a lack of expertise or experience, or because senior management simply does not provide the support and room for doing so. The following framework based on research of role types of communications practitioners illustrates this distinction between 'technicians' and 'managers' or 'strategists' and offers, in this respect, a useful way of considering how and where practitioners may contribute to both the formulation and implementation of strategy.

As indicated in Table 4.1, Broom and Smith,[29] the originators of role research among communications practitioners, suggest four types of roles which practitioners may fulfil within organizations: 'communications technician', 'expert prescriber', 'communications facilitator' and 'problem-solving process facilitator'. Research has indicated that the more *strategic* roles of 'communications facilitators' and 'problem-solving process facilitator' are to a greater degree enacted when senior management values and appreciates the input of communications practitioners, and when the communications practitioner him/herself is capable – in terms of having the required business knowledge and intelligence – of enacting it.[30]

This distinction between role types is thus important because it will largely determine the extent to which practitioners are likely to participate in the strategic decision-making process within organizations, and thus contribute directly to the formulation of corporate strategies. As said, whether practitioners enact a strategic role within the organization depends on a number of factors, including the environment and the political context within the organization (as further discussed in Chapter 6), but perhaps most importantly, it depends on the knowledge that the practitioner has of strategy making and of the role of corporate communications therein.

A basic distinction can be made at this point between 'strategic' and 'craft' approaches to communications.[31] A strategic approach allies with the strategic practitioner roles outlined above and suggests that practitioners understand how communications not

Table 4.1   Roles of communications professionals and their strategic input

Role	Description	Strategic role
Communication technician	Production of communications 'products' for organizations and dealing with the media.	Little if any involvement in the process of defining organizational problems and solutions. Practitioners just produce communications products and implement programmes, often without the full knowledge of organizational motivation, larger organizational goals or intended results.
Expert prescriber	Regarded as the authority on communications problems and solutions. Communications issues are defined and programmes run, but independently from senior management.	Communications is compartmentalized, often apart from the mainstream of the organization. Communications practitioners may work only periodically with senior management (e.g. crisis situations).
Communication facilitator	Practitioners act as liaisons, interpreters and mediators between the organization and its stakeholders, communicating and maintaining a dialogue.	Emphasis on providing management and stakeholders with the information they need to make decisions of mutual interest. Communications practitioners occupy a boundary-spanning role – linking organizations and stakeholders and thereby improving the quality of decisions by facilitating communications.
Problem-solving process facilitator	Practitioners collaborate with other managers to define and solve organizational problems.	Practitioners are recognized as part of the strategic management team, engaged in the formulation of strategies. Incorporates the boundary-spanning function of corporate communications.

only contributes but also fully participates in the achievement of strategic corporate objectives. This means, among other things, that communications practitioners not only understand corporate strategy making, including the concepts, tools and financial terms that are used within it,[32] but also that they are able to identify communications issues at the level of corporate strategy – at the level of the whole organization and its business operations – and develop an integrated communications strategy for it. A craft approach to communications management, in contrast, resonates with the 'technician' roles outlined above, and suggests that the role and practice of communications is refined to being a tactical support function concerned with producing and disseminating communications materials simply to effectuate and announce corporate and managerial decisions made higher up within the organization. A craft approach to managing communications then also suggests that the subject of communications strategy is thought of in tactical terms as simply campaign planning.

A strategic approach to communications thus requires that practitioners have an understanding of strategic management and corporate strategy making and that they know how they can integrate and link communications counsel and strategy into it. This in itself asks for a process or framework of connecting or integrating corporate and communications strategies, such as the one outlined above in Section 4.3. But it also means that many communications practitioners, who until now have been cast in a craft orientation, need to change or shift somewhat in their approach to their work. For one, rather than fencing with terms such as 'environmental scanning' and quickly reporting some observed communications trends (for instance by gathering newspaper clippings), practitioners at all times need to see the bigger picture and work towards corporate and not merely communications-functional ends, and provide useful environmental data, counsel and tactical input for this.

Challenge 2: Senior management support.   Senior managers, of course, need to allow communications to play its strategic part, and recognize its lead or support role within corporate and market strategies. This means, among other things, that managers see communications as a strategic instrument, and corporate communications as a strategic management function, rather than as a simple set of tactics. Relegating communications to tactics often happens when senior managers are actually unsure what the communications function brings to the strategic management of the organization. This is pertinent in organizations where decision makers are uncertain about the value of corporate communications to their decision making, as well as to the achievement of the corporate strategy as a whole. Put differently, senior managers of an organization need to recognize and value the input of communications practitioners if the corporate communications function is to develop its strategic scope and play its critical role in the strategic management of the organization.

Value recognition – the value placed upon corporate communications by senior managers – appears therefore, as much research has documented,[33] to be directly related to the input of corporate communications practitioners in strategic management before decisions are made. Ways of achieving such value recognition for communications are manifold and range from expert advice and counselling of senior management to showing the function's accountability in delivering communications results with stakeholders and arranging work processes in a cost-effective manner.[34]

Challenge 3: Organizational arrangements.   Related to the two points mentioned that communications practitioners should have the ability to enact a strategic role and that senior management should support and allow them to do so, a third issue is the need for organizational arrangements that support strategic corporate communications management. This refers to a range of organizational mechanisms and structures, such as the inclusion of the senior communications practitioner in the organization's management team or executive board, consolidating different communications disciplines into separate and visible departments, cross-functional coordination mechanisms (e.g. teams, networking platforms) that allow different communications practitioners to work together, and organizing and accrediting communications at the corporate level as a staff function, instead of placing it as a support function within the organization's operating units.

4.5.   Chapter summary

Traditional accounts of communications management have treated the subject in a rather narrow and tactical way and have equated it with campaign planning. But communications has additional strategic and important dimensions within the entire corporate strategy of an organization, and thus within the overall strategic management of the interactions between an organization and its environment. The chapter has made an attempt to describe these strategic dimensions of communications and outlined a process that may guide its use and help implement it. This process builds from the understanding that corporate communications is a 'boundary-spanning' function between the organization and stakeholders in its environment, and that it needs to contribute to the achievement of corporate and/or market strategies that target those stakeholder parties if it is to have a genuine strategic role.

However, a number of challenges exist for the corporate communications function to be put to its fullest strategic use, including the need for communications practitioners who can think and act strategically – at the level of the corporate and/or market strategy – and senior managers valuing and including corporate communications for its strategic input into decision making. Only when these challenges are fully met and overcome will communications staff be included in decision making at the senior management level, and will corporate communications strategies be integrated within the overall corporate and market strategies of the organization.

It also follows from these deliberations that communications strategy cuts across different hierarchical layers, as well as different departments (e.g. marketing, public relations) of the organization, which points to questions about how organizations can design structures that enable communications practitioners to interact and coordinate their work, and to have a strategic input into corporate and market strategies. The following chapter, Chapter 5, answers these questions in detail. Academic research and cases are sourced to outline the various ways in which communications may be organized so as to ensure its strategic input into decision making and its strategic role within the management of relationships between an organization and its stakeholders.

Key terms

Communications effects	Organization-environment analysis
Communications strategy	Process effects
Competitive forces	Stakeholder analysis
Corporate strategy	Stakeholder mapping
'Craft' communications	Strategic action
DESTEP	Strategic analysis
Differentiation competitive strategy	Strategic intent
Evaluation	Strategy
Low cost competitive strategy	SWOT
Market and competitor analysis	Value recognition
Marketing strategy	Zero-based media planning

Notes

[1]Shrivastava, P. (1986), 'Is strategic management ideological?', *Journal of Management*, 12, 363–377.

[2]See for instance Mintzberg, H. (1989), 'Strategy formation: schools of thought', in Frederickson, J. (ed.), *Perspectives on Strategic Management*. San Francisco, CA: Ballinger;

Mintzberg, H., Ahlstrand, B., and Lampel, J. (1998), *Strategy Safari: The Complete Guide Through the Wilds of Strategic Management*. London: Prentice Hall/Financial Times; or Elfring, T., and Volberda, H.W. (2001), 'Schools of thought in strategic management: fragmentation, integration or synthesis', in Volberda, H.W., and Elfring, T. (eds), *Rethinking Strategy*. London: Sage, pp. 1–25.

[3]Mintzberg, H. (1987), 'The strategy concept: five Ps for strategy', *California Management Review*, 30 (1), 11–24.

[4]Johnson, G. (1988), 'Rethinking incrementalism', *Journal of Strategic Management*, 6, 75–91, p. 80.

[5]Cornelissen, J.P., and Thorpe, R. (2001), 'The organisation of external communications disciplines in UK companies: a conceptual and empirical analysis of dimensions and determinants', *Journal of Business Communications*, 38 (4), 413–438, p. 429.

[6]Steiner, G.A., Miner, J.B., and Gray, E.R. (1982), *Management Policy and Strategy*. New York: Macmillan, second edition, p. 6.

[7]Rumelt, R.P., Schendel, D.E., and Teece, D.J. (1994), 'Fundamental issues in strategy', in Rumelt, R.P., Schendel, D.E., and Teece, D.J. (eds), *Fundamental Issues in Strategy: A Research Agenda*. Boston, MA: HBS, p. 22.

[8]Grunig, J.E., and Repper, F.C. (1992), 'Strategic management, publics and issues', in Grunig, J.E. (ed.), *Excellence in Public Relations and Communications Management*. Hillsdale, NJ: Lawrence Erlbaum Associates, pp. 122–123.

[9]White, J., and Dozier, D.M. (1992), 'Public relations and management decision-making', in Grunig, J.E. (ed.), *Excellence in Public Relations and Communications Management*. Hillsdale, NJ: Lawrence Erlbaum Associates, p. 92.

[10]Ibid. (1992).

[11]Moss, D., and Warnaby, G. (2000), 'Strategy and public relations', in Moss, D., Vercic, D., and Warnaby, G. (eds), *Perspectives on Public Relations Research*, pp. 59–85. London: Routledge, pp. 591–85.

[12]Grunig and Repper (1992).

[13]Webster, P.J. (1990), 'Strategic corporate public relations: what's the bottom line?', *Public Relations Journal*, 46 (2), 18–21, p. 18.

[14]Mintzberg, H. (1994). *The Rise and Fall of Strategic Planning*. New York: The Free Press Whittington, R. (1993), *What Is Strategy – and Does It Matter?* London: Routledge.

[15]See for instance Cutlip, S.M., Center, A.H., and Broom, G.H. (1985), *Effective Public Relations*. London: Prentice Hall, fifth edition; or Argenti, P.A. (1998), *Corporate Communication*. Boston: McGraw-Hill, second edition.

[16]Vercic, D., and Grunig, J.E. (2000), 'The origins of public relations theory in economics and strategic management', in Moss, D., Vercic, D., and Warnaby, G. (eds), *Perspectives on Public Relations Research*. London: Routledge, pp. 49–58.

[17]Eden, C., and Ackermann, F. (1998), *Making Strategy: The Journey of Strategic Management*. London: Sage.

[18]Johnson, G., and Scholes, K. (1993), *Exploring Corporate Strategy: Text and Cases*. Hemel Hempstead: Prentice Hall, third edition.

[19]Porter, M.E. (1985), *Competitive Advantage: Creating and Sustaining Superior Performance*. New York: The Free Press.

[20]Mitchell, R.K., and Agle, B.R. (1997), 'Toward a theory of stakeholder identification and salience: defining the principle of who and what really counts', *Academy of Management Review*, 22 (4), 853–887.

[21]This management brief was based on Agle, B.R., Mitchell, R.K., and Sonnenfeld, J.A. (1999), 'Who matters to CEOs? An investigation of stakeholder attributes and salience, corporate performance, and CEO values', *Academy of Management Journal*, 42 (5), 507–525, and Mitchell, R.K., Agle, B.R., Wood, D.J. (1997), 'Toward a theory of stakeholder identification and salience: defining the principle of who and what really counts', *Academy of Management Review*, 22 (4), 853–886.

[22]Hamel, G., and Prahalad, C.K. (1989), 'Strategic intent', *Harvard Business Review*, May–June, 63–76, p. 64.

[23]Dowling, J., and Pfeffer, J. (1975), 'Organizational legitimacy: social values and organizational behavior', *Pacific Sociological Review*, 18, 122–136.

[24]Ibid. (1975).

[25]Jones, J.P. (1992), *How Much Is Enough?* New York: Lexington Books; Rossiter, J.R., and Danaher, P.J. (1998), *Advanced Media Planning*. Boston: Kluwer.

[26]Deighton, J. (1996), 'Features of good integration: two cases and some generalizations', in Thorson, E., and Moore, J. (eds), *Integrated Communications: Synergy of Persuasive Voices*. Mahwah, NJ: Lawrence Erlbaum Associates, 243–256; Schultz, D.E. (1999), 'Integrated marketing communications and how it relates to traditional media advertising', in J.P. Jones (ed.), *The Advertising Business: Operations, Creativity, Media Planning, Integrated Communications*. London: Sage, 325–338; Cornelissen, J.P. (forthcoming), 'Change, continuity and progress: the concept of integrated marketing communications and marketing communications practice', *Journal of Strategic Marketing*, 11, 27–234.

[27]Cutlip, S.M., Center, A.H., and Broom, G.H. (2000), *Effective Public Relations*. London: Prentice Hall, seventh edition.

[28]This case study was based on Walton, S., and Huey, J. (1993), *Sam Walton: Made in America – My Story*. New York: Bantam Books; Weir, T. (2000), 'Does Wal-Mart rule?', *Supermarket Business Magazine*, 55 (11); Arnold, S.J., Handelman, J., and D.J. Tigert (1996), 'Organizational legitimacy and retail store patronage', *Journal of Business Research*, 35, 229–239; and Arnold, S.J., Kozinets, R.V., and Handelman, J. (2001), 'Hometown ideology and retailer legitimation: the institutional semiotics of Wal-Mart flyers', *Journal of Retailing*, 77, 243–271.

[29]Broom, G.M., and Smith, G.D. (1979) 'Testing the practitioner's impact on clients', *Public Relations Review*, 5 (3), 47–59. See for a comprehensive discussion of role types Dozier, D.M., and Broom, G.M. (1995), 'Evolution of the manager role in public relations practice', *Journal of Public Relations Research*, 7, 3–26.

[30]Dozier and Broom (1995); Moss, D., Warnaby, G., and Newman, A.J. (2000), 'Public relations practitioner role enactment at the senior management level within UK companies', *Journal of Public Relations Research*, 12 (4), 277–307.

[31]Dozier, D.M., Grunig, L.A., and Grunig, J.E. (1995), *Manager's Guide to Excellence in Public Relations and Communications Management*. Hove: Lawrence Erlbaum Associates.

[32]Moss, et al. (2000).

[33]Lauzen, M.M. (1995), 'Public relations manager involvement in strategic issue diagnosis', *Public Relations Review*, 21, 287–304; Spicer, C.H. (1997), *Organizational Public Relations: A Political Perspective*. Mahwah, NJ: Lawrence Erlbaum Associates.

[34]Grunig, J.E., and Grunig, L.A. (1998), 'The relationship between public relations and marketing in excellent organizations: evidence from the IABC study', *Journal of Marketing Communications*, 4 (3), 141–162.

Chapter 5
The Organization of Communications: Theory and Practice

Central themes

- There is an increased interest in the subject of communications organization on both the academic and practitioner side as a result of the integration trend and the rise of corporate communications as a guiding philosophy for managing communications.

- The overall organization of communications consists of the vertical structure – the departmental arrangement and location of communications disciplines within the organization's hierarchy – and the horizontal structure – the coordination mechanisms that are laid over departments and across disciplines.

- There are differences of opinion as to whether factors within the power structure of the organization or its environment determine (and therefore explain) the vertical and horizontal structuring of communications.

- Regardless of what *explains* structures, the vertical structure that seems to work for most companies (with the exception of small firms) is to have an independent communications department at a central place within the organization, which includes all communications disciplines except for marketing communications disciplines, which are placed under marketing.

- Regardless of what *explains* structures, companies often opt for having sufficient horizontal structures in place exercised through a range of coordination mechanisms including conference and networking facilities, project teams, process documentation, job rotation and council meetings.

5.1 Introduction

Recent years have seen an increased interest in the subject of the organization of communications disciplines on both the academic and practitioner side as a result of the integration trend identified in Chapter 2 and the increased importance of corporate communications for contemporary organizations. This trend signalled that whereas communications had previously been organized and operated in a rather fragmented manner, different organizational forms and coordination mechanisms were now needed that would integrate the work of various communications practitioners and, when pulled together, would enable the communications function as a whole to have an input into strategic decision making at the corporate level. Many practitioners have effectively called for a drastic overhaul of the way in which public relations and marketing communications are organized in the face of the turbulence and change in the marketing and communications landscape throughout the 1990s because of fragmented audiences, wider stakeholder concerns, media proliferation and the relative decline of mass media advertising.[1] Whether such new organizational forms have since appeared is one of the central themes of this chapter. But, regardless of whether such a change in communications organization has occurred, the subject has reappeared firmly on the agenda of academics and practitioners alike and has become more salient and significant than before.

   The chapter therefore aims to address the subject of communications organization in a comprehensive manner, sourcing the extant research evidence as well as cases from practice. The general structure of the chapter is as follows. First, I will discuss in Section 5.2 the different perspectives that have been brought to bear upon the subject of communications organization, its general importance to the corporate communications function and the organization as a whole, and the different elements of organizational structure that can be distinguished. Then I will discuss two of these structural elements in greater detail in Sections 5.3 and 5.4: the vertical structure, which includes the hierarchy of authority in which communications staff are placed and the way in which they are organized into departments, and the horizontal structure, which encompasses cross-functional and lateral coordination mechanisms that exist over and above departmental structures to streamline and integrate work processes of communications staff. Then, in Section 5.5, I will explain how and why organizations differ in the way in which they have organized their communications (that is, differences in vertical and horizontal structures across organizations), and address the question of whether there is a best 'fit' between the type of organization (i.e. small business, multinational firm, public organization, professional service organization) and organizational form.

   Being structured in this way, the chapter should thus provide the reader not only with a clear overview of the various ways in which communications can be organized, but also with an understanding of which organizational form suits a particular company best.

5.2   Perspectives on communications organization

The subject of communications organization is important as it not only determines to a large extent whether the communications function is enabled to provide strategic input into decision making at the corporate level, but also whether the communications activities that are carried out at various places within the organization are streamlined and integrated in a cost-effective manner. In other words, the way in which communications is organized carries important strategic and political dimensions and is also crucial for the effective support and integration of communications activities.

Traditional and contemporary views on communications organization

Despite being of such importance, historical evidence upon the subject of communications organization, in terms of the way in which different communications disciplines were located and structured within companies in the past, is rather limited. The marketing historian Hollander, with his historical study of the market orientation of US firms, is one of the few exceptions and observed that in the 1950s and 1960s the different marketing communications disciplines of advertising, promotions, selling and publicity were functionally separated within the organization, but he suggested nonetheless that 'the indications are that advertising, sales, promotion and merchandising people in industry worked together more closely than is commonly thought'.[2] In the 1970s, there was equally little systematic empirical research into communications organization, although there were some commentary pieces written by practitioners that again stressed the functional separation of communications disciplines, a feat that was generally seen as detrimental to the effective functioning of communications as a whole. Writing in 1973, Cook, one of these communications professionals, argued in this respect that companies should consolidate their entire communications function, bringing together various external communications disciplines, such as advertising, public relations, promotions and issues management, into a central organizational function, with the purpose of increasing the *organizational autonomy* of communications within the organization.[3] Following in Cook's footsteps, many academics in the 1980s and 1990s equally started discussing the *traditional division of communications responsibilities* into separate disciplines. Don Schultz and his colleagues from Northwestern University, for instance, took issue with what they called the *functional silos* of communications that had emerged within many organizations because of this division of communications into separate disciplines. They argued that in the 1970s and 1980s, because of an emphasis on functional specialism, there had been a trend towards dividing and splitting communications disciplines and organizing them apart, which had led to each discipline protecting its financial and specialist 'turf' and to an ineffective use of communications as fragmented and conflicting messages were being sent out.[4]

The views expressed on the subject of communications organization in the 1980s and 1990s all voice this concern that dividing communications and organizing it in a functional manner by discipline or speciality leads to 'fragmentation', 'functional silos', 'stovepipes' and 'Chinese walls' between communications disciplines,[5] and that companies should move to other more integrated forms of organizing communications that would enable communications professionals from marketing communications, public relations and internal communications to collaborate and coordinate their work. The philosophy of corporate communications, when it got a foothold within communications practice in the early 1990s, equally prescribed an alternative form of organizing communications to ensure the autonomy of the function and its strategic input into decision making, as well as to enable practitioners from different disciplines to work together and align their communications products (messages, campaigns, etc.). The recommendations that came out of it were the following:[6]

1. **Consolidating and centralizing communications disciplines into a single department**: the general idea in this regard is to bring a range of communications disciplines together into a single department so that knowledge and skills of practitioners can be shared, specialist expertise is enhanced, and the autonomy and visibility of the communications function within the organization is secured. Some communications disciplines might still be organized as

separate units or devolved to other functional areas (e.g. finance, human resources), but the general idea here is to consolidate a sufficient number of communications disciplines into a single department so that communications can be strategically managed from a central corporate perspective.

2. **Locating the communications department within the organizational hierarchy with access to decision makers**: a second recommendation was to place this single communications department within easy reach of senior managers who are members of the decision-making team, so that the strategic input of communications into corporate strategy is secured. In practice, this implies that the communications department is a staff function at corporate headquarters from where it can advise the senior decision-making team, and that the most senior communications practitioner has a direct reporting or advisory relationship to the CEO or even a seat on the executive board or senior management team.

3. **Implementing cross-functional coordination mechanisms**: it was also recognized that, while a range of communications disciplines may have been consolidated into a single department, further cross-functional integration over and above departments (for instance, between the communications and marketing departments) was needed because most of the work related to communications cuts across different knowledge and skills domains. The suggestion therefore was for companies to implement cross-functional coordination mechanisms such as teams and council meetings between professionals working in different communications disciplines and departments, which would lead to a sharing and cross-fertilization of expertise, a greater understanding on the part of practitioners of each others knowledge and skills, an increased ability to cope with complex, dynamic environments, and the design of tonally and visually consistent communications programmes.

Vertical and horizontal structure

These three prescriptions point to a particular way in which communications disciplines can, and perhaps should, be organized within contemporary companies. They therefore also suggest what the vertical and horizontal structure of communications organization should look like. The *vertical structure* refers to the way in which tasks and activities (and the disciplines that they represent) are divided and arranged into departments – the departmental arrangement – and located in the hierarchy of authority within an organization. The solid vertical lines that connect the boxes on an organization chart depict this vertical structure and the authority relationships involved (see Figure 5.1 below). Within such vertical lines, the occupant of the higher position has the authority to direct and control the activities of the occupant of the lower position. A major role of the vertical lines of authority on the organization chart is thus to depict the way in which the work and output of specialized departments or units are coordinated *vertically*; that is by authority in reporting relationships.

The first two prescriptions mentioned above refer to the vertical structure. The third prescription, on the other hand, refers to the *horizontal structure*: the structures

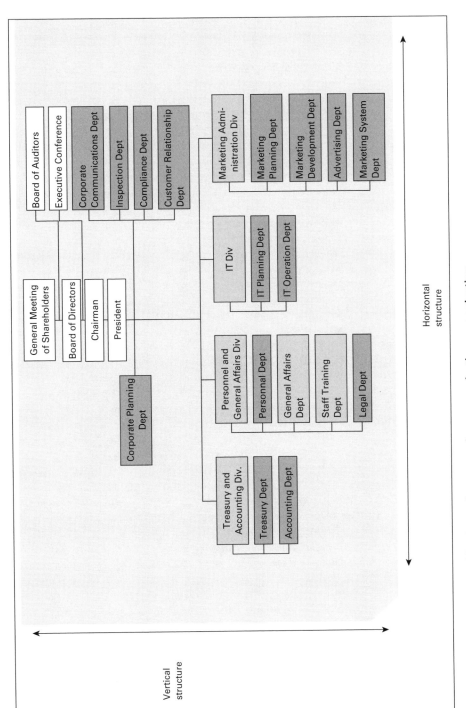

Figure 5.1   The vertical and horizontal structure in communications organization

that are laid over the vertical structure to coordinate and integrate functionally separated tasks and activities. Vertical structure divides each organization's primary tasks into smaller tasks and activities, with each box on the organization chart representing a position assigned to undertake a unique, detailed portion of the organization's overall mission. Such vertical specialization, and the spreading out of tasks over different departments, however, requires some coordination or integration of work processes. This coordination or integration is achieved through a horizontal structure, which ensures that tasks and activities, while spread out over departments, are combined into the basic functions (i.e. human resources, finance, operations, marketing, and communications) that need to be fulfiled within the organization. Horizontal structure can take various forms, including multidisciplinary task or project teams, formal lines of communication, standardized work processes, council meetings or the use of 'czars' (senior professionals working as integrators between departments), and is not normally displayed within an organization chart. Figure 5.1 shows the vertical and horizontal structure of a mid-size Japanese corporation in the financial services industry. The vertical structure of this organization shows that corporate communications is placed quite high within the organization as an independent staff department advising the president (CEO) and chairperson of the corporation. The horizontal structure, which for this corporation most likely involves formal collaborative ties connecting the corporate communications department with the advertising and general affairs departments, cannot, as mentioned, be directly read from the organization chart.

The above three prescriptions also suggest that with a few exceptions (e.g. small businesses), organizations would be wise to use both vertical and horizontal structures for organizing communications. The obvious reasoning behind this is that although bringing communications specialists together *vertically* into one or a few departments may lead to enhanced efficiency, the ability to develop specialized, distinctive capabilities, and ease management through the centralization and consolidation of communications activities, it may not lead to coordination between communications disciplines and with other functional areas (e.g. marketing) outside those departments, it risks 'turf wars', functional myopia and over-specialization. A horizontal structure overlaying the vertical structure is therefore needed for coordinating disparate communications tasks and activities, which also recognizes that communications with key stakeholders might emerge from various places within the organization and that the process of developing and executing communications programmes is therefore essentially cross-functional or cross-disciplinary.[7]

Seen in this light, many academic researchers have in recent years started to argue that there should be a balance or trade-off between differentiation (vertical structure) and coordination or integration (horizontal structure). On the one hand, it is argued, communications disciplines should still be consolidated into one or a few departments or units, as too much differentiation and dispersion of communications into several small units misses potential interactions between the disciplines, dilutes the technical sophistication and knowledge base of communications, and might lead to a more tactical, 'craft' orientation within communications. The communications scholars Grunig and Grunig point out in this regard that many separate communications units are likely to contribute mainly to tactical routine operations and are less likely to participate in strategic planning and management.[8] In other words, the

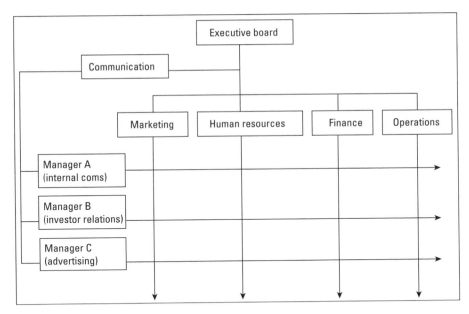

Figure 5.2   A matrix structure of communications organization

autonomy and functional expertise of communications needs to be secured through vertical structuring into one or a few departments. But, on the other hand, as many academic researchers have equally suggested in recent years, there is a need for much greater coordination and collaboration through horizontal structures working across departments and linking communications with other functional areas within the organization. The marketing communications scholars Gronstedt and Thorson,[9] for instance, have responded to this quest for a balance or trade-off between differentiation and integration by proposing a matrix structure where vertical and horizontal structures coexist in the dual reporting relationships that any individual communications practitioner in the matrix has. A matrix structure, Gronstedt and Thorson suggest, enables a company to enjoy both the depth of specialized knowledge that the functional departments facilitate and the collaboration across the disciplines through the horizontal structure. Figure 5.2 illustrates such a matrix structure within a simple 'functional' organization chart in which communications is organized as a *staff department* (as in Figure 5.1), and where individual communications managers report to both communications and another department (marketing, human resources, finance or operations) that they serve.

Sections 5.3 and 5.4 report on the evidence from academic research and practitioner cases on the vertical and horizontal structuring of communications across different types of companies. Section 5.5 then elaborates from this in discussing what explains structure and, in a more prescriptive sense, which organizational form suits a particular company (i.e. manufacturing or service company, small business, public organization, professional service organization, multinational corporation) best.

5.3   Vertical structure

To reiterate, communications organization consists of a vertical and horizontal structure. The vertical structure refers to the way in which different communications disciplines are arranged into departments, and the formal reporting relationships that these departments abide by. The horizontal structure, which is discussed in Section 5.4, refers to the cross-functional mechanisms that are horizontally laid over departments and connect communications practitioners with one another and with professionals from across the organization.

In recent years there has been a lot of discussion around the departmental arrangement of communications and the reporting relationship of the communications department. Ultimately, the stakes of this discussion are about the professional status of corporate communications (*vis-à-vis* other established functions such as human resources, marketing and finance) and its strategic involvement in decision making at the highest corporate level. Claims that have been made to this effect include the arguments that different communications disciplines *should be consolidated* in a single department, and that the head of this department *should report directly to the CEO or the senior management team* (or be a member of this team) to bolster and secure the functional expertise as well as the strategic involvement of corporate communications in decision making. The scholars Broom and Dozier characterized this involvement in organizational decision making as perhaps most important to the communications practitioner than any other measure of professional growth.[10]

The following paragraphs discuss the extant research on the departmental arrangement of communications and the reporting relationships involved within large manufacturing and service companies, before moving on to a more general discussion of the vertical structuring of communications across different types of companies: the small business, the multinational corporation, the public organization and the professional service organization.

The departmental arrangement of communications

There are in principle many different ways in which organizations can arrange their communications disciplines, and the staff responsible for them, into departments. Depending on the range of communications disciplines (e.g. advertising, publicity, community relations, corporate advertising, crisis communications, internal communications, financial communications, government relations, investor relations, issues management, lobbying, promotions, sponsorship and public affairs) present in a company, such disciplines can be brought together into one or two central communications departments, be devolved as stand-alone units (e.g. a governmental affairs unit), or be subordinated to other functions such as marketing, human resources or finance. Given these organizing options open to companies, much academic research has in recent years aimed to describe and explain how different communications disciplines are mapped on to organizational units or departments, and whether this mapping reveals tendencies towards consolidation or, alternatively, towards a dispersion of communications responsibilities.

these studies have moved beyond this simple observation and have started to explain why across companies and continents such consolidation exists. The following three sets of reasons figure most prominently as explanations.

1. Staff versus line.   A traditional explanation for having a central communications department separate from marketing is that certain areas of communications fall outside the operational and more tactical orbit of the marketing department.[17] Marketing is a so-called line function concerned with producing, distributing and promoting the company's products within selected markets, which includes marketing communications (advertising, promotions, publicity and selling). All other communications disciplines have a more general corporate (rather than product) focus, and are also more supportive and advisory in nature rather than being directly involved in the core business process of bringing products to markets. These other communications disciplines (e.g. issues management, investor relations, media relations, public affairs and government relations) have therefore been brought together into a separate staff department as a staff function. A *staff function* is a function where the manager has no direct executive power over the primary process or responsibility for it, but fulfils an advisory role, based on specific expertise, to all departments within the organization (see Figure 5.1 for an illustration). A *line function* such as marketing, in comparison, is concerned with the primary operating activities of the company. As a staff department, communications is enabled to counsel the CEO and the senior management team, and to support and assist line managers with strategic communications advice, whereas when it would have been organized as a line department (or incorporated into, for instance, marketing), communications would be cast in the role of a tactical support function or production unit supporting the primary operating activities.

2. Domain similarity and resource dependencies.   A second explanation for the grouping of communications disciplines into communications and marketing departments is that this reflects astute domain similarities and task dependencies between certain disciplines. *Domain similarity* is defined as the degree to which two different individuals or disciplines share similar goals, skills or tasks. *Resource dependence* is the dependence of a practitioner in one communications discipline on obtaining resources (e.g. advice, assistance or communications products) from another discipline to accomplish his or her objectives. The explanation provided here is that separate communications and marketing departments exist as the practitioners and disciplines within each department share the same technical skills, knowledge and a focus on either corporate or marketing stakeholders. The disciplines in each department are as a result highly dependent on each other's knowledge, skills and resources. The survey findings of the UK study of the Centre for Corporate and Public Affairs supports this explanation in that managers of communications and marketing departments suggested that the domains of their respective departments while showing some overlap are sufficiently distinct (indicating significant differences in the skills of practitioners, the work performed by the unit, the operating goals of the unit, and the sources from which the departments obtain their funding) to warrant a departmental separation.[18] In this sense, as the organization theorist Pfeffer has suggested, this departmental separation into communications and marketing, with the latter carrying

the responsibility for marketing communications, can be seen as rational in that 'the process of grouping activities, roles, or positions in the organization [serves] to coordinate effectively the *interdependencies* that exist ... the implicit goal of the structuring process is achieving a more rationalized and coordinated system of activity'.[19]

3. Economies of scale. A third and final explanation is that there is a certain economic rationale behind bringing disciplines together into departments. The point here is that it is relatively expensive to have stand-alone units for different communications disciplines, as it raises the costs of coordinating tasks and responsibilities. In contrast, when disciplines are taken together into one or a few departments, it may not only enhance the functional expertise and skills base of communications professionals within those departments, but it may also ease coordination and minimize the necessity and cost associated with cross-unit interaction.

As a result of these economies of scale, a discipline will normally only be separated out and organized as a separate unit when it is of critical and growing importance to a company, and comes to engross a critical mass of communications practitioners as a result. This happened, for instance, with the discipline of investor relations in large US corporations, which, given the importance of informing shareholders (who can make or break a company) and the financial community, came to incorporate more staff, and was in many companies eventually split up and departmentized as a stand-alone unit. A study by Rao shows that of all the Fortune 500 industrial companies only 16 per cent (84 cases) had investor relations departments in 1984, but that by the end of 1994 they had spread to 56 per cent (270 cases) of the sample.[20]

Reporting relationships

Different communications departments and units may have different reporting relationships. The manager of a communications services unit may be found, for instance, to report to the head of the marketing department, whereas an investor relations unit may, for instance, have a dual reporting relationship to the finance and communications departments. Such reporting relationships are of course largely determined by the departmental arrangement of communications – that is, where communications disciplines (as a separate department or unit, or as subordinated to another department) are placed within the organization's hierarchy. Academic research in this area has been particularly concerned with identifying to whom the communications department reports: whether directly to the CEO and senior management team, or to another department at a lower level in the hierarchy.

The guiding idea in this regard was that a direct reporting relationship to the CEO may be seen as an indication that there is indeed a broad, growing recognition among corporate executives and corporate boards that the ability to succeed will depend upon the corporation's ability to communicate effectively with its stakeholders, and that therefore the communications function is recognized as an absolute, integral part of the top management function. White and Mazur add that such a direct reporting relationship is also important as it leads to excellent communications management as senior management is counselled on issues, and stakeholder and tactics are used and are added to the extant responsibilities of one or a few of the 'functional' managers, often the marketing manager.

The multinational corporation. The key issues around communications, and the organization of it, are substantially different for multinationals than those facing the small business. Here the company is likely to be diverse in terms of both products and geographic markets. It may be that the company is in a range of different types of business in the form of subsidiary companies within a holding company structure, or divisions within a multidivisional structure. Therefore, issues of structure and control at the corporation, and relationships between businesses and the corporate centre, are usually a major strategic issue for multinational firms. One key structural consideration in organizing communications is, as Argenti suggests, to have 'all communications focused by centralizing the activity under one senior officer at a corporation's headquarters or to decentralize activities and allow individual business units to decide how best to handle communications'.[28] Centralization of all communications responsibilities by placing the majority of communications professionals in a staff department at the corporate centre perhaps has advantages in terms of greater corporate control and coordination of all communications programmes to stakeholders, ensuring consistency and achieving greater efficiency as research and communications materials can be shared. Decentralization, devolving communications responsibilities to departments within the separate business units, requires a larger apparatus of personnel, but delivers advantages as communications can be attuned to the specifics of the business unit and the geographic market and stakeholders that it serves. Decisions over whether to centralize or decentralize communications are often also based on the identity structure of a company: centralization is likely to be greater in the case of a monolithic identity structure (where the company and its business units carry the same name), while decentralization is often preferred for endorsed and branded identity structures (where the business units profile their own distinct names). The rationale behind this is that in branded and endorsed identity structures, greater leverage can be given to communications practitioners within the individual business units in their communications to markets and stakeholders.[29] A related issue in this regard is the extent to which the centre adds to or detracts from the value of its businesses. For the communications staff department at the corporate centre, this means that it must deliver value-added advice and assistance to the communications practitioners in the individual business units if it wants to secure a receptive environment for its involvement. Van Riel suggests that this requires the department to move beyond a technician view of communications, where it is seen as part of organizational routine and overheads and just deals with programmed decisions such as using weekly news briefings and publishing the monthly employee newsletter. Rather, practitioners within the corporate staff department need to provide expert and strategic advice and develop useful tools such as an overall communications strategy, so that the communications activities of the different parts of the company can be coordinated, and so that individual business units see their part in the overall communications strategy.[30] The case study in Box 5.1 illustrates some of these challenges in communications organization facing multinational companies.

Box 5.1   Case study: Sara Lee/DE – organizing communications in a multinational corporation[31]

Sara Lee/DE, headquartered in Utrecht, the Netherlands, is a subsidiary of Chicago-based Sara Lee Corporation, and is a global group of branded consumer packaged goods companies. The DE part of the Sara Lee/DE name goes back to the Douwe Egberts (DE) brand, a Dutch coffee and tea producer that was taken over by Sara Lee in 1978. Initially, the situation for the organization that formerly traded under the DE name changed little through the take-over. But, early in the 1980s, Sara Lee also acquired the Dutch company Intradel, a household and body care merchant, and decided to merge this newly acquired company with the existing DE organization. Having merged these two companies operating in very different sectors, Sara Lee finally decided in 1989 to change the structure of the newly formed organization. A corporate holding was established carrying the name Sara Lee/DE with two divisions: Coffee and Tea, and Household and Body Care. Together, these divisions now (in 2003) encompass around a hundred business units operating in more than 40 countries. Within this holding structure, responsibilities are devolved to each of these business units so that local businesses can respond to and meet local market needs in the best possible way.

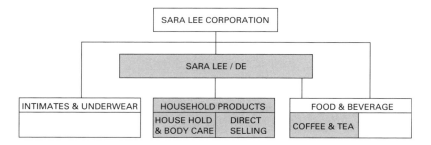

As a result of the restructuring in 1989 communications responsibilities became split into a central corporate public relations department at the group level of Sara Lee/DE, and smaller communications departments and professionals being placed within the various business units.

The split seemed a logical division of tasks, and is typical for many multinational corporations, but almost immediately brought clear tensions with it about responsibilities and procedures concerning communications. Particularly in the area of media relations, managers and professionals from across the organization duly talked with the press on their own initiative, in the absence of clear procedures for media relations.

These tensions and debates about responsibilities and procedures have since led to the implementation of two formal initiatives that aim to ensure that the central corporate public relations department maintains its policy making and coordinating role in an organization where communications responsibilities are largely decentralized to the level of the individual business units. The first initiative, supported by the executive board, is that corporate public relations offers the general strategic framework for communications to business units. This basically means that the general corporate strategy of the Sara Lee/DE company is translated into a set of communications values and procedures by the corporate public relations department, which are then passed on to communications practitioners within the individual business units. These practitioners in turn develop their own communications plans, but need to adhere to these values and procedures. As the chairman of the executive board once said: 'the corporate public relations department offers the frame, and professionals within the business units each deliver a picture for it'. The second formal initiative is that the corporate public relations department not only supports and counsels the executive board on organization-wide communications, but also is designated as an internal consultancy practice that the individual business units can turn to for advice and assistance. As an internal consultancy, the department operates on a project basis for communications practitioners in the business units, giving them value-added, expert communications advice or assisting and helping them with developing and executing communications plans. The corporate public relations department is, for this purpose, staffed with three expert consultants (each specializing in an area of communications) alongside the head of the department, an editor, a production manager and two personal assistants.

Through these two initiatives, Sara Lee/DE seeks to balance the coordination and management of communications issues at the central level, at the level of the whole organization, with its decentralized management structure in which individual business units manage their own communications plans. Individual business units are still responsible for their own communications plans, but these two initiatives are seen to ensure a greater coordination and collaboration across the organization, which leads to consistency of communications and a better profiling of the corporation as a whole.

Questions for reflection

1. To what extent are these tensions between a central communications department at group level and local communications practitioners at the level of individual business units typical and therefore generally descriptive of all multinational corporations? Which multinational corporations fall outside this characterization?
2. To what extent do you believe Sara Lee/DE has implemented suitable initiatives to deal with these tensions? What would you have done differently?

The public sector organization.   An effective streamlining of communications activities is just as important to organizations within the public sector as in commercial firms. The public sector involves many different types of organizations, including national-ized companies (e.g. utilities), government agencies and departments (e.g. the ministry of defence), and public service organizations (e.g. hospitals and schools). The larger organizations in the public sector (as opposed to, for instance, small government agencies) traditionally have a strong presence close to senior management and policy making of 'public' communications disciplines (e.g. media relations, publicity) that are used to inform the general public, and traditionally little marketing communications. This is a result of the direct or indirect control or influence exercised from outside the organization by government in particular. With budgets being allo-cated by government and missions imposed, there was traditionally little incentive for public organizations to develop extensive marketing programmes, let alone think in marketing terms about the products and services that they deliver. But, increasingly, organizations that were once within the public sector are either being privatized, or that changes are carried out within them because the government sees benefits in requiring public organizations to become more sharply focused on markets, and specifically on customer requirements and competitive pressures. Many public organizations have therefore developed marketing expertise in recent years, and have brought marketing communications professionals in-house. Often these professionals are incorporated into the staff communications department, from the viewpoint that marketing communications needs to be aligned with the other communications of the organization that are aimed at informing and gaining acceptance among stakeholders for the public good that the organization delivers. Alternatively, the professionals in marketing communications may be departmentized as a separate service unit and placed in the 'line' of the organization near the core operating units, or placed under marketing (when the organization has set up such a department).

The professional service organization.   Traditionally-based values are often of particular importance in professional service organizations where professional advice has traditionally been seen as more important than revenue earning capability. To a large extent this was the case in medicine, accountancy, law and other professions. Therefore, many of these organizations consisted of either a simple functional structure built around the expertise – and the products and services associated with it (often defined as 'practice areas') – of their professionals and a number of supporting departments (finance, human resource, and research and development), or more loose network structures in the case of larger, geographically dispersed professional service organizations. The latter network structure is often the case in private sector professional service firms with global acumen and a partnership structure (i.e. partners managing and/or owning local branches) in place. Either way, the structure of professional service organizations is typically geared towards the development and nurturing of specific professional expertise (whether in law, accountancy, medicine or management consultancy) and the acquisition of clients through direct selling or referral, and therefore lacks separate, fully developed marketing or communications departments. As with the small business, communications and marketing responsibilities, if they exist, are typically added to and integrated within existing responsibilities of professionals in each of the firm's practice areas. Some professional service organizations have, however, in recent years added a small communications unit to their supporting departments, usually charged with assisting in the acquisition of clients through the production of communications materials (website, brochures, etc.).

5.4   Horizontal structure

The horizontal organization involves a whole raft of coordination mechanisms that companies implement to integrate the work processes that are carried out in disparate parts of the organization. In the area of communications, horizontal mechanisms are furthermore important as these enable companies to respond quickly and effectively to emergent issues or shifting priorities of stakeholder groups, and allow for the exercise of control and ensuring that consistent messages are being sent out through all the various communications channels to stakeholders. A final point stressing the importance of horizontal structure is that it may off-set the potential disadvantages (functional silos, compartmentalization and 'turf wars') of the vertical structure, allowing for cross-functional work processes, integration and sufficient flexibility. Academic research has identified a number of elements of horizontal structure such as teamwork, council meetings and documentation of work processes.

Overview of horizontal structures

Recruitment, training and job rotation.   A first element that needs to be emphasized is that the horizontal integration of communications work processes starts with the profile and training of the communications practitioners within the company. When these practitioners have a more general outlook and understanding of the communications profession, and know how work processes need to be integrated, they will look beyond their own departmental boundaries and start appreciating other communications disciplines and the professionals working with them. Recruitment is therefore important as it can select practitioners who not only have an ability to work in teams, to appreciate different communications disciplines, and fit into the company culture, but also have a 'generalist' focus (instead of a purely specialist focus on a particular communications discipline) that leads to strategic, integrated and holistic thinking.[32] Training is also important as communications practitioners who receive ongoing skills training in different communications disciplines are generally found to be better able to integrate their work with people working in other communications disciplines. An additional mechanism to support integration among communications practitioners is job rotation. The benefits of rotating communications professionals among different work tasks and/or among different business units of the company are increased appreciation for colleagues in other communications professions, personal networks within the company, and identification with the company, rather than with occupational and technical specialization. Identification with the company is important, as it may lead to practitioners thinking more strategically about what communications can contribute to the company and the achievement of corporate objectives.

Recruitment and training of practitioners is thus important for the horizontal integration of work, but, beyond this personal level of the communications professional, there are a number of further horizontal structures and processes of coordination within and across departments: teamwork, process documentation, open communication and networking platforms, council meetings and communications guidelines.

Teamwork.   Multifunctional teams are an important mechanism for the coordination and integration of work of different communications disciplines.[33] Teams can be further distinguished within the natural work team, as permanent teams that work together on an ongoing basis (e.g. a cross-company investor relations team), or as task force teams, created on an ad hoc basis for specific projects (e.g. an internal communications team that guides a corporate restructuring). Task force teams are also assembled when an issue or crises emerges in the company's environment, and an adequate response needs to be formulated and communicated to key stakeholders. It is important for both the natural work teams and task force teams that team members with complementary skills are selected, that practitioners are trained in teamwork, that the whole team has authority to make decisions and implement suggestions, and that the team follows a step-by-step process in its work (from analysis and planning to action and evaluation).

Process documentation. The processes of integration across disciplines and departments can also be identified and documented in order to be improved. Companies can use various tools to document processes in visual and comprehensive formats, such as flow charts, process maps and checklists. Such process documentation creates a shared understanding among all communications practitioners about the processes of integration, institutionalizes processes of integration thus making the organization less dependent on certain individuals, facilitates continuous improvements of the processes of integration, enables communications practitioners to benchmark their processes against other companies, and creates opportunities for cycle-time reduction. Traditionally, however, communications practitioners are unaccustomed to defining work tasks in terms of process steps. Many of them do not think the analytical and disciplined approach of documenting and standardizing processes is conducive to creativity. This was also the reaction of communications staff in Philips, the global electronics manufacturer, when the company decided its process documentation exercise was to be carried through with all its functions and departments, including corporate communications. Senior managers argued that, even if the development of communications programmes is a unique creative process, there were some process steps that communications professionals always follow, and these steps should be identified, documented and improved on. Routine processes and repetitive steps in the company's communications process have since been documented and standardized in flow-charts and worksheets, which the company believes has not stifled creativity, but has cut redundancies in the coordination process (e.g. too many meetings or approvals previously built in) and has made the horizontal organization of communications across the company more streamlined, professional and, in light of the cost reductions received, more accountable.

Open communications and networking platforms. In addition to documented work processes, which are explicit and formal, integration also often occurs through more informal channels. Much of the interaction among communications practitioners takes place informally, in the electronic mail system, over the phones and in the hallways. Companies can facilitate such informal communications by placing communications professionals physically close to one another (in the same building), by reducing symbolic differences like separate parking lots and cafeterias, by establishing an infrastructure of e-mail, video conferences and other electronic communication channels, and by establishing open access to senior management. In large organizations, it is also important that communications practitioners from different disciplines (e.g. marketing communications, internal communications) frequently gather at internal conferences and meetings, where they can get to know one another, network and share ideas.

Council meetings.   Council meetings are often seen as critical to the coordination of communications practitioners from different departments working in different business units.[34] A council meeting usually consists of representatives of different communications disciplines (e.g. public relations, internal communications, marketing communications), who meet to discuss the strategic issues concerning communications and to review their past performance. Typically, ideas for improved coordination between communications disciplines bubble up at such council meetings, and the council assigns a subcommittee or team to carry them out. Most of the coordination of communications across many larger companies takes place in these council meetings and the subcommittees and teams that emerge from them. Generally, communications councils support coordination by providing opportunities for communicators to develop personal relationships among each other, coordinating communications projects, sharing best practices, learning from each other's mistakes, learning about the company, providing professional training, improving the status of communications in the company, and making communications professionals more committed to the organization as a whole. For all of this to happen, it is important that the council meeting remains constructive and participative in its approach towards the coordination of communications (instead of becoming a control forum or review board that strictly evaluates communications campaigns), so that professionals can learn, debate and eventually decide on the strategic long-term view for communications that is in the interest of the organization as a whole.

Corporate vision and communications strategy.   Processes of coordination and integration of communications can also be supported with a strong vision and formulated strategy by senior communications practitioners. Senior communications practitioners need to meet with CEOs and senior executives to help clarify the company's strategies and reach agreement on how communications can strategically support them, and what performance measures their progress should be evaluated against. From this, a communications strategy (Chapter 4) can then be developed, which not only describes the strategic role of communications within the overall corporate and market strategies of the company, but also articulates the input, activities and performance expected of individual practitioners and communications disciplines from across the organization.

Communications guidelines.   A final mechanism for horizontally integrating work processes of communications practitioners involves the use of communications guidelines. Such guidelines may range from agreed upon work procedures (whom to contact, formatting of messages, etc.) to more general design regulations on how to apply logotypes and which PMS colours to use. Often companies have a 'house style' book that includes such design regulations, but also specifies the core values of the corporate identity. Ericsson, the mobile phone manufacturer, has a 'global brand book' that distils the corporation's identity in a number of core values that communications practitioners are expected to adhere to and incorporate in all of their messages to stakeholders. Ericsson also convenes a number of workshops with communications practitioners across the organization to familiarize these practitioners with the Ericsson identity, the brand book, and the general work procedures that come with their job.

The above-mentioned mechanisms apply to the coordination and integration of work among practitioners from different communications disciplines. But it is important to note that corporate communications and the management of stakeholders spirals to other functions as well. Horizontal procedures and arrangements for the coordination of work processes between communications practitioners and professionals in, for instance, human resources or finance, therefore equally need to be put in place. This might take the form of simply a meeting between senior managers of communications, human resources and finance to sound out the issues, and align their strategies accordingly. FedEX fits this picture, where the director of communications meets once a year individually with all of the company's senior managers to discuss their communications needs. As he explains, 'we need to understand what the business priorities are, in order to align corporate communications with them. Otherwise we will be relegated to a mouthpiece, a media impression generating machine'.[35]

It might, however, also be that there are more concrete interdependencies and work processes between communications and other management functions, which require more structural horizontal arrangements. The implementation of work teams connecting these functions might be an option in such cases, and it perhaps also requires that communications managers approach professionals from these other functions as their 'customers'. Hewlett-Packard's corporate communications staff, for instance, have even developed a database to profile their internal 'customers' to better meet their needs. Telefonica, the global telecommunications firm, equally has such an arrangement where the corporate reputation department counsels 'clients' – i.e. all other functions within the company (including finance, human resources, operations and marketing) – on stakeholders issues, and assists and supports each of these functional areas in the development of stakeholder management programmes.

Horizontal structure in different contexts

Academic research on the use of horizontal coordination mechanisms across different companies has been scant. There is thus very little systematic evidence from research that documents whether and how companies may be seen to use some of the horizontal mechanisms outlined above. Case studies and evidence from practice are equally limited, but the few existing case studies do indicate that generally not enough horizontal structures are in place to assist communications practitioners in the carrying out and integration of their work. In small businesses, one might in fact expect little formal horizontal structures such as teams and communications guidelines, as personnel can easily, and often informally, liaise with one another and solve the communications problem at hand. But large organizations in both the private and public sectors generally need more elaborate horizontal structures, such as council meetings and teams. Particularly in multidivisional firms operating across geographical borders, horizontal structures are not a luxury but an absolute necessity. Nonetheless, in many large organizations not enough attention is being paid to the use of horizontal structures, as there is often among managers and practitioners a preoccupation with the vertical structure of bringing disciplines together into departments. Gronstedt, author of an influential study into horizontal structures in eight best-practice US firms, challenges this preoccupation and suggests that there should be less focus on 'who is in charge?' and 'who belongs to what department?' and rather an emphasis on developing more knowledge about horizontal processes and structures of integration. As he emphasizes the importance of horizontal structures: 'integrated communication is not necessarily about putting public relations, marketing communications and other communications professionals into a single department, but about integrating their [work] processes'.[36] Gronstedt therefore suggests that each company should have a *sufficient* or fair number of horizontal mechanisms in place, as this not only leads to better coordination of the work of communications practitioners, but also to more job satisfaction, greater identification with the company, and generally more competent professionals.

5.5   What explains structure?

Vertical and horizontal structures of communications organization may vary across companies. Because of historical precedents, powerful coalitions, organizational size or environmental factors, companies might differ in how communications disciplines are arranged into departments, in terms of whether they have a central, independent communications department, and also in the degree and kind of coordination mechanisms that have been installed between communications disciplines and departments. The nature of these differences was documented in detail in Sections 5.3 and 5.4, which dealt with differences in vertical and horizontal structures across different types of companies. At this point it is worth mentioning that there is a lot of academic debate about why there are such differences in communications organization across companies, in terms of what factors seem to determine vertical and horizontal structures, and whether there is an 'optimal' or best way of organizing communications for different types of companies (i.e. whether the company is a small business, manufacturing/ service firm, public organization, professional service organization or multinational corporation).

Explaining structure: contingency versus power-control

The debate about what determines structure centres on two different schools of thought: contingency and power-control theory.[37] Both offer alternative frameworks for studying and explaining organizational structure. Contingency theory, first of all, is a so-called structural-functionalist theory of organizational structure suggesting that organizations are very much dependent on the constellation of environmental factors affecting organizations at any point in time. This perspective was initially developed in the 1960s in the works of Chandler (1962) and Lawrence and Lorsch (1967), among others.[38] The situational factors affecting organizational structure such as environmental (in)stability, technology, size and strategy that they studied came to be called contingency factors, and the related body of work came to be called contingency theory. Here the basic principle is that of interdependency. Companies are seen to adapt their formal organizational structure to align it with factors in their environment.[39] A characteristic of contingency theory is that, as a theory, it assumes that such structural, deterministic relationships between contingency factors and structure can be found and that, as contingency factors broadly differ by classes of organizations, it therefore also accounts for differences across different types of organizations.

This latter point distinguishes contingency theory, which argues that variation in structures is thus dependent on mechanisms in the environment, from theories such as 'political choice' or 'power-control', which in contrast, argue against determinism and the existence of structural relationships between an organization and its environment.[40] These political frameworks challenged the determinism inherent in contingency theory, as they sought to replace contingency theory with approaches that focus often on individual perception, belief and choice, as well as conflict and power struggles between classes or groups within the organization. A particular example of this strand of organization theory is the 'political choice' theory of organizational structure, which posits that people exercise choice rather than bowing to situational dictates. Hence, this theory rejects the notion that a functional structure will be chosen and suggests that organizational structure is often counter-productive and only serves the interests of certain organizational members (i.e. powerful coalitions). Yet another theory, power-control theory, does not go as far as to deny any form of functionalism, but stresses the importance of managerial perceptions and actions mediating between the environment and the structures within a company. This theory, initially framed by Child in 1972, now represents a separate and powerful school of thought in management and organization research. Power-control theory states that organizational structures are partly determined by or related to conditions within a company's environment, but also partly result from managerial choices. Decisions over organizational structure are influenced by managerial perceptions, so that the preferences, interest and power of managers also affect which structure is chosen. Comparing these two perspectives suggests that contingency theory focuses for its explanation of organizational structure on material or 'objective' factors such as size and technology in the company's environment, rather than on 'subjective' or political factors such as ideas, perceptions and norms, as power-control theory does. And in terms of managerial choice, contingency theory implies a relatively high level of determinism where managers are seen as having to adopt the organizational structure required by a company's environmental conditions. The power-control theory, in contrast, assumes a larger variance in structures and hence a friction between environment and structure possible because of the decisive influence and variant nature of managerial perceptions and actions.

The contingency perspective on communications organization.   The contingency or environmental perspective on communications organization emerged with the work of Kotler and Mindak in 1978.[41] Observing increased dependencies and overlap between public relations and marketing, Kotler and Mindak argued for a more contingent view relating alternative relational concepts of public relations and marketing to factors such as organizational size and business sector. They for instance suggested that for some companies, particularly retail and manufacturing companies, it might be more effective to closely align marketing and public relations so as to reduce interdepartmental conflict and problems of coordination. Since Kotler and Mindak's groundbreaking work, a number of academic researchers have since followed the contingency path for research into communications organization including Schneider, Van Leuven and Cornelissen.[42] Van Leuven, for instance, researched whether the structuring of the company and its communications department varies or is contingent upon relationships between the company and its outside environment.

The power-control perspective on communications organization. The power-control perspective on communications organization is largely associated with the group of academic researchers of the IABC Excellence study into public relations. These researchers, including James Grunig, Larissa Grunig and Dozier, argued that earlier studies from a contingency perspective had produced little if any explanatory evidence of why communications is actually organized across organizations as it is. This group of academics critiqued Schneider's study in particular, which had taken an environmental perspective towards explaining the structural variation of organizations but had provided only a minimal explanation for the structuring of the communications department.[43] Such weak and insignificant links between environment and organizational structure subsequently led these researchers to suggest the power-control perspective as a more viable theoretical framework to research and explain structural variations of communications. For exactly these reasons, Larissa Grunig motivated the turn to the power-control perspective, which suggests 'that organizations do what they do because the people with the most power in the organization – the dominant coalition – decide to do it that way'.[44] The rationale here, from the power-control perspective, is that the lack of contingent relations between environment and structure indicates the considerable latitude of choice among the dominant coalition of senior managers, permitting them to devise structures and organizational responses that in the light of environmental needs 'satisfice' rather than 'optimize'.[45] The idea is thus that perceptions and choices of senior managers within the company, which are influenced by intra-organizational power and the forming of coalitions, are the main determinants of the structuring of communications. In other words, as research within the power-control paradigm suggests the structuring of communications is dependent upon the intra-organizational power of the communications function in terms of the valuable resources and knowledge that it holds (which other departments are dependent upon) and its perceived value by the dominant coalition within a company.

In summary, both the contingency and power-control perspectives offer alternative theoretical frameworks for studying and explaining the way in which communications is vertically and horizontally structured within companies. Both have been supported with some empirical data in research, and go some way towards explaining the variance in structures discussed in Sections 5.3 and 5.4. The *size of the organization*, for one, clearly explains some of the variance in vertical structures across companies. Small businesses generally have communications responsibilities located with one or a few managers in other functional areas (marketing, human resources) within the organization. When organizations grow larger, however, and adopt a multidivisional structure (with each division catering for a certain product-market combination), the proportion of communications personnel it contains equally increases, and communications disciplines will be taken together into departments or separate units. This is particularly evident in the consistent findings that in large manufacturing and service companies communications disciplines are arranged into separate communications and marketing departments. Second, the *domain similarities and resource dependencies* between disciplines, as discussed above, may be seen to account for the departmental arrangement of communications, for whether communications disciplines are taken together or split up into separate departments. Both these elements – size, and domain similarities and resource dependencies – are factors in a company's internal and external environment, and thus point to a contingency explanation of communications structure. At the same time, however, the location of communications departments in the *hierarchy of the organization* seems to be associated with managerial discretion. When senior managers value communications for its input into decision making, the senior communications manager may be promoted to a seat on the executive board or management team, or, alternatively, may be working in a close reporting relationship with senior managers. In other words, the reporting relationship, and particularly the variance in whether the senior communications manager just reports to the CEO and executive team or whether he is really a member of that dominant coalition, can be more aptly explained with power-control theory. Box 5.2 proceeds from these observations and explanations, and provides a management brief of key steps in deciding upon an effective organizational structuring of communications.

Box 5.2   Management brief: steps in organizing communications

In January 1982, AT&T agreed to divest itself of the wholly owned Bell operating companies that provided local exchange services following an antitrust suit by the US government. Divestiture took place on 1 January 1984; the regional business units became independent Bell companies separate from the AT&T company, which from then on would focus on the long-distance telephone market. This new focus required a new corporate identity and logo (a stylized globe and the monogram AT&T) and a more aggressive marketing strategy of the AT&T company, so that it would successfully compete in the intensely competitive long-distance telephone market. The divestiture also meant a change in the way in which communications was organized and managed. In the original company structure, a small staff communications department at group headquarters had acted only in an advisory capacity to communications professionals in the regional Bell business units, as communications was largely decentralized. But with the change to the AT&T company, and the separation from the regional business units, a more centralized approach to communications was taken to guard and control the monolithic AT&T brand. The staff communications department was enlarged and charged with company-wide decision-making power over communications. In 1995 another new structure was announced. AT&T decided that because of few synergies between its communications and manufacturing businesses, it would restructure into three separate publicly traded companies: a systems and equipment company (which became Lucent Technologies), a computer company (which was named NCR), and a communications services company (which kept the AT&T name). Again, communications staff were reshuffled across the three different companies, but the central communications department was kept in place. And in 2000 and 2001, the AT&T company was once again subject to a restructuring into a family of separate publicly held companies: AT&T Wireless, AT&T Broadband and AT&T. This obviously meant that more communications staff would once again be placed in the separate companies, and that responsibilities would to a large extent be devolved to them. But the central communications department, whose director by now had become a member of the executive team, was kept in place and still heads the communications council that works across the three companies and deals with strategic issues around AT&T's positioning as 'the world's networking company'.

As the restructuring in AT&T's recent history shows, the organization of communications may equally be changed, adapted and restructured over time. With each change and at any point in time, however, senior managers and communication practitioners need to reflect and evaluate whether the organizational structure for communications is still effective and lean in the light of the communications resources (i.e. disciplines and professionals) that the company possesses. Three key steps are essential in such an evaluation exercise.

1. *Identify and characterize the present and anticipated communications resource.* The first step in considering and evaluating the structuring of communications is to identify what communications disciplines there actually are in the company, and whether any new disciplines and expertise (e.g. social responsibility reporting) are expected in the near future. Once all of these disciplines are identified, managers should further characterize them. Do these disciplines serve to communicate to stakeholders about the company as a whole, about its products, or both? And which of these disciplines provide advice and general counsel alongside more operational tactics and techniques? And how many people are working in each of these disciplines? Once the range and scope of all communications disciplines have been identified, managers can start to consider and reflect how these disciplines might be best organized.

2. *Arrange disciplines into departments in an efficient and effective manner.* Managers need to ask themselves whether the current way in which disciplines are taken together into departments reflects the interdependencies between these disciplines in terms of resource dependencies (whether disciplines are highly dependent on one another for knowledge, skills or materials) or domain similarities (whether disciplines share objectives, stakeholder groups, tactics and skills), and whether the departmental arrangement is thus *effective*. If this is not the case, the company may not capitalize fully on its communications resources, as these are not shared, and therefore may not fully tap its communications expertise. Managers also need to ponder whether the departmental arrangement is *efficient* in that it reflects clear economies of scale. If, for instance, too many independent units have been created without any valid reasons, this proves costly and inefficient. The trade-off with the departmental arrangement is thus to create the minimum required number of departments, which also secures effectiveness in that disciplines with interdependencies are pooled.

3. *Determine the need for coordination across departments.* The final step, once disciplines have been put into departments, is to identify the amount and the nature of interaction between departments, and how this interaction can best be facilitated and coordinated. When there is a steady flow of interaction between certain departments, say between a marketing department in a business unit and a staff communications department at group headquarters, there is a need for a horizontal coordination mechanism, such as a work team or communications guidelines. The type of horizontal structure to use depends not only on the amount of interaction, but also on the nature of this interaction;

when the interaction is about clear and standard issues, work procedures or guidelines can be used, when the interaction is more varied and equivocal it rather requires face-to-face meetings and consultation in a council meeting, committee or task force team.

Taken together, these three steps point to an effective and efficient structuring of communications, and provide guidelines for practitioners in evaluating their current structuring of communications, whether any change in structure is needed and what this change may then look like. As with most management and corporate communications problems, organizing communications does not involve 'right' or 'wrong' answers or general principles, but these three steps may nevertheless be an aid to senior managers and communications staff in deciding upon an appropriate structure for communications.

5.6   Chapter summary

The subject of communications organization carries important strategic and political dimensions; the way in which communications is structured not only determines whether communications activities that are carried out at various places within the organization are coordinated in a cost–effective manner, but also whether the communications function is enabled to provide strategic input into corporate decision making. In fact, the fullest strategic use of corporate communications in many ways stands or falls with an effective structuring of communications, with the presence of a consolidated communications department with ready access to the decision-making coalition, and with the use of horizontal mechanisms to align the work and communications products of practitioners from different departments. Fortunately, as this chapter has suggested, many companies do have such consolidated departments placed at a high location in the organization's hierarchy. This high location, however, often consists of a direct reporting relationship from the senior communications manager to the CEO or executive board rather than this manager actually having a seat on the executive board. The reason for this, as mentioned, is the still considerable lack of understanding and lack of commitment to communications among many senior managers, but also the incompetence of many communications practitioners to meet the needs of senior managers in ways that contribute to the accomplishment of organizational objectives and that affect the bottom line. The following chapter takes a closer look at the competencies of communications practitioners.

Key terms

Centralization	Dominant coalition
Contingency	Economies of scale
Coordination mechanism	Executive/senior management team
Council meeting	Horizontal structure
Departmental arrangement	Line function
Domain similarity	Matrix structure

Power-control

Procedures and guidelines

Process documentation

Reporting relationship

Resource dependence

Staff function

Team

Vertical structure

Notes

[1]Gronstedt, A. (1996A), 'Integrated communications at America's leading total quality management corporations', *Public Relations Review*, 22 (1), 25–42; Caywood, C.L. (1997), 'Introduction', in Caywood, C.L. (ed.), *The Handbook of Strategic Public Relations and Integrated Communications*. New York: McGraw-Hill, pp. xi–xxvi.

[2]Hollander, S.C. (1986), 'The marketing concept: a déjà vu', in Fisk, G. (ed.), *Marketing Management Technology as a Social Process*. New York: Praeger, pp. 3–29.

[3]Cook, J. (1973), 'Consolidating the communications function', *Public Relations Journal*, 29 (6–8), 28.

[4]Schultz, D.E., Tannenbaum, S.I., and Lauterborn, R.F. (1993) *The New Marketing Paradigm: Integrated Marketing Communications*. Lincolnwood: NTC Publishing; Schultz, D.E. (1996), 'The inevitability of integrated communications', *Journal of Business Research*, 37, 139–146.

[5]See for instance Gronstedt (1996A); Prensky, D., McCarty, J.A., and Lucas, J. (1996), 'Integrated marketing communication: an organizational perspective', in Thorson, E., and J. Moore (eds), *Integrated Communication: Synergy of Persuasive Voices*. Mahwah, NJ: Lawrence Erlbaum Associates, pp. 167–183.

[6]See for instance Argenti, P.A. (1998), *Corporate Communication*. Boston: McGraw-Hill, second edition; Dozier, D.M., and Grunig, L.A. (1992), 'The organization of the public relations function', in Grunig, J.E. (ed.), *Excellence in Public Relations and Communication Management*. Hillsdale, NJ: Lawrence Erlbaum Associates, pp. 395–417; Moss, D., Warnaby, G., and Newman, A.J. (2000), 'Public relations practitioner role enactment at the senior management level within UK companies', *Journal of Public Relations Research*, 12 (4), 277–307; Stewart, D.W. (1996), 'Market-back approach to the design of integrated communications programs: a change in paradigm and a focus on determinants of success', *Journal of Business Research*, 37, 147–153; Schultz, Tannenbaum and Lauterborn (1993).

[7]Heath, R.L. (1994), *Management of Corporate Communication: From Interpersonal Contacts to External Affairs*. Hillsdale, NJ: Lawrence Erlbaum Associates; Gronstedt, A. (1996b), 'Integrating marketing communication and public relations: a stakeholder relations model', in Thorson, E., and Moore, J. (eds), *Integrated Communication: Synergy of Persuasive Voices*. Mahwah, NJ: Lawrence Erlbaum Associates, pp. 287–304.

[8]Grunig, J.E., and Grunig, L.A. (1998), 'The relationship between public relations and marketing in excellent organizations: evidence from the IABC study', *Journal of Marketing Communications*, 4 (3), 141–162.

[9]Gronstedt, A., and Thorson, E. (1996), 'Five approaches to organize an integrated marketing communications agency', *Journal of Advertising Research*, 36 (2), 48–58.

[10]Broom, G.M., and Dozier, D.M. (1986), 'Advancement for public relations role models', *Public Relations Review*, 12, 37–56.

[11]Post, J.E., and Griffin, J.J. (1997), 'Corporate reputation and external affairs', *Corporate Reputation Review*, 165–171; Hutton, J.G., Goodman, M.B., Alexander, J.B., and Genest, C.M. (2001), 'Reputation management: the new face of corporate public relations?', *Public Relations Review*, 27, 247–261.

[12]Hunter, T. (1997), 'The relationship of public relations and marketing against the background of integrated communications: a theoretical analysis and empirical study at US American corporations'. Masters Thesis (unpublished), University of Salzburg (Austria).

[13]Grunig and Grunig (1998), 154.

[14]Cornelissen, J.P., and Thorpe, R. (2001), 'The organization of external communication disciplines in UK companies: a conceptual and empirical analysis of dimensions and determinants', *Journal of Business Communication*, 38 (4), 413–438.

[15]Van Ruler, B., and De Lange, R. (2003), 'Barriers to communication management in the executive suite', *Public Relations Review*, 2, 145–158.

[16]Marion, G. (1998), 'Corporate communications managers in large firms: new challenges', *European Management Journal*, 16 (6), 660–671; and Tixier, M. (1998), 'Corporate communications: conception and structure in some European, American and Asian countries', *Journal of Communication Management*, 3, 363–379.

[17]Kitchen, P.J., and Moss, D.A. (1995), 'Marketing and public relations: the relationship revisited', *Journal of Marketing Communications*, 1 (2), 105–119; Van Riel, C.B.M. (1995), *Principles of Corporate Communication*. London: Prentice Hall.

[18]Cornelissen and Thorpe (2001).

[19]Pfeffer, J. (1978), *Organizational Design*. Arlington Heights: Harlan Davidson, p. 25.

[20]Rao, H. (1997), 'The rise of investor relations departments in the Fortune 500 industrials', *Corporate Reputation Review*, 1 (1/2), 172–177.

[21]White, J., and Mazur, L. (1995), *Strategic Communications Management: Making Public Relations Work*. Wokingham: Addison-Wesley.

[22]Wright, D.K. (1995), 'The role of public relations executives in the future of employee communications', *Public Relations Review*, Fall, 181–198.

[23]Post and Griffin (1997); Cornelissen and Thorpe (2001); Marion (1998); Tixier (1998); Van Ruler and De Lange (2003).

[24]Troy, K. (1993), *Managing Corporate Communications in a Competitive Climate*. New York: Conference Board.

[25]Bevan, S. (1997), 'PR resumes its seat on Inchcape's board', *PR Week*, 30 May, 2.

[26]Moss, Warnaby and Newman (2000), 299.

[27]Osborne, J. (1994), 'Getting full value from public relations', *Public Relations Journal*, October/November, 64.

[28]Argenti (1998), p. 50.

[29]Körver, F., and Van Ruler, B. (2003), 'The relationship between corporate identity structures and communication structures', *Journal of Communication Management*, 7 (3), 197–208.

[30]Van Riel (1995), pp. 144–146.

[31]This case was based on Den Haan, J.J. (2002) 'De communicatie bij Sara Lee/DE: corporate communicatie in een decentrale organisatie', *Communicatie Cases*, 11, 9–24, and corporate documents from the Sara Lee/DE website (www.saralee-de.com).

[32]Stewart (1996); Lauer, L.D. (1995); 'Will we need a whole new breed of professional?', *Communication World*, August.

[33]See, for instance, Duncan, T., and Moriarty, S.E. (1998), 'A communication-based marketing model for managing relationships', *Journal of Marketing*, 62 (April), 1–13.

[34]Van Riel (1995), Dolphin (1999), *The Fundamentals of Corporate Communications*. Oxford: Butterworth-Heinemann, p. 73.

[35]Gronstedt (2000), *The Customer Century: Lessons from World-class Companies in Integrated Marketing and Communications*. London: Routledge, p. 180.

[36]Gronstedt (1996a), p. 40.

[37]Cornelissen, J.P., and Lock, A.R. (2000), 'The organizational relationship between marketing and public relations: exploring paradigmatic viewpoints', *Journal of Marketing Communications*, 6 (4), 231–245.

[38]Chandler, A.P. (1962), *Strategy and Structure*. Cambridge MA: MIT Press; Lawrence, P.R., and Lorsch, J.W. (1967), *Organization and Environment: Managing Differentiation and Integration*. Boston: Division of Research, Graduate School of Business Administration Harvard University.

[39]Burrell, G., and Morgan, G. (1979), *Sociological Paradigms and Organizational Analysis: Elements of the Sociology of Corporate Life*. London: Heinemann. Educational Books; Donaldson, L. (1996), *For Positivist Organization Theory: Proofing the Hard Core*. London: Sage; Donaldson, L. (1999), 'The normal science of structural contingency theory', in Clegg, S., and Hardy, C. (eds), *Studying Organization: Theory and Method*. London: Sage, pp. 51–70.

[40]Child, J. (1972), 'Organizational structure, environment and performance: the role of strategic choice', *Sociology*, 6 (1), 2–22; Child, J. (1997), 'Strategic choice in the analysis of action, structure, organizations and environment: retrospect and prospect', *Organization Studies*, 18 (1), 43–76; Silverman, D. (1970), *The Theory of Organizations: A Sociological Framework*. London: Heinemann; Weick, K.E. (1979), *The Social Psychology of Organizing*. Reading, MA: Addison-Wesley, second edition.

[41]Kotler, P., and Mindak, W. (1978), 'Marketing and public relations, should they be partners or rivals?', *Journal of Marketing*, 42 (10), 13–20.

[42]Schneider (aka Grunig), L.A. (1985), 'The role of public relations in four organizational types', *Journalism Quarterly*, 62 (3), 567–576; Van Leuven, J. (1991), 'Corporate organizing strategies and the scope of public relations departments', *Public Relations Review*, 17 (3), 279–291; Cornelissen, J.P., Lock, A.R., and Gardner, H. (2001), 'The organisation of external communication disciplines: an integrative framework of dimensions and determinants', *International Journal of Advertising*, 20 (1), 67–88; Cornelissen and Thorpe (2001); Cornelissen, J.P. and Harris, P. (2004), 'Interdependencies between marketing and public relations as correlates of communication organisation', *Journal of Marketing Management*, 20, 1–2, 237–264.

[43]Grunig, J.E., and Grunig, L.A. (1989), 'Toward a theory of the public relations behavior of organizations: review of a program of research', in Grunig, J.E., and Grunig, L.A. (eds), *Public Relations Research Annual – volume one*. Mahwah, NJ: Lawrence Erlbaum Associates, pp. 27–63; Grunig, L.A. (1992), 'How public relations/communication departments should adapt to the structure and environment of an organization … and what they actually do', in Grunig, J.E. (ed.), *Excellence in Public Relations and Communication Management*, Hillsdale, NJ: Lawrence Erlbaum Associates, pp. 467–481; Dozier and Grunig (1992), p. 431.

[44]Grunig, L.A. (1992), 'Power in the public relations department', in Grunig, J.E. (ed.), *Excellence in Public Relations and Communication Management*. Hillsdale, NJ: Lawrence Erlbaum Associates, pp. 483–501, p. 483.

[45]Dozier and Grunig (1992).

Chapter 6
Communications Practitioners: Theory and Practice

Central themes

- Communications practitioners carry out a variety of tasks and activities and are often cast in the role of technician or manager. In the role of a communications technician, a practitioner focuses on the production of communications products for organizations and implements decisions made by others. In the role of a communications manager, a practitioner is involved in strategic decisions, or helps management to do so, makes communications programme decisions and is held accountable for that programme's success or failure.

- While practitioners can be cast in these general roles, it is important to note that all practitioners enact elements of both the manager and technician roles that are simply useful abstractions for understanding the wide range of activities that practitioners perform in their daily work.

- Both technician and manager roles are needed within practice, although for the strategic use of communications within companies the onus lies on the enactment of the manager role.

- As a practice and occupation, communications management often has *not* been characterized as a true profession primarily as it is judged to lack a sufficient body of knowledge, as well as intellectual expertise and skills that are unique to it, and are also valued within organizations and accredited by peer groups (other managers, practitioners from established professions, etc).

- Further development of the practice and occupation of communications management is needed to enable communications to fulfil its managerial role in the strategic interests of the organization, and is dependent on training and education, the development of a knowledge base, a reflective approach of practitioners and a supportive organizational environment.

6.1   Introduction

Chapters 4 and 5 have discussed the importance of the strategic use of communications within an organization, and what this requires in terms of the *process* of strategy making as well as the way in which communications staff and their tasks are *structured*. This chapter examines another critical element within the strategic management of communications: the *people* working in communications. What people bring to the communications job in terms of expertise, competencies and skills is a crucial element in the effective functioning and use of communications, and for the value that is assigned to it by other managers within the company.

This chapter provides a detailed look at the practice of communications and the people working within it. It starts with an overview of the roles and activities carried out by practitioners in Section 6.2. Based on these roles and activities, practitioners have often been characterized as either managers or technicians. This distinction between technicians and managers is important as it not only captures the nature of the work and the views that these practitioners themselves have of it, but also explains and suggests how the communications function is regarded by others (i.e. as a strategic management function or as a low-level support function) and whether it has any involvement in corporate decision making. From this overview of roles and activities performed by practitioners, Section 6.3 then moves on to discuss the general state of the practice and occupation of communications management at the start of the twenty-first century and attempts to answer whether it can be characterized as a true profession (as, for instance, the professions of medicine, law, accounting, etc.). Although the jury is still out on this, this section attests that communications has not yet evolved into a full-blown profession as it still lacks a comprehensive body of knowledge and the type of education that would provide practitioners with rigorous intellectual expertise and skills that not only are unique to it, but are also valued within organizations and accredited by peer groups (other managers, practitioners from established professions, etc.) and society at large. The final part of Section 6.3 picks up from these observations on the state of communications as an occupation and suggests ways in which it can be further developed, and also what this requires of the parties (i.e. practitioners themselves, teachers and trainers, senior managers, professional associations and academic researchers) involved. One particular area of concern, for example, is that the higher education sector has not sufficiently responded to the needs of practitioners to be equipped with management competencies and a business frame of reference alongside their tactical communications skills (writing, editing, graphics, etc.). Calls for a more management-oriented framework for educating practitioners have been heard for decades, yet few university public relations, advertising or business communications courses today include more than token business-focused course work, if any at all. Educating students and practitioners so that they become business-literate with a specialized knowledge of, and skills sets in, communications (and thus know how communications can be used within and for the purpose of organizations) is, however, essential for the development of communications as a *management function* and as a full-grown profession.

Taken together, the chapter should thus provide the reader not only with a clear overview of the various activities and roles performed by practitioners, but also with an understanding of the state of the practice and occupation of communications and of ways in which it can be further developed.

6.2 The roles and practices of communications practitioners

On a day-to-day basis, practitioners working in communications are engaged in a broad variety of activities ranging from, for instance, editorial work, internal counselling, handling of inquiries, gathering information, looking at data from research, talking to press contacts, drafting communications plans, delivering presentations, producing communications materials (brochures, visuals, etc.), and administrative tasks within the department. The job of communications practitioners, at various levels of seniority, thus consists of a broad range of activities that in its scope and variety not only varies with the tasks that have been assigned to a communications department (i.e. whether the department is a service unit or is involved in counselling and decision making at the senior management level), but also with the range of issues and enquiries from stakeholders that are directed to communications practitioners for handling. In companies where stakeholder groups indeed wage many claims upon the organization and raise issues that require a response, practitioners often work at an unrelenting pace to counsel management, draft resolutions and policy documents, and respond to and communicate with those outside stakeholder groups.

As in many other organizational jobs, practitioners often work at a fast pace and under pressure on a whole range of different tasks and activities.[1] While these activities may be characterized by variety and brevity, and thus differ from practitioner to practitioner, academic research has established that despite this variety practitioners can generally be cast in two broad role types: managers and technicians. These general roles are based upon the outlook of a practitioner upon the job and the *general* range of activities that he or she performs.

Communications managers and technicians

Katz and Khan in 1978 initially identified the importance of the role concept in organizations. They defined organizations as role systems and 'role behaviour' as 'recurring actions of an individual interrelated with the actions of others so as to yield a predictable outcome'.[2] An organizational role is, of course, an abstraction; a conceptual order imposed on the many activities performed by individuals in organizations to make sense of organizational behaviour and explain its causal factors and its consequences. Working with the role concept, Glen Broom pioneered roles research in communications to explain the pattern of activities performed by practitioners. Using a battery of 24 self-reporting measures of roles activities, Broom conceptualized four dominant theoretical roles, which he argued captured the main patterns of activities that communications practitioners perform.[3] These four theoretical practitioner roles comprised:

1. **The communications technician role**: in this role, the practitioner provides the specialized skills needed to carry out communications programmes. Rather than being part of the management team, technicians are concerned with preparing and producing communications materials for the communications effort of the organization.

2.   **The expert prescriber role**: in this role, the practitioner operates as the authority on both communications problems and their solutions. The client or management is often content to leave communications in the hands of the 'expert' and to assume a relatively passive role.
3.   **The communications facilitator role**: this role casts the practitioner as a sensitive 'go-between' or information broker. The practitioner serves as a liaison, interpreter and mediator between the organization and its stakeholders.
4.   **The problem-solving process facilitator role**: in this role, practitioners collaborate with other managers to define and solve communication and stakeholder problems for the organization. Unlike the expert prescriber role, here practitioners work with management and are more likely to play an active part in strategic decision making.

Reflecting on these four role types, Broom also observed that the expert prescriber, communications facilitator and problem-solving process facilitator roles were closely correlated, but quite distinct from the communications technician role. David Dozier equally suggested that these four practitioner roles could be reduced to more general 'manager' and 'technician' roles because the expert prescriber, the communication facilitator and the problem-solving process facilitator roles all represented a broader managerial role. Reworking Broom's data, Dozier identified two *major* conceptual roles: communications technician and communications manager.

1.   **Communications technician**: communications practitioners are characterized as technicians if their work focuses on such activities as writing communications materials, editing and/or rewriting for grammar and spelling, handling the technical aspects, producing brochures or pamphlets, doing photography and graphics, and maintaining media contacts and placing press releases. Dozier and Broom define a technician as 'a creator and disseminator of messages, intimately involved in production, [and] operating independent of management decision making, strategic planning, issues management, environmental scanning and program evaluation'.[4] In other words, a technician tactically implements decisions made by others and is generally not involved in management decision making and strategic decisions concerning communications strategy and programmes.
2.   **Communications manager**: practitioners enacting the manager role predominantly make strategy or policy decisions and are held accountable for programme success or failure. These practitioners are primarily concerned with externally oriented, long-term decisions, rather than solving short-term, technical problems. Activities within the manager role include counselling management at all levels in the organization with regard to policy decisions, courses of action and communications, taking into account their public ramifications and the organization's social or citizenship responsibilities, making communications programme decisions, evaluating programme results, supervising the work of others, planning and managing budgets, planning communications programmes and meeting other executives. Communications managers also typically use research as the bedrock of their work, employ environmental scanning to monitor the organization's environment and help it manage relationships with key stakeholders. And because they possess needed intelligence gained from research,

managers are more likely to participate in the organization's decision making and strategic planning.

While the manager and technician roles are very distinct in terms of the activities performed within them, it is important to note that these two general roles are conceptual abstractions. In other words, manager and technician role activities are different, but neither mutually exclusive nor in opposition to each other. As Dozier and Broom point out: 'all practitioners enact elements of both the manager and technician roles which are themselves simply useful abstractions for studying the wide range of activities that practitioners perform in their daily work'.[5] As such, senior communications managers, for instance, do not exclusively occupy themselves with managerial tasks as they are often still engaged in handling routine technical communications tasks (media relations, publicity, the production of in-house newspapers, etc.). Nonetheless, the concept of *predominant role types* has proved useful in thinking about and studying roles in communications practice. If a practitioner enacts activities of the manager role set with greater frequency than activities of the technician role set, then this practitioner can be categorized as a manager. Such categorization is helpful not only in understanding the tasks and activities carried out by practitioners, but also for explaining practitioner involvement in decision making and for thinking about the further professional development of communications practitioners.

The strategic importance of roles

First of all, the concept of two dominant role types – managers and technicians – is helpful *in capturing and explaining daily behavioural patterns of individual practitioners*. The two roles are important theoretical concepts because they explain how people behave in carrying out their job responsibilities and predict the result of that action. Academic research on roles in communications practice[6] has, for instance, examined how the roles communications personnel play relate to variables such as environmental uncertainty, size of the department, gender and length of professional service. Environmental uncertainty, for instance, implies that when decisions about organizational responses to the environment become more novel and non-programmed, practitioner roles change from technician to manager. Practitioners working in organizations faced with such uncertain environments then shift activities from generating communications to making strategic decisions – or helping management to do so. Equally, the size of the communications department matters: for practitioners to focus on managerial tasks they usually require a support team to release them from technical tasks. Hence, manager roles tend to be found more often in larger communications departments (i.e. more than five or six people). A third factor, and the one often igniting the most response, is that gender determines role enactment. In various studies it has been observed that women were more likely than men to perform the technician role. According to some this just reflects the widespread influx of women into the communications profession (who start their careers working in technician roles) that is here today, although for others it indicates a glass ceiling for women who are disadvantaged in terms of career advancement (as they are hindered from progressing to manager roles). And, finally, the length of professional service of

the practitioner explains the adoption of either the manager or technician role by practitioners. Generally, practitioners tend to enter the profession by performing largely technician roles and it is only as practitioners become more experienced and move up the management hierarchy in organizations that they are typically able to adopt manager roles.

Thinking about manager and technician role types is not only helpful in capturing what activities practitioners are engaged in and explaining why they do so, but is also important as it suggests what the *consequences of role enactment* are. In particular, predominant manager role enactment is positively related to participation in management decision making. The enactment of management and technician roles thus also indicates whether, as a consequence of role enactment, communications departments participate in strategic decision making of the dominant coalition or simply execute decisions made by others. In a management-oriented communications department one or a few senior communications managers oversee a range of management and decision-making oriented activities, including analysis and research, the formulation of communications objectives for the organization, the design of short-term and long-term organizational philosophies, and counselling of senior management. In contrast, practitioners enacting the technician role are predominantly located in a peripheral department; technicians do not participate in management decision making, but only make programme decisions necessary to the internal functioning of their department. These practitioners are concerned with day-to-day operational matters (providing services such as writing, editing, photography, media contracts and production of publications), and they carry out the low-level communications mechanics necessary for implementing decisions made by others. In other words, *the enactment of the manager role is crucial for communications to be involved in management decision making concerning the overall strategic direction of the organization.* When communications practitioners are involved at the decision-making table, information about relations with priority stakeholders gets factored into the process of organizational decision making and into strategies and actions.[7] This would mean, among other things, that senior communications practitioners are actively consulted concerning the effects of certain business actions (e.g. staff lay-offs, divestiture) on a company's reputation with stakeholders, and even have a say in the decision making, instead of being called in after the decision was made to draft a press release and deal with communications issues emerging from it.

This enactment of the manager role, however, requires that practitioners are able to couch the importance and use of communications in the context of general organizational issues and objectives. This requires on the part of the practitioner knowledge of the industry or sector in which the organization operates and of the nature of the strategy-making process, as well as a strategic view of how communications can contribute to corporate and market strategies and to different functional areas within the company[8] (see also Chapters 4 and 5). In other words, instead of a 'craft' approach to communications that is skills-based and focuses on the production of communications materials, manager role enactment requires that a practitioner is able

> to bring thoughtfully conceived agendas to the senior management table that address the strategic issues of business planning, resource allocation, priorities and direction of the firm. Instead of asking what events to sponsor and at what cost, [practitioners] should be asking

which customer segments to invest in and at what projected returns … instead of asking how to improve the number of hits to the website, [practitioners] should be asking who their key stakeholders are and how to get more interactive with them.[9]

Manager role enactment, however vital to the strategic use of communications and its involvement in decision making, depends on a number of factors, such as the size of the department and environmental uncertainty (as mentioned above), but perhaps most importantly it depends on the *willingness* and *ability* of practitioners. As for their willingness, some practitioners, it needs to be remarked, still have little aspiration to enact the manager role, as they have built their careers around technical specializations and skills and exhibit high levels of job satisfaction in the stability of technician role enactment over time. A recent survey among practitioners even found that the majority of respondents were happiest performing the 'down and dirty' tasks, such as writing, editing and production of news releases and publications. According to the same survey, only 21 per cent of the respondents stated that managing, planning and working with top management represented the parts of the job they liked best.[10]

Apart from their willingness, practitioners must of course also be able to enact the manager role. This ability depends on crucial experience gained in communications 'on the job', as well as training and education in a number of areas.

- A first area includes *communications competence and skills*: a practitioner enacting the manager role needs to master the use of communications techniques and skills (writing, editing, etc.) just as technicians, but importantly also needs to know about different communications disciplines and how these can be integrated into a comprehensive strategy for the organization.
- A second area includes *management competence and skills*: manager role enactment requires an intimate knowledge of managerial processes of decision making and strategy development, and of the role and use of communications in organizational development and change. Requisite management skills at the manager level are the ability to consult, counsel, lead, plan, organize, galvanize support and reflect upon strategic actions.
- A third area includes *competence and skills in research and environmental scanning*: communications managers distinguish themselves from technicians in that they base their actions on data that are gathered systematically and check whether they have achieved their objectives. Technicians, on the other hand, go straight to work and do not anticipate or check what they have done, either during or after the task. Knowing about different research techniques, so that one can read and interpret research reports, as well as having the skills to set up and conduct research and environmental audits is thus crucial to manager role enactment.
- And a fourth and final area is *general knowledge of the organization and the industry or business sector* in which the company operates: a manager needs to have an intimate understanding of the organization – its structures, cultures and working conditions – as well as of the industry and environment of a company including the trends and issues within it.

Practitioners who are expected to enact the manager role, however, do not always meet these requirements for competencies and skills in each of these areas. Many communications practitioners still lack the requisite knowledge and skills to fully enact the manager role, particularly in areas such as financial management, the strategy-making process, and the use of communications in organizational development and change. As a result, these practitioners and the communications disciplines that they represent may be sidelined by companies and treated as a peripheral management discipline – one viewed as unimportant to the overall functioning of the corporation. Pincus, Rayfield and Ohl refer in this regard to a belief commonly held among some parts of senior management that communications adds little to corporate perfor-mance[11] as it is a 'fluffy' discipline that is insufficiently focused on the practicalities and demands of the business. Practitioners in senior positions who are expected to enact the manager role thus bear a responsibility to show and communicate the value of communications in terms of what it contributes to the organization.

> There is a lot of bemoaning in the hallways of marketing and communications offices of how CEOs 'don't understand communications', when the real problem is that marketing and communications professionals do not understand the intricacies of business manage-ment well enough to become part of the governing coalition.[12]

In other words, the development of practitioners into full managers is, as we have seen, crucial to the status accorded to communications and its input into management decision making. To make this developmental shift, practitioners, particularly those who come from a communications technician background, need to be trained and educated to become fully knowledgeable and skilled as communications managers. In this sense, thinking in terms of technician and manager roles and what competencies and skills are needed in each capacity thus also suggests a trajectory of professional development in terms of what is needed of practitioners within organizations if they want to progress from technician to manager roles (see Box 6.1). This professional development from technicians to managers is important at the local level – at the level of individual organizations – but is also central to the development of the practice and occupation of communications management as a whole, in terms of whether this occupation acquires professional status. The next section of this chapter picks up on this latter point and suggests ways in which the occupation can be further developed, and also what this requires of the different parties (i.e. practitioners, teachers and trainers, senior managers, professional associations and academic researchers) involved.

Box 6.1   Management brief – using role types for professional development programmes

KPN, the Dutch telecommunications provider operating in Western Europe, decided in 2003 to audit its communications workforce on their competencies and skills. The audit was conducted to determine the strength of the communications workforce, and areas for development, and to provide an input into a professional development programme for practitioners. Central to the audit was assessment of practitioners on three key competencies and skills areas: (1) the knowledge and use of communica-tions theory, processes and tactics, (2) the knowledge and use of management and organization theory, processes and tactics, and (3) the knowledge and skills concerning research and environmental scanning. Detailed scorecards for measuring the knowledge and skills for each practitioner in each of these areas were subsequently drawn up, and the audit was conducted.

The results of the audit revealed that the workforce was generally knowledgeable and also skilled in communications management, but that there was not enough differentiation between the different profiles or roles of practitioners. When cast in their official roles of technician (at either a junior or senior level) or manager, there was not enough differentiation between practitioners performing manager and technician roles. That is, in some areas such as strategic planning and communications strategy development, managers were not particularly more knowledgeable than their technician counterparts. Senior management therefore decided to sharpen the profiles of their managers and technicians, and to draw up a formal chart of what knowledge and skills are required at each level: junior technician, senior technician, manager/advisor, manager/executive. In this way, it became clear what was required of practitioners in any one role, and also what training and development was needed to support practitioners in their professional development.

6.3   The status and development of the communications profession

Virtually all organizations, with the exception of small businesses, have one or more communications practitioners working within them. These practitioners, as we have seen, carry out various tasks and activities, and in the general patterns of activities that they undertake can be characterized as technicians or managers. In other words, the practice or occupation of communications management thus simply *exists* as an inevitable part of organizations, with thousands of practitioners being employed in communications roles in companies across the world. This observation, of course, simply asserts that communications is practised in large measure across organizations, which furthermore begs the more qualitative question of whether the current way in which it is practised is valued and can be characterized as a true and full-grown profession.

Communications management as a profession

To answer whether the way in which communications is nowadays practised can be qualified as a profession, instead of as a mere occupation, one of course first needs to have a clear picture of what a profession actually entails. Wylie suggests that interdisciplinary guidelines for a 'profession' as opposed to a mere occupation generally include requirements for (a) a well-defined body of scholarly knowledge, (b) completion of some standardized and prescribed course of study, (c) examination and certification by a state as an authoritative body, and (d) oversight by a state agency which has disciplinary powers over practitioners' behaviours.[13] Reflecting upon professionalism in the practice of communications, Nelson added that professionalism is furthermore characterized in (a) practitioners being guided by professional values in their work, (b) membership of a professional organization, (c) professional norms that regulate the practice, (d) an intellectual tradition underpinning it, and (e) a constant development of technical skills.[14] Other criteria that have been mentioned by writers and commentators on professionalism in communications include intellectualism, a code of ethics, a comprehensive self-governing professional body, greater emphasis on public service than self-interests such as profits, and performance of a 'unique and essential service based on a substantial body of knowledge'.[15] Judged by these different writings, there is no evidently mutually shared understanding or strict definition of standards of professional performance in communications management. While there is some overlap and consensus regarding criteria – the familiar troika of (a) existence of a body of knowledge, (b) a code of ethics to guide the practice, and (c) certification of the practice being most often mentioned as the defining characteristics of a profession – there is still, as far as academic writings on the subject go, no strict set of criteria with which to judge the occupation of communications management and its professional acumen.

Nonetheless, as with other professions (e.g. medicine, law, accountancy) it is reasonable to suggest that an occupation is seen and judged as a profession when it is socially valued and recognized as such. This generally happens when practitioners in an occupation address a need or solve a problem through their specific competencies and skills that are (a) critical (to individuals, organizations, society at large) and therefore valued, (b) difficult to substitute or emulate, and (c) recognized, and possibly protected (by codes of practice, or through certification by the occupation's governing body, state agencies or companies themselves), as such.[16] In other words, professionalism is not just about solving problems and executing solutions in a way that others (outside the occupation) cannot, but also about 'convincing others about the legitimacy of these solutions and the practitioner's right to deal with the problem in the first place'.[17] As such, a fully-fledged and mature profession is characterized by:

1. the articulation of a domain of expertise;
2. the establishment of monopoly in the market for a service based on that expertise;
3. the ability to limit entry to the field;
4. the attainment of social status and recognition; and
5. systematic ways of testing competence and regulating standards.

Against the background of these five criteria, the occupation of communications management is indeed acquiring some of the attributes of a profession: its domain of expertise is gradually being circumscribed, and practitioners have acquired expert skill sets in a number of different communications specialities and techniques. In fact, many practitioners have now grown into full masters of communications techniques, as they know how to secure media coverage, prepare press releases, write speeches, write and design brochures, produce video news releases, lobby representatives in government, stage a special event, or prepare an annual report. The body of knowledge of communications management is, however, far less developed, primarily as theory and formal education are lagging behind, and as practitioners, perhaps because of historical precedent, continue to regard communications as a vocation.

Table 6.1   Practitioners' views about the qualities needed in communications

'Personality is important … you are flitting daily from one thing [or] another, so you need your
   wits about you'
'One has to have lateral thinking like Edward de Bono'
'Common sense [is important]. You need to be reasonably practical … You need to be able
   to communicate'
'Critical ability [is important, as are] … [being] persuasive in writing and verbally …, integrity …,
   personal courage …, [and] a sense of humor … it doesn't matter if they can write a press release.
'[Practitioners should be] ideas men who … wish to change things, and that's what I mean by
   being creative'
'People [who] speak up, who dress nicely, who've got something intelligent to say [can be
   successful] … The old slap-dash approach is just not good enough … Personality and good
   interpersonal skills [are important]'
'Credibility [is important] … People who can operate at a senior level on very sensitive
   topics [can be successful] …, so the ability to have those relationships is more important,
   in a way, than technical training … There is a personality requirement … Salesmanship is a
   crucial skill for the top people in consultancy … In the noncommercial area, the key skill is
   persuasiveness'
'More character than anything else [is important] …, getting along with clients, … being relatively
   intelligent, a streetwise intelligence, … [and] a sense of humor … [to be able to] come up with
   ideas and think at a bit of a tangent [is important]'

Table 6.1 presents some practitioners' views on their occupation, and illustrates that
the job of the communicator is often vocationally defined by personality and social
characteristics (including elements such as 'courage', 'discretion', 'empathy', 'handling
people', 'creative', 'up to speed', 'energetic', 'attitude of mind'), which are often seen
as subjective and intuitive, as well as by technical skills (writing, editing, etc.), which
can be learnt.[18]

   In a sense, the effect of such a vocational view of the occupation is that the practice of communications is characterized by being gifted in the use of communications techniques and tactics, but that insufficient attention has been given to the
development and nurturing of specific professional knowledge that would lead to a
distinct domain of expertise. The result is that communications as yet does not qual-
ify as a profession, which is evident in the fact that many senior managers are still
unsure about the value of communications (as opposed to other functions) and often
just use it for tactical purposes rather than for its specific knowledge, that people with
little formal education can enter the occupation, and that communications continues to be under threat from other functions (e.g. marketing, human resources) that
may encroach upon its domain.

   In recent years, many commentators have agreed that in the process of professionalization, the field of communications is developing and has shown considerable
progress, as it now possesses its own professional associations (such as the International
Association of Business Communicators (IABC) or the Institute of Practitioners in
Advertising), ethical codes of conduct and professional guidelines, as well as skills
training and education courses.[19] But these commentators have also concurred that
the field still lacks a well-grounded and distinct domain of expertise that is difficult to
emulate and thus raises barriers for entry to novices and practitioners from other

functions. James Grunig has suggested that it is exactly this feat – that professional knowledge requirements increase with the development into a profession – that is lagging behind and hindering us from considering communications management as a fully-fledged profession. And, he suggests, only a body of knowledge allows practitioners to take a mindful and more managerial approach to the practice (rather than a fly-by-the-seats-of-the-pants approach)[20] and would have the practice subsequently attain recognition from other professionals. Or as Jacquie L'Etang recently put it:

> The development of a body of knowledge not only increases the ability of the [communications] practice to base decisions on sound knowledge but also provides external vitality that is essential in the post-industrial world.[21]

The development of a body of knowledge is thus the crucial plank in the field's quest for professional status. It is the body of knowledge that can provide the cognitive core to the occupation, bolster practitioners' expertise and competencies and help define their field of jurisdiction.

Professional development

The body of knowledge that is required for professional status involves more extensive expertise and knowledge of how communications can be put to use in and for organizations. Such expertise and knowledge goes considerably further than just a skills-based understanding of different communications disciplines and techniques, to a broader understanding of the organizational context and purpose to which communications is put. Different parties are involved in this professional development of communications, and each bears responsibility in furthering communications on the road towards a respected and valued profession. These parties are (1) higher education, (2) professional associations, (3) academic researchers, (4) senior managers within organizations, and (5) communications practitioners themselves.

1. Higher education. The higher education sector (universities and polytechnic institutions) bears a particular responsibility in instiling in students the view that communications is a strategic managerial function, rather than a craft or technical support function for other management functions. For over a decade, academics and practitioners have been calling for a more management-oriented framework for educating practitioners. Yet, few university public relations, advertising or business communications courses today require much more than token business-focused course work or experiential opportunities. In fact, most require no business training whatsoever, as their grounding remains housed in communications or journalism schools.

Further professional development of communications, however, requires communications students to become business literate and develop an understanding of how communications can support critical business processes and be used within the strategic management of the organization. This suggests that higher education programmes must continue to develop superior communications skills in students, but they must frame these technical skills in principles of strategic management, research, and ethics and social responsibility.[22] As Cropp and Pincus recently suggested:

practitioners will need the tactical skills that they have always needed (e.g. writing, graphics, media relations). But in addition they will be expected to possess a 'business' frame of reference and set of competencies not historically typical of all professionals. In essence, they will need to think, make decisions, and communicate as savvy and believable members of their organization's management teams. Tomorrow's practitioners – and scholars, for that matter – must be able to understand not only public relations and communication strategies and tactics but also economic and organizational change strategies.[23]

Communications practitioners need a thorough preparation for their roles, a preparation that should be as rigorous and demanding as the preparation expected of professionals in other management areas. In a recent commentary piece, the former director of the Cranfield School of Management argued that for this reason more needs to be done to encourage communications practitioners to take part in general management education and to develop their professional knowledge and qualifications.[24]

In comparison with other specialists, [communications] practitioners may be relatively less qualified in terms of their specific preparation for the roles they play. In other areas of management, such as financial management, senior managers may have professional qualifications, gained through rigorous preparation, and general management qualifications such as the MBA. It has long been recognized that the preparation of senior PR, public affairs or corporate communications managers may have been much less thorough – a general first degree and some relevant experience, perhaps in journalism or politics.[25]

The responsibility for a more rigorous preparation lies in part with the higher education sector, which may need to revamp its curricula and programmes with more intellectual substance and business knowledge. In doing so, the practice of communications may in time come to be defined more by its domain of expertise and formal education than by its techniques, and through more rigorous education may be advanced to a level comparable to that of established professions, such as accountancy or law.

2. Professional associations.   Professional associations such as the Public Relations Society of America (PRSA) or the Institute of Practitioners in Advertising play an important role in the professional development of communications. Besides their roles as political representative bodies (to government, industry and society at large), professional associations also provide their own practitioner members with learning and networking opportunities, with an understanding of best practices, and with professional norms and values. In fact, quite a number of these professional associations have been rather successful in that many of their practitioner members across the US, UK and Europe are now guided by ethical guidelines and professional norms, as well as by well-established standards in skills (in writing, editing, etc.).[26]

Many of these professional associations have also discussed, often in their own national contexts, the professional status of communications over the years in terms of what criteria appropriately determine professional qualification and how the practice can be monitored and adjudicated to ensure appropriate professional training and behaviour.[27] Discussion has often been in this regard about the licensing or certification of practitioners in communications. In the UK, for instance, there has been an ongoing discussion of entry criteria and licensing in the Institute of Public

Relations (IPR). In 1998, the IPR even introduced a new diploma qualification as the basis for entry to membership of the IPR. The motivation behind this development was to achieve 'chartered status' for which the IPR would have to demonstrate that 50 per cent of its members held an approved qualification and met acceptable academic and work qualifications. In the US, there has equally been an ongoing discussion around licensing and certification of practitioners, and whether professional associations should be in the business of according and protecting this for the field of communications as a whole (and not just for its own members). Edward Bernays has been the most vocal proponent for licensing of practitioners in the US as a way to enhance credibility in communications practice and to elevate the practice to a profession.[28] Although legislation to introduce licensing in public relations and communications management was subsequently introduced in Bernays' home state of Massachusetts in the early 1990s, no other US state has yet adopted licensing of practitioners as a standard. Others have vigorously opposed licensing in the practice, including the PRSA and the IABC.[29] The opposition reasons that given the current state of professional development, and the huge differentiation in practitioners' competencies and skills in particular, systematic accreditation and licensing is not yet possible, and that furthermore government involvement through legislation would be ineffective, restrictive, unwelcome and superfluous. The general idea behind this is that first of all practitioner standards must be raised across the board, a development in which professional associations can play a part, before a full-force accreditation, let alone licensing, of practitioners can set in.

3. Academic researchers.   In the process of expanding the body of knowledge and thus the domain of expertise of communications, academics have an obvious stake. The academic James Grunig even suggests that communications cannot be practised as a profession, rather than a mere occupation, unless practitioners have a body of knowledge based on scholarly research available to them.[30] Academic research on communications management has, as mentioned in Chapter 1, increased over the last two decades or so, and academic theorizing and research is now even seen by many as maturing in its theoretical scope, the sophistication of its analysis and the many new insights that it has brought. The progress of academic research notwithstanding, there is still a huge range of academic questions that need to be addressed concerning the use of communications within strategic management – particularly questions about the way in which communications can be effectively used within organizational development and change programmes – and also greater efforts need to be made on the part of academics to communicate their concepts and findings to practitioners. In the past, practitioners have often been unaware of developments in theory and research, because of insufficient links between the worlds of academia and practice, and as many theories and research are couched in general and abstract terms and therefore often difficult to understand for practitioners. When cast in such abstract terms, practitioners may then feel that theory and research do not appear to provide anything useful or relevant to their day-to-day affairs.

Therefore, what seems to be needed for further professional development is not only to increase the level of academic research into crucial questions in communications management (i.e. questions concerning the role of communications in strategic management and organizational development), but also to foster greater links between academics and practitioners (through, for instance, conferences, associations, practitioner journals) so as to better communicate and explain academic theories and knowledge to practitioners.

4. Senior managers. For practitioners to develop themselves beyond their 'craft' communication skills, and effectively move into more manager role related activities (such as management counselling, support for organizational change trajectories, etc.), there of course needs to be a supportive organizational environment for doing so. A supportive organizational environment means, among other things, that senior managers recognize the role of communicators as broader than just skilfully disseminating messages, and that they enable practitioners to develop themselves by getting involved in management assignments, and through training and job rotation. Jon White and Laura Mazur have suggested in this regard that senior managers should give senior communicators central strategic and visible roles in assisting the formulation of corporate strategy and should spare them to engage in advising, research and evaluation rather than having them stretched by keeping up with the day-to-day operations.[31]

5. Practitioners. While opportunities for development need to be provided by the other parties mentioned above, practitioners themselves also need to rise to the occasion. One important point in this respect is that practitioners, as a group, may need to reframe their occupation as a management function, rather than as a creative–artistic or craft job. The perceptions and self-belief that communications is creative–artistic and a largely technical activity hinders the progression into management ranks and further professional development. Traditionally, however, this has been the dominant view of communications with practitioners, who prefer the intuitive and creative aspects of the communications process and even appear to avoid the activities associated with the managerial role.[32]

A further shift into manager roles is, however, needed not only for organizations but also for the communications profession as a whole. In this sense, practitioners have to take charge to train and educate themselves in matters concerning research, environmental scanning and the strategic management of organizations. Jon White recently suggested therefore that the fully qualified practitioner now needs to possess not just creative skills and a good personality, but also managerial and organizational knowledge and negotiating abilities.[33] Moreover, practitioners may also need to become more 'reflective' in their approach to the communications job than they have been in the past. James and Larissa Grunig's study into 'excellent' practitioners shows that excellent practitioners are the ones who increasingly have enjoyed some education, but also continually read, study and learn – through books, scholarly journals and professional publications. These practitioners think and approach their work as reflective practitioners by thinking, searching the literature, and planning and evaluating what they do (see also Chapter 1), and approach each decision by searching for research-based knowledge or do research themselves to create the knowledge they need.[34]

Together, these different parties may increase and solidify the body of knowledge of communications management, and in doing so may advance what is now still seen by many as an occupation into a full profession. The body of knowledge of communications management, it has been argued, needs to be specifically built around the managerial use of communications in and for organizations, as this will provide practitioners with a domain of expertise that is legitimately theirs, difficult to emulate and also valued by senior managers within the organization. In this sense, professional development is directly tied in with a further enactment of the manager role across organizations. Several studies have indicated in this regard that enactment of the managerial role is associated with multiple benefits: enhanced expertise, greater status within the organization, lower possibility of encroachment (i.e. being taken over by another function or department), and a powerful indicator of an expert and strategic approach to communications management.[35] Such a link between manager role enactment and professional development does not devalue the role of skilled technicians, but nonetheless suggests that technician activities need to be embedded within a larger domain of expertise and associated activities (i.e. environmental scanning, programme evaluation, issues management, strategic planning) directed towards how communications can be put to use in and for organizations. In other words, as Dozier and Broom have suggested, technical activities continue to be vital to communications management, but are not ends in themselves and rather need to be embedded in manager role enactment.

Recent studies suggest that many practitioners also realize themselves that the greatest stride in professional development comes with the development of further expertise and the enactment of the manager role, which would also define communications management more by its expertise and strategic use, rather than by its skills and techniques. Indeed, there seems to be a growing sense among practitioners that they should now take on this professionalization agenda, and start enacting the manager role through reflective and experiential learning on the job or through learning from formal education and training provided by the higher education sector and professional associations.

An across-the-board move into manager role enactment would also suggest that considerably more emphasis is placed on competencies (i.e. knowledge that is difficult to emulate) rather than simply skills, as has been the focus in the past. This, in turn, not only would provide a cognitive base in the form of expert knowledge of the field of communications, and an associated increase in status and legitimacy (i.e. acceptance of its role and acknowledgment of its standards of practice), but also would provide greater barriers for entering communications practice. In the past, the focus on skills created relatively low barriers for entry, as these could be relatively quickly learned, with the result that people with various backgrounds and with little formal education were often found within communications practice. Adding a set of competencies as expected and required of practitioners would greatly raise the barrier for entry, comparable to other, more established professions, as it would stipulate the need for more knowledge and skills (acquired through formal education, training or on the job experience) before one qualifies as a full professional and is also seen by others as such.

6.4   Chapter summary

Although the field of communications has already come a long way in its development towards a profession, it still largely fails to receive the recognition and status afforded to other management disciplines. In many organizations, communications is still regarded as an afterthought, a duty for delegation or as a peripheral management discipline. A central reason for why this has been the case is the stage of professional development that many practitioners are still at, operating largely as technicians and located in a peripheral department that may support but does not directly participate in management decision making. The importance of manager role enactment was therefore discussed in the chapter, in terms of what it entails and what different parties (e.g. higher education, professional associations, academics, senior managers) can contribute in this process of professional development of practitioners into communications managers. As it stands, the role of the communications manager is still quite embryonic in many organizations across the globe, pointing the way towards the future and towards further development in communications management.

Key terms

Body of knowledge	Occupation
Certification	Practitioner role
Code of ethics	Problem-solving process facilitator
Communications facilitator	Profession
Competence	Professional association
Environmental scanning	Professional standards
Expert prescriber	Reflective practitioner
Issues management	Skill
Licensing	Technician
Manager	Vocation

Notes

[1]Mintzberg, H. (1994), 'Rounding out the manager's job', *Sloan Management Review*, 36 (1).

[2]Katz, D., and Kahn, R.L. (1978), *The Social Psychology of Organizations*. New York: Wiley, second edition, p. 1.

[3]Broom, G.M. (1982), 'A comparison of sex roles in public relations', *Public Relations Review*, 8 (3), 17–22.

[4]Dozier, D.M., and Broom, G.M. (1995), 'Evolution of the manager role in public relations practice', *Journal of Public Relations Research*, 7, 3–26, p. 22.

[5]Ibid. (1995), p. 5–6.

[6]Toth, E.L., Serini, S.A., Wright, D.K., and Emig, A.G. (1998), 'Trends in public relations roles: 1990–1995', *Public Relations Review*, 145–163; Moss, D., Warnaby, G., and Newman, A.J. (2000), 'Public relations practitioner role enactment at the senior management level within UK companies', *Journal of Public Relations Research*, 12 (4), 277–307; Wrigley, B.J. (2002), 'Glass ceiling? What glass ceiling? A qualitative study of how women view the glass ceiling in public relations and communications management', *Journal of Public Relations Research*, 14 (1), 27–55; Dozier, D.M. (1992), 'The organizational roles of communications and public relations

practitioners', in Grunig, J.E. (ed.), *Excellence in Public Relations and Communication Management*. Hillsdale, NJ: Lawrence Erlbaum Associates, pp. 327–355.

[7]Lauzen, M.M. (1995), 'Public relations manager involvement in strategic issue diagnosis', *Public Relations Review*, 21, 287–304.

[8]Moss et al. (2000); Cropp, F., and Pincus, D.J. (2001), 'The mystery of public relations: unraveling its past, unmasking its future', in Heath, R.L. (ed.), *Handbook of Public Relations*. Thousand Oaks, CA: Sage, pp. 189–204.

[9]Gronstedt, A. (2000), *The Customer Century: Lessons from World-class Companies in Integrated Marketing and Communications*. London: Routledge, p. 203.

[10]McGoon, C. (1993), 'Life's a beach for communicators', *Communication World*, 10 (1), 12–15.

[11]Pincus, J.D., Rayfield, B, and Ohl, C.M. (1994), 'Public relations education in MBA programs: challenges and opportunities', *Public Relations Review*, 20 (1), 55–74.

[12]Gronstedt (2000), p. 204.

[13]Wylie, F. (1994), 'Commentary: public relations is not yet a profession', *Public Relations Review*, 20, 1–3.

[14]Nelson, R.A. (1994), 'The professional dilemma', *PR Update*, 1 November.

[15]Sallot, L.M., Cameron, G.T., and Weaver Lariscy, R.A. (1998), 'Pluralistic ignorance and professional standards: underestimating professionalism of our peers in public relations', *Public Relations Review*, 24 (1), 1–19, p. 3; see also Cameron, G.T., Sallot, L.M., and Weaver-Larsicy, R. (1996), 'Developing standards of professional performance in public relations', *Public Relations Review*, 22 (1), 43–61.

[16]L'Etang, J. (1999), 'Public relations education in Britain: an historical review in the context of professionalization', *Public Relations Review*, 25 (3), 261–289.

[17]Pieczka, M., and L'Etang, J. (2000), 'Public relations and the question of professionalism', in Heath, Robert L. (ed.), *Handbook of Public Relations*. Thousand Oaks, CA: Sage pp. 223–235.

[18]These practitioner quotes were taken from Pieczka and L'Etang (2001), p. 235.

[19]Pieczka and L'Etang (2000).

[20]Grunig, J.E. (2001), 'The role of public relations in management and its contribution to organizational and societal effectiveness', Speech delivered in Taipei, Taiwan, 12 May 2001.

[21]L'Etang, J. (2002), 'Public relations education in Britain: a review at the outset of the millennium and thoughts for a different research agenda', *Journal of Communication Management*, 7 (1), 43–53, p. 51.

[22]Clutterbuck, D. (2001), *Linking Communication Competence to Business Success: A Challenge for Communicators*. San Francisco: International Association of Business Communicators; Grunig (2001); Grunig, J.E., and Grunig, L.A. (2002), 'Implications of the IABC Excellence Study for PR education', *Journal of Communication Management*, 7 (1), 34–42.

[23]Cropp and Pincus (2001), p. 201.

[24]Murray, L. (2002), 'Public relations and communication management: suitable subjects for management education?' *Journal of Communication Management*, 7 (1), 9–13.

[25]Ibid. (2002), p. 12.

[26]Sallot et al. (1998); Cameron et al. (1996).

[27]Hainsworth, B.E. (1993), 'Commentary: professionalism in public relations', *Public Relations Review*, 19 (4), 311–313.

[28]Bernays, E.L. (1993), 'The future of public relations: is licensing the answer?', *Journal of Corporate Public Relations*, 3, 8–10.

[29]See Cameron et al. (1996), p. 45.

[30]Grunig (2001).

[31]White, J., and Mazur, L. (1995), *Strategic Communications Management: Making Public Relations Work*. Wokingham: Addison-Wesley.

[32]Dozier and Broom (1995).

[33]White, J. (2002), 'Editorial', *Journal of Communication Management*, 7 (1), 6–8, p. 6.

[34]Grunig and Grunig (2002), p. 41.

[35]Dozier and Broom (1995).

PART 3
Retrospect and Prospect

Part 1 of the book circumscribed theory and practice perspectives on corporate communications, introduced the theoretical concepts, and provided a historical sketch of the emergence and increasing importance of the corporate communications function within contemporary organizations. Part 2 of the book progressed from the theoretical overview presented in the first part and focused on the current practice and practicalities concerning corporate communications around three major themes: strategy, structure and people. The chapters in Part 2 also indicated that in terms of the way in which communications is currently practised, organized and staffed, further professional development and changes are in fact needed.

The short chapter in the final part of the book picks up on those ruminations and weaves many of the book's strands together into a number of scenarios and challenges for the future development of the field.

Chapter 7
The Future of Corporate Communications

Central themes

- There are a number of strategic, structural and staffing challenges that need to be faced and overcome within each organization for communications to be treated as a strategic management function.

- One further important challenge for communications practitioners is to show and communicate their added value to senior management to secure their strategic input and status within the organization.

- When these challenges are met the future for communications in organizations looks bright – well on its way towards a fully recognized and visible management function. The alternative scenario faced by communications practitioners and their departments is to be relegated or continue to be treated as a tactical support function for other management functions.

7.1   Introduction

This brief chapter reviews and integrates the strands, ideas and arguments from the previous chapters into a number of challenges and a vision for communications management in the future. The previous chapters have described in detail the changes that have occurred in communications practice. Chapter 2 outlined the different market, organizational and communications drivers that have led to a new way of viewing communications. This view embodies a more integrated conception, which advocates seeing the whole range of communications disciplines and activities in conjunction, instead of narrower, specialist approaches. Corporate communications, as we have seen, is a perspective on communications management, and a way of practising it, that departs from this integrated perspective. Seen in a *historical* light, and against the background of the evolution of communications management, the concept of corporate communications presents a new, integrated perspective of managing communications where communication is connected to corporate objectives and ultimately serves the organization as a whole. Perspectives of communications management that preceded corporate communications had never to such an extent advocated an intimate connection between communications and the overall corporate strategy of the organization. Rather, prior perspectives in both the marketing and public relations literatures had simply emphasized the artistries and creativity involved in producing communications materials and the tactics (media planning, budgeting, and so on) employed when planning a communications campaign.

The corporate communications philosophy of managing communications thus presented a break with the past, particularly in its premise of viewing and developing communications as a fully fledged management function within the organization. Such a view of communications also required a new theoretical vocabulary and concepts that would allow practitioners to enact their managerial roles, and to have a strategic input into corporate strategy making. The key concepts of stakeholder, identity and reputation that have emerged to this end may indeed enable practitioners to couch and communicate the use of communications in more general, corporate and organization-wide terms. In a more general sense, these three concepts are also indicative of the *theoretical change* that corporate communications has brought and its suggestion to base and ground communications, as a *management* function, to a greater extent than before in management theory and thought instead of vocational skills-based or communications knowledge alone.

The chapters in Parts 1 and 2 of the book have elaborated in quite some detail on the different managerial theories and frameworks for managing, structuring and staffing communications within an organization. These chapters have also suggested, based on evidence from academic research and practice, that there may still be a gap between the stated aspiration of corporate communications to practise communications as a management function and the actual reality. In many companies across the world, communications practitioners still enact largely technician roles, generally wary of the strategic importance and contribution that communications can make to the organization. This is unfortunate, as today's business climate indeed requires such a strategic input from communications within the overall strategic management of the company. Further *professional development* of practitioners and a number of structural and practical changes are, as the book has already suggested, therefore needed for the corporate communications function to come to full fruition and to play its part as a management function in each and every organization.

The following section of this brief chapter picks up on this point and suggests a number of scenarios and challenges for the future development of the field.

7.2   The challenges ahead

In terms of the way in which communications is currently still practised, organized and staffed in many organizations, further professional development and changes are needed. The guiding idea in this regard is to have an across-the-board developmental shift from a 'craft' orientation to communications, characterized by technician role enactment and communications service departments or units carrying out low-level communication mechanics, to a strategic management function. As a management function, communications practitioners would then enact managerial roles by participating in strategic decision making of the dominant coalition and by overseeing a range of management and decision-making oriented activities including analysis and research, the formulation of communications objectives for the organization, the design of short-term and long-term organizational philosophies, and counselling of senior management. This developmental shift can be more clearly circumscribed and pinpointed with a number of challenges in the three central areas of communications practice that the chapters in Part 2 of the book described: strategy, structure and people. Each of these challenges needs to be met by practitioners with appropriate strategies in order to develop and sustain communications as a strategic management function.

Challenge 1 (strategy): communications programmes need to be linked to corporate and/or market objectives to show the wider contribution and added value of communications to the corporation.

Strategy 1: this first challenge is about ensuring that communications has a wider organizational remit than just a tactical or operational orbit in terms of crafting and running communications campaigns. Adaptive strategies that practitioners can follow to this end include: (a) thinking and reflecting upon the wider organizational consequences of their work, (b) starting to build an intimate understanding of the organization, (c) couching the use and effect of communications in terms of wider organizational consequences and contributions with the stakeholder, identity and reputation concepts, (d) developing expertise on the role and use of communications in organizational development and change trajectories, (e) developing communications programmes from the mission and vision of the organization, (f) developing expertise on corporate, market and communications strategy formation.

Challenge 2 (structure): communications needs to be structured and organized in a way that enables an effective coordination of communications staff and activities, and with ready access to corporate decision makers.

Strategy 2: This challenge refers to the need for communications, in order to fulfil its strategic potential, to be structured in such a way that it is a visible and autonomous management function within the organization (rather than communications being fragmented or relegated to support units) and whereby senior communications practitioners are involved (in an advisory or executive capacity) with the decision makers or dominant coalition (CEO and the executive team) of the organization. For practitioners, this challenge means that they have to vie for one or a few departments of communications within the organization with a direct reporting relationship to the CEO. Adaptive strategies that practitioners can follow in this regard include: (a) convincing the dominant coalition that senior managers need ready access to communications advice on stakeholder, identity and reputation issues, and (b) showing the cost of a fragmentation of communications into separate units or delegation to other functions (instead of having one or a few departments) in terms of loss of expertise and control, inconsistent images, and inefficiency because of the costs of greater cross-unit interaction.

Challenge 3 (people): communications practitioners to a greater degree than before need to enact the manager role.

Strategy 3: the third and final challenge suggests that many more practitioners now need to enact the manager role, and thus embed their technical and programmatic activities in the context of research, strategic planning and the overall corporate strategy of the organization. Strategies for practitioners here lie in the area of professional development including: (a) job rotation, (b) receiving training in the strategy process and financial management, (c) education in research and monitoring, communications counsel and advice, management and control of administrative tasks within the department, and (d) adopting a generally reflective approach towards communications practice and its contribution to the organization.

Together, these three challenges suggest an interrelated set of changes for further development. Shifting to a strategic approach of linking communications programmes to overall corporate objectives is intimately related to a structural location of communications close to the executive board and to manager role enactment, and vice versa. Each of these three challenges, ideally, needs to be met in the near future to enable communications to play a strategic role within the management of the organization, and thus to have the corporate communications philosophy come to full fruition. This, of course, may not be an easy task, because of established power relationships and a traditional craft tradition among practitioners or, indeed, historical precedents. Nonetheless, change and development is needed.

A general theme running through all of these challenges, and the suggested changes and development, is to show the *added value* of communications to the organization. Each and every function or set of disciplines within a corporation is evaluated and scrutinized by senior management for its contribution to the organization and to the achievement of corporate objectives. When the contribution or added value of a particular function to the organization is high and visible, it is more likely that the function will be granted input into strategic decision making. To illustrate, the function of human resources (HR) has recently been criticized by senior managers for not being sufficiently focused on the practicalities and demands of the business, and thus does not warrant any strategic input. Vivienne Hines, a consultant with Deloitte and Touche, argued to this effect in a recent piece in the *Financial Times* that 'for HR to be seen as a commercial part of the business, HR leaders, on the board or not, need to quantify and communicate the contribution they make'.[1]

The same goes for communications, which as every other function (human resources, finance, marketing, etc.) is measured with the same stick. Capturing and quantifying the contribution of communications to the organization and to the commercial bottom line is thus key, although unfortunately not yet commonplace. In a recent survey in the US, only 48 per cent of those practitioners interviewed used measurement and evaluation. And in an Institute of Public Relations study in the UK only 28 per cent of those practitioners interviewed found using techniques to assess communications was worthwhile at all.[2] Instead of using research to quantify results, practitioners, it seems, often rather fence with the idea that, whether or not results are quantified and visible, organizations cannot in any case do without communications.[3] In a recent commentary piece, one practitioner, referring to CEOs who question the bottom line and cost of communications, even said that they only have to look at the millions of dollars, pounds or euros lost by corporations which have disinherited the trust and confidence of one or more key stakeholders.[4] That may indeed be so, but in order to be judged as accountable and as adding value to the organization, communications practitioners would, however, be wise to continuously measure the reputation of the organization with stakeholder groups (see Chapter 3), and to quantify the effect that communications has had upon them.

In other words, communications practitioners need to work at the image that they have with senior managers by quantifying and actively communicating their added value. Pincus et al. refer to a belief commonly held among senior management that they believe that communications adds little to corporate performance and is often described and seen as 'fluffy'.[5] This is the image that needs to be worked on and debunked by communications practitioners, so as to avoid being sidelined and communications being treated as a peripheral management discipline – one unimportant to the overall successful functioning of the corporation.

These are the challenges that lie ahead for communications practitioners and that in essence determine whether communications will effectively evolve into a strategic management function for most, if not all, organizations across the globe, or whether it remains to be cast in the role of a technical support function. This book has argued that such evolution and further development into a management function is indeed needed, in the light of the historical changes in communications practice and the stakeholder society and business climate faced by many corporations today.

7.3   Chapter summary

This brief chapter has discussed the challenges faced by communications practitioners for securing their strategic involvement in the organization, and also indicated ways of meeting them. Communications management has made considerable progress in recent years in the sophistication of its practices and the quality of people working within it, but further development, the chapter suggested, is still needed. When practitioners rise to the occasion and meet the challenges described, the prospect for the practice of communications and its strategic acumen is bright. If, however, they fail to do so, communications is likely to be cast in the role of a support function rather than a management function within organizations across the globe.

Notes

[1]Hines, V. (2002), 'Human resources is not fluffy', *Financial Times*, 29 January, 9; see also Skapinker, M. (2002), 'A higher status for the people person', *Financial Times*, 29 January, 9.

[2]Dolphin, R.R. (2000), *The Fundamentals of Corporate Communication*. Oxford: Butterworth-Heinemann.

[3]Fleisher, C.S., and Burton, B. (1995), 'Taking stock of corporate benchmarking practices: panacea or Pandora's box', *Public Relations Review*, Spring, 1–19.

[4]Finlay, J.R. (1994), 'The tasks and responsibilities of public affairs', *Business Quarterly*, 58, 105–110.

[5]Pincus, J.D., Rayfield, B., and Ohl, C.M. (1994), 'Public relations education in MBA programs: challenges and opportunities', *Public Relations Review*, 20 (1), 55–74.

Glossary of Corporate Communications and Other Communications Terms

4 Ps	Product, price, promotion (marketing communications) and place (distribution)
Above the line	All media that remunerate agencies on the basis of commission (e.g. advertising)
Account management	The process by which a communications (PR, advertising) or marketing agency or supplier manages the needs of a client (corporation)
Accountability	An evaluation of the contribution of functions or activities against their costs
Added value	The increase in worth of an organization's product or services as a result of a particular activity – in the context of communications, the activity might be effective stakeholder dialogue
Ambient media	Originally known as 'fringe media', ambient media are communications platforms that surround us in everyday life – from petrol pump advertising to advertising projected on to buildings to advertising on theatre tickets, cricket pitches or even pay slips
Advertisement	A paid-for dedicated space or time in which only the advertiser is represented
Advertising	The process of gaining the public's attention through paid media announcements
Advertising agency	An agency specializing in advertising and other marketing communications on behalf of a client organization
Advertising campaign	A planned use and scheduling of advertising over a defined period of time
Advertising media	Paid-for communications channels such as newspaper (print) or television
Advertorial	An editorial feature paid for or sponsored by an advertiser
Advocacy advertising	Advocacy advertising expresses a viewpoint on a given issue, often on behalf of an institution or organization
Ansoff matrix	Model relating marketing strategy to the general strategic direction. It maps product-market strategies – e.g. market penetration, product development, market development and diversification – on a matrix showing new versus existing products along one axis and new versus existing markets along the other

Asymmetrical communication	A process of communication where the one party (e.g. an organization) attempts to influence and persuade another party in line with its own interests
Attitude	A learned predisposition towards an object (e.g. organization, product), person or idea
Audience fragmentation	The process or trend whereby audience segments become more heterogeneous and divided (and therefore more difficult to reach with a mass marketing approach)
Audit	*See* Communications audit
Awareness	Measure of a proportion of target audience which has heard of the organization, product or service.
BCG matrix	Boston Consulting Group matrix based on market share and market growth rate
Below the line	Non-media advertising or promotion when no commission has been paid to the advertising agency. Includes direct mail, point of sale displays and give aways
Body of knowledge	The state of acquired knowledge related to a profession, discipline or practice
Brand	The set of physical attributes of a product or service, together with the beliefs and expectations surrounding it – a unique combination which the name or logo of the product or service should evoke in the mind of the audience
Brand acceptance	The condition wherein an individual, usually a customer, is well disposed towards a brand and will accept credible messages
Brand awareness	The condition wherein an individual, usually a customer, is aware of the brand
Brand equity	The notion that a respected brand name adds to the value of a product (and therefore generates returns to an organization upon customer purchase)
Brand image	The perception of a brand in the eyes of an individual, usually a customer
Brand loyalty	Extent to which individuals, usually customers, repurchase (or utilize) a particular branded product or service
Brand management	The process by which marketers attempt to optimize the marketing mix for a specific brand
Brand positioning	The way in which a brand is communicated to its target market, describing the attributes and values of the brand and its added value/appeal relative to its customers and the competition
Brand(ed) identity	A structure whereby businesses and product brands of an organization each carry their own name (without endorsement by the parent company) and are seemingly unrelated to each other
Business communications	The (vocational) discipline of writing, presenting and communicating in a professional context

Business plan	A strategic document showing cash flow, forecasts and direction of a company
Business strategy	The means by which a business works towards achieving its stated aims
Business-to-business	Relating to the sale of a product for any use other than personal consumption. The buyer may be a manufacturer, a reseller, a government body, a non-profit-making institution or any organization other than an ultimate consumer
Business-to-consumer	Relating to the sale of a product for personal consumption. The buyer may be an individual, family or other group, buying to use the product themselves, or for end use by another individual
Buzz	Media and public attention given to a company, its products or services
Centralization	Bringing tasks and/or activities together as the responsibility of one person or department in an organization
CEO	Chief executive officer
Certification	A formal test or document attesting the quality of someone's professional conduct
Channels	The methods and media used by a company to communicate and interact with its stakeholders
Channel noise	Confusion caused by too many messages trying to be delivered at one time
Clutter	The total number of message competing for attention of the audience; usually mentioned in the context of excessive amounts of communications
Cob-web method	A technique whereby individuals rate an organization on a number of selected attributes, which are then visually represented in the form of a wheel or web with eight or more scaled dimensions
Code of ethics	A professional code prescribing certain ethical principles and good practice
Communications	The internal and external communications techniques and media that are used towards internal and external groups
Communications audit	A systematic survey of members of a target audience (often members of the media or potential customers) to determine awareness of or reaction to a product, service or company
Communications facilitator	A practitioner acting as a liaison, mediator or interpreter between the organization and its stakeholders
Communications strategy	The general set of communications objectives and related communications programmes or tactics chosen by an organization in order to support the corporate and/or market strategies of the organization

Competence	Knowledge of a certain (professional) area that is difficult to emulate
Competitive advantage	The product, proposition or benefit that puts a company ahead of its competitors
Competitive forces	The competitors and competitive threats posed to an organization in a particular market or market segment
Competitors	Companies that sell products or services in the same marketplace as one another
Consumer	An individual who buys and uses a product or service
Consumer behaviour	The buying habits and patterns of consumers in the acquisition and usage of goods and services
Consumer research	Research into the characteristics, changes, usage and attitudes of consumers
Contingency theory	A branch of theory that suggests that variations in structure are determined and explained by factors in an organization's environment
Continuous research	Research conducted constantly to pick up trends, issues, market fluctuations, etc
Coordination mechanism	A mechanism by which activities and tasks are coordinated within an organization
Copy	The written words (storyline, formatting, etc.) to appear in a communications medium (press release, commercial, etc.)
Copy date	The date by which a publication or medium requires copy
Copy testing	Research into reactions and responses to written copy
Copywriting	Creative process by which written content is prepared for communications material
Corporate advertising	Advertising by a firm where the corporate entity, rather than solely its products or services, is emphasized
Corporate citizenship	Expressions of involvement of an organization in matters concerning society as a whole
Corporate communications	The function and process of managing communications between an organization and important stakeholder groups (including markets and publics) in its environment
Corporate identity	The profile and values communicated by an organization; the character a company seeks to establish for itself in the mind of its stakeholders, reinforced by consistent use of logos, colours, typefaces, and so on.
Corporate image	The way a company is perceived, based on a certain message and at a certain point in time; the immediate set of meanings inferred by an individual in confrontation or response to one or more signals from or about a particular organization at a single point in time
Corporate objectives and goals	(Precise) statement of aims or purpose

Corporate reputation	An individual's collective representation of past images of an organization (induced through either communication or past experiences) established over time
Corporate social responsibility (CSR)	Actions that do not have purely financial implications and that are demanded or expected of an organization by society at large, often concerning ecological and social issues
Corporate strategy	The general direction taken by a company with regard to its choice of businesses and markets and approach of its stakeholder groups
Council meeting	A meeting of representatives of different (communication) disciplines who meet to exchange views or to make policy
Coverage	Percentage of target audience which has the opportunity to be confronted with the communications message at least once
Craft communications	An artistic-creative approach to communications with an emphasis on the production and dissemination of communication materials
Crisis (crisis management)	A point of great difficulty or danger to the organization, possibly threatening its existence and continuity, and that requires decisive change
CSR	Corporate social responsibility
Culture	The general values and beliefs held and shared by members of an organization
Customer	A person or company that purchases goods or services (not necessarily the end consumer)
DAGMAR	Defining advertising goals for measured advertising response – a model for planning advertising in such a way that its success can be quantitatively monitored
Database	A collection of information about relevant data (e.g. information about past, current and potential customers)
Database marketing	Whereby customer information, stored in an electronic database, is utilized for targeting marketing activities. Information can be a mixture of what is gleaned from previous interactions with the customer and what is available from outside sources
Decoding	Process where the receiver converts the symbolic forms transmitted by the sender
Demographics	Information describing and segmenting a population in terms of age, sex, income, and so on, which can be used to target communications campaigns
Departmental arrangement	The administrative act of grouping or arranging disciplines, activities and people into departments
Depth interview	An interview, usually one-to-one, exploring deeper motivations and beliefs
Desk research	Using publicly available and previous data (e.g. on certain issues, markets)

DESTEP	Demographic, economic, social, technological, ecological and political analysis. A broad analysis of macro factors that may impinge upon an organization's business and operations
Differentiation (competitive strategy)	A competitive strategy whereby the unique and added value of a product or service is emphasized (which then warrants a premium price)
Direct mail	Delivery of an advertising or promotional message to customers or potential customers by mail
Direct marketing	All activities that make it possible to offer goods or services or to transmit other messages to a segment of the population by post, telephone, e-mail or other direct means
Direct response	Communications (e.g. advertising) incorporating a contact method such as a phone number, address and enquiry form, website identifier or e-mail address, with the intention of encouraging the recipient to respond directly to the advertiser by requesting more information, placing an order, and so on
Distribution channels	The process and ways of getting the goods from the manufacturer or supplier to the user
Domain similarity	The degree to which two individuals or disciplines share similar goals, skills or tasks
Dominant coalition	The group of people, usually the executive or senior management team, within an organization making the important decisions (concerning the direction and focus of the firm, etc.)
Economic market stake	A stake held by those who have an economic interest in an organization, such as employees, customers, suppliers and competitors
Economies of scale	The greater efficiency associated with groupings of larger size
Encoding	The process of putting information into a symbolic form of words, pictures or images
Endorsed identity	A structure whereby businesses and product brands of an organization are endorsed or badged in communications with the parent company name
Environmental scanning	The process whereby the environment of an organization is continuously scanned for issues and trends, usually in relation to important stakeholder groups
Equity stake	A stake of direct ownership in an organization (e.g. stockholders, directors)
Evaluation	The process of assessing communications effects, often against predetermined corporate, marketing and communications objectives

Exchange	The process by which two or more parties give up a desired resource to one another
Execution	The act of carrying something out (usually a set of planned for communications programmes)
Executive team	The senior management team of an organization, typically led by the chief executive officer, responsible for the overall management and strategic direction of the firm
Expert prescriber	A practitioner who is responsible for the design and management of communications programmes; in an independent capacity from senior management
External analysis	Study of the external environment of an organization, including factors such as customers, competition and social change
FMCG	Fast moving consumer goods – such as packaged food, beverages, toiletries and tobacco
Focus group	A tool for market, communications and opinion research where small groups of people are invited to participate in guided discussions on the topic being researched
Forecasting	Calculation of future events and performance
Frequency	Average number of times the target audience will have the opportunity to be confronted with a certain communications message
Full service agency	An agency that specializes in a whole range of communications disciplines and can assists the client in the full process of communications planning and execution
Geodemographics	A method of analysis combining geographic and demographic variables
Global brand	A brand that has world-wide recognition (e.g. Coca-Cola)
Goal	The primary and direct result a company is attempting to achieve through its communications efforts
Horizontal structure	The structures that are laid over the vertical structure to coordinate and integrate functionally separated tasks and activities
IABC	International Association of Business Communicators
IC	Integrated Communications
Image	An individual's perceptions of an organization, product or service at a certain point in time
IMC	Integrated marketing communications
Industrial goods	Products/resources required by industrial companies
Influencer stake	A stake held by those who have no economic or equity involvement in an organization, but want to influence public opinion or the direction of the organization, such as consumer advocates and environmental groups

Infomercials	An advertising commercial that p information
Integrated marketing communications (IMC)	A concept favouring the combined ț multiple marketing communications ing, direct marketing, sales promotio
Integration (integrated communications)	The act of coordinating all commu corporate identity is effectively and consisu.u., nicated to internal and external groups
Intentional communications	A message that an organization intends to convey
Intermediary	Any individual/company in the distribution channel between the supplier and final consumer
Internal analysis	The study of a company's internal resources in order to assess opportunities, strengths or weaknesses
Internal communications	All methods (internal news letter, intranet) used by a firm to communicate with its employees
IPO	Initial public offering
IPR	Institute of Public Relations
Issues (issues management)	An unsettled matter (which is ready for a decision) or a point of conflict between an organization and one or more publics
Kelly grids	*See* Repertory grids
Laddering	A research technique whereby people's opinions are represented as means-end chain; used to infer the basic values and motivations that drive people
Legitimacy	Here: conformity of an organization to public standards, norms and values
Licensing	The act of formally accrediting an agency or professional, often done by a professional association or legal body
Life cycle	Stages through which a product or brand develops (*see* PLC)
Lifestyle	Research classification based on shared values, attitudes and personality
Likert scale	Research scale that uses statements to indicate agreement or disagreement
Line extension	Extending existing brands to other products in the same product category
Line function	An organizational function that is directly involved in the core and operational business process (i.e. the line) of producing products and bringing them to market (e.g. marketing)
Logo	A graphic, usually consisting of a symbol and/or group of letters, that identifies a company or brand
Low cost (competitive strategy)	Competitive strategy where the lower cost of a product or service is emphasized

cro environment	The external factors that affect a company's planning and performance, and are beyond its control (e.g. socio-economic, legal and technological change)
Management communications	Communication between managers and employees; restricted to dyads and small groups
Manager (communications manager)	A practitioner who makes strategy or programme decisions concerning communications, and is held accountable for programme success or failure; engages in research, strategic planning and management of communications
Market	A defined group for whom a product is or may be in demand (and for whom an organization creates and maintains products and service offerings)
Market development	The process of growing sales by offering existing products (or new versions of them) to new customer groups (as opposed to simply attempting to increase the company's share of current markets)
Market orientation	Steadfast adherence to the marketing concept; an approach in which customer needs and wants are the underlying determinants of an organization's direction and its marketing programmes
Market penetration	The attempt to grow one's business by obtaining a larger market share in an existing market
Market research	The gathering and analysis of data relating to marketplaces or customers; any research which leads to more market knowledge and better-informed decision making
Market segmentation	The division of the marketplace into distinct subgroups or segments, each characterized by particular tastes and requiring a specific marketing mix
Market share	A company's sales of a given product or set of products to a given set of customers, expressed as a percentage of total sales of all such products to such customers
Market structure	The character of an industry, based on the number of firms, barriers to entry, extent of product differentiation, control over price, and the importance of non-price competition
Marketing	The management process responsible for identifying, anticipating and satisfying customer requirements profitably
Marketing audit	A comprehensive and systematic review and appraisal of every aspect of a firm's marketing programme, its organization, activities, strategies and people

Marketing communications	All methods (advertising, direct marketing, sales promotion, personal selling and marketing public relations) used by a firm to communicate with its customers and prospective customers
Marketing concept	The process by which the marketer responds to the needs and wants of the consumer
Marketing mix	The combination of marketing inputs that affect customer motivation and behaviour. These inputs traditionally encompass four controllable variables: the 4 Ps
Marketing objective	A market target to be achieved reflecting corporate strategy
Marketing public relations	The use of what are traditionally seen as public relations tools (media, free publicity) within marketing programmes; used to reach marketing objectives
Marketing strategy	The set of objectives that an organization allocates to its marketing function in order to support the overall corporate strategy, together with the broad methods chosen to achieve these objectives
Matrix structure	A structure where a professional has a dual reporting relationship. This structure aims to foster both functional expertise and coordination at the same time
MBA	Master in Business Administration
Media	Members or tools for disseminating the news; unbiased third parties (press representatives); communication channels for a certain campaign
Media coverage	Mention in the media of a company, its products or services
Media plan	Recommendation for a media schedule including dates, publications, TV regions, etc.
Media relations	The function or process of gaining positive media attention and coverage
Media schedule	Records of campaign bookings made or a proposal (with dates, costs, etc.) for a campaign
Merchandising	Traditionally in-store promotion and displays
Micro environment	The immediate context of a company's operations, including such elements as suppliers, customers and competitors
MIIS	Management Intelligence and Information System – system of collecting and examining environmental and/or market data
Mission	A company's overriding purpose in line with the values or expectations of stakeholders
Mission statement	A company's summary of its business philosophy and direction
Monolithic identity	A structure whereby businesses and product brands of an organization all carry the same corporate name

Multinational	A corporation whose operational and marketing activities cover multiple countries over the world
Neo-classical economic theory	A branch of theory that considers organizations from an economic and profit-making perspective
NGO	Non-governmental organization
Niche marketing	The marketing of a product to a small and well-defined segment of the market place
Noise	*See* Channel noise
Non-verbal communications	Transmission of a message without the use of words or language
Objective	A company's defined and measurable aims for a given period
Occupation	A person's temporary or regular employment
Organizational identity	The shared values and sense-making of people within an organization
Organization-environment analysis	A process of analysis that focuses on the organization – its strengths and weaknesses – and on factors and trends in its environment
OTH	Opportunities to hear – number of opportunities a target consumer has of hearing an advertisement
OTS	Opportunities to see – number of opportunities a target consumer has of seeing an advertisement
PR	*See* Public relations
Partnership promotion	Joint promotions aiming to achieve additional exposure
Perception	The way a corporation/product/event/stimulus is received and evaluated by an individual
Personal selling	One-to-one communication between a seller and prospective purchaser
Persuasion	A means by which a person or organization tries to influence and convince another person to believe something or do something, using reasoning and coaxing in a compelling and convincing way
Pitch	Prepared sales presentation by an agency to a client organization, usually one-on-one
PLC	Product life cycle – supposed stages of a product (e.g. birth, growth, maturity and decline)
POS	Point of sale – the location, usually within a retail outlet, where the customer decides whether to make a purchase
Porter's five forces	An analytic model developed by Michael E. Porter. The five forces in terms of which the model analyses businesses and industries are: buyers, suppliers, substitutes, new entrants and rivals

Portfolio (and portfolio analysis)	The set of products or services that a company decides to develop and market. Portfolio analysis is the process of comparing the contents of the portfolio to see which products or services are the most promising and deserving of further investment, and which should be discontinued
Positioning	The creation of an image for a company, product or service in the minds of stakeholders, both specifically to that entity and in relation to competitive organizations and offerings
Power-control theory	A branch of theory that suggests that variations in structures are determined and explained by the views and relationships of the powerful dominant coalition within an organization
Practitioner role	The general set of activities performed by a practitioner
Press agentry	The use of press agents, promoters and publicists to promote and publicize an organization and its products or services through the media, often used to describe communications during the early decades of the twentieth century
Press kit	Several press deliverables combined in one package (usually a folder)
Press release	A paper or electronic document submitted to the media with the intent of gaining media coverage
Problem-solving process facilitator	A practitioner who collaborates with other managers to define and solve organizational problems
Procedures and guidelines	General prescriptions on the design and management of communications programmes
Process documentation	The documentation of works processes, often in visual and comprehensive formats, such as flow charts, process maps and checklists
Process effects	An audit of the effectiveness and efficiency in which communication programmes are developed, managed and run
Profession	A vocation or calling that involves some branch of advanced learning or science (e.g. the medical profession)
Professional association	A trade body representing a particular profession or occupation
Professional standards	The standards by which someone is judged as professional; i.e. competent, skilled and ethical in his/her professional practice
Production orientation	A primary focus of business on the efficient development and assembly of products – characteristic of the early twentieth century
Proposition	The message that the advertiser wants the customer to focus upon

Projective technique	Qualitative research technique by which an individual is asked to respond to ambiguous stimuli such as vague statements or objects, designed to measure feelings, opinions, attitudes and motivations
PRSA	Public Relations Society of America
Psychographics	A base for segmentation derived from attitude and behavioural variables
Public affairs	The public policy aspect of corporate communications
Public information	The use of writers and publicists to inform and reassure the general public of corporate practices, often used to describe communications before the Second World War
Public relations	The function or activity that aims to establish and protect the reputation of a company or brand, and to create mutual understanding between the organization and the segments of the public with whom it needs to communicate
Publicity	Media coverage
Public	People who mobilize themselves against the organization on the basis of some common issue or concern to them
Publicly syndicated rankings	Rankings of the reputation of organizations that are published on an annual basis by various associations or agencies
Pull strategy	Pull communications, in contrast to push communications, addresses the customer directly with a view to getting them to demand the product, and hence 'pull' it down through the distribution chain. It focuses on advertising and above the line activities
Push strategy	Push communications relies on the next link in the distribution chain (e.g. a wholesaler or retailer) to 'push' out products to the customer. It revolves around sales promotions – such as price reductions and point of sale displays – and other below the line activities
Q-sort	An oral interview technique where respondents are asked to sort cards (e.g. with company statements on them) and are then asked to motivate
Qualitative research	Research that does not use numerical data but relies on interviews, focus groups, repertory grid, etc. usually resulting in findings that are more detailed but also more subjective than those of quantitative research
Quantitative research	Research that concentrates on statistics and other numerical data, gathered through opinion polls, customer satisfaction surveys, and so on
Reach	The percentage or number of people exposed to a media vehicle at least once

Recall	Used by researchers to establish how memorable a certain communications message was
Receiver	In communications theory the party receiving the message
Reflective practitioner	A practitioner who is mindful about his/her own professional conduct; and continuously reflects upon his/her own performance
Repertory grid	A technique for representing the attitudes and perceptions of individuals, also called Personal Construct Technique. The technique can be useful in developing market research (and other) questionnaires
Reporting relationship	The person or department to whom a certain practitioner reports about his/her performance and activities
Reputation	*See* Corporate reputation
Resource dependence	The dependence of a practitioner in one communications discipline on obtaining resources (e.g. advice, assistance, communication products) from another discipline to accomplish his or her objectives
Return on investment (ROI)	The value that an organization derives from investing in a project
Sales orientation	A primary focus of business on the selling of products – characteristic of the 1950s and beyond
Sales promotion	A range of techniques used to engage the purchaser. These may include discounting, coupons, guarantees, free gifts, competitions, vouchers, demonstrations, bonus commission and sponsorship
Sampling	The use of a statistically representative subset as a proxy for an entire population (e.g. in order to facilitate quantitative market research)
Secondary research	*See* Desk research
Segmentation	*See* Market segmentation
Selective attention	Where receivers notice only some of the message presented
Selective distortion	To see and hear differently from the message presented
Selective exposure	Idea that individuals only expose themselves to certain messages
Selective perception	The process of screening out information that is not of interest, and retaining information of use
Sender	In communications theory the party sending the message
Share of voice	Calculation of a brand's share of media expenditure in a particular category
Shareholder value	The worth of a company from the point of view of its shareholders
Skill (communications skills)	The ability to produce or craft something (e.g. a written document by way of writing skills)

Slogan	Frequently repeated phrases that provide continuity in messages and campaigns of a certain corporation, its products or services
SMART objectives	Objectives that are specific, measurable, achievable, realistic and timely
SME	Small to medium sized enterprise – variously defined: according to one EU definition, it must employ under 250 people, have either a turnover of less than 40 million € or net balance sheet assets of less than 27 million € and not be more than 25% owned by a larger company
Socio-economic theory	A branch of theory that considers organizations from a societal and normative perspective alongside its economic performance
SRI	Socially responsible investment
Spin	The attempt to manipulate the depiction of news or events in the media through artful public relations – often used with derogatory connotations
Sponsorship	Specialized form of sales promotion where a company will help fund an event or support a business venture in return for publicity
Staff function	An organizational function (e.g. communications) that carries no direct executive power over the primary operational process or responsibility for it, but that fulfils an advisory role to other functions within the organization
Stakeholder	Any group or individual that can affect or is affected by the achievement of the organization's objectives
Stakeholder analysis	A process of analysis aimed at identifying, prioritizing and understanding stakeholders of an organization
Stakeholder audit	A systematic survey of stakeholders to determine the nature of the relationship, issues and possible reactions to corporate actions
Stakeholder mapping	An analytical tool whereby stakeholder groups are identified and their relationship to the organization becomes visually represented in a map
Strategic action	The translation of the strategic intent or chosen strategic option into action
Strategic analysis	The process of characterizing, analysing and benchmarking the position of an organization in its environment
Strategic intent	The possible courses of strategic actions open to an organization (as informed by strategic analysis); often articulated in corporate and marketing objectives
Strategic management function	A management function with an input into the strategic direction of the organization

Strategies	The ways or means in which the corporate objectives are to be achieved and put into effect
SWOT	A method of analysis that examines a company's strengths, weaknesses, opportunities and threats. Often used as part of the development process for a corporate or marketing plan
Symmetrical communication	A process of communication between organizations and stakeholders where the interests of both are balanced, accommodated and harmonized
Tactics	Specific action items to support strategies and objectives
Target audience	The key groups or individuals that a company wants to receive with its communications messages
Target market	The segment of a market at which marketing efforts are directed
Targeting	The use of market segmentation to select and address a key group of potential purchasers
TAT	Thematic apperception test
Team	A temporary or permanent grouping of individuals (from different disciplines) charged with a certain task or project
Technician (communications technician)	A practitioner who in his/her day-to-day work focuses primarily on programmatic and tactical communications activities such as writing, editing, producing brochures, etc. A technician thus tactically implements decisions made by others
Telemarketing	The marketing of a product or service over the telephone
Through the line	Mixture of below and above the line communications
Tracking	Surveying attitudes and perceptions (images and reputations) of individuals to an organization, products or services on a continuous basis
Trademark	Sign or device, often with distinctive lettering, that symbolizes a brand
Transparency	The state where the image or reputation of an organization held by stakeholder groups is similar to the actual and/or projected identity of an organization
Triple bottom line	A phrase referring to 'people, planet and profits'; emphasizes the social and ecological responsibilities of organizations alongside their economic or profit-making responsibility
Unintentional communication	Message that an organization does not intend to convey
USP	Unique selling proposition – The benefit that a product or service can deliver to customers that is not offered by any competitor, one of the fundamentals of effective marketing and business

Value recognition	The value placed upon communications by senior managers
Vertical structure	The way in which tasks and activities are divided and arranged into departments and located in the hierarchy of authority within an organization
Vision	The long-term aims and aspirations of the company for itself
Vocation	A trade or profession
Word-of-mouth	The spreading of information through human interaction alone
Zero-based media planning	A review of media options during communications planning based on research, analysis and insight, not habit and preference

Index

NOTE: page numbers in *italic type* refer to boxes, figures or tables. Page numbers in **bold type** refer to glossary terms.